向海而生
古罗马海港的传说

PORTUS
THE SEA OF THE ANCIENT ROMANS

宁波中国港口博物馆
中国（海南）南海博物馆　编著
天禹文化集团有限公司

文物出版社

图书在版编目（C I P）数据

向海而生：古罗马海港的传说 / 宁波中国港口博物馆，中国（海南）南海博物馆，天禹文化集团有限公司编著. —北京：文物出版社，2019.10

ISBN 978-7-5010-6272-0

Ⅰ. ①向… Ⅱ. ①宁… ②中… ③天… Ⅲ. ①历史文物 – 介绍 – 古罗马②海洋 – 文化研究 – 古罗马 Ⅳ. ① K885.46 ② P7-05

中国版本图书馆 CIP 数据核字（2019）第 191110 号

向海而生：古罗马海港的传说

编　　著：宁波中国港口博物馆
　　　　　中国（海南）南海博物馆
　　　　　天禹文化集团有限公司

装帧设计：北京博简文化发展有限公司
责任编辑：刘永海
特约编辑：齐　方
责任印制：张道奇
特约校对：刘宣谷

出版发行：文物出版社
社　　址：北京市东直门内北小街 2 号楼
邮　　编：100007
网　　址：http://www.wenwu.com
邮　　箱：web@wenwu.com
经　　销：新华书店
制版印刷：雅迪云印（天津）科技有限公司
开　　本：889 毫米 ×1194 毫米　1/16
印　　张：13
版　　次：2019 年 10 月第 1 版
印　　次：2019 年 10 月第 1 次印刷
书　　号：ISBN 978-7-5010-6272-0
定　　价：268.00 元

主办单位 Organizers

宁波中国港口博物馆	China Port Museum
中国（海南）南海博物馆	China (Hainan) Museum of the South China Sea
罗马国家博物馆	National Roman Museum
罗马考古、艺术品和景观监管局	Special Superintendent of Archeology, Fine Arts, and Landscapes of Rome
坎皮佛莱格瑞考古公园	Campi Flegrei Archaeological Park - Archaeological Museum of the Campi Flegrei in the Castle of Baia
阿皮亚古道考古公园	Appia Antica Archaeological Park - Antiquarium of Lucrezia Romana
圣塞维拉航海博物馆	Santa Marinella Civic Museum - Museum of the Ancient Sea and Navigation

协办单位 Co-organizers

中国博物馆协会展览交流服务平台	Chinese Museums Association Exhibition Exchange Center
天禹文化集团有限公司	Tianyu Cultural Group Co., Ltd.
ChinaMuseum International 有限公司	ChinaMuseum International S.r.l.
n!studio Asia 工作室	n!studio Asia
EaWe 项目公司	EaWe Project
Archquadro 联合设计公司	Archquadro Associati

支持单位 Supporters

意大利文化遗产与活动部	Ministry of Cultural Heritage and Activities (Italy)
中意文化合作机制	Italy - China Cultural Forum

特别鸣谢 Acknowledgement

国家水下文化遗产保护宁波基地	National Underwater Cultural Heritage Protection Center, Ningbo Base
宁波市文物考古研究所	Ningbo Institute of Cultural Relics and Archaeology

展览委员会 / EXHIBITION COMMITTEE

中国

展览总策划
冯　毅
辛礼学
胡　波

展览统筹
陈卫立
章佩岚
钱　茜

宁波中国港口博物馆
展览协调：吴　凤
展陈设计：吴　凤　王文武
内容辅助：毕显忠　杜　宁　李　蜜
展览宣传：杜　宁
公共教育：刘玉婷　宿艳娇
参展人员：李永歌　曹　莹　周　怡　郑艺媛
张凯学　翟常青

中国（海南）南海博物馆
展览协调：李东风
展陈设计：郑睿瑜　齐天俏
展览宣传：朱　磊　李婧瑜
公共教育：陈小冰　孙梦圆　杨　娜
参展人员：陈子晗　符晓遥　李　剑　李其仁
田钟钰

天禹文化集团有限公司
展览协调：唐　磊　郭子凤　许雅璐
内容编辑：齐　方

The Chinese Committee

The Organizer of the Exhibition
Feng Yi
Xin Lixue
Blair Hu

The General Coordination of the Exhibition
Chen Weili
Zhang Peilan
Qian Qian

China Port Museum
Exhibition Coordination : Wu Feng
Exhibition Design: Wu Feng, Wang Wenwu
Content Assistance: Bi Xianzhong, Du Ning, Li Mi
Exhibition Promotion: Du Ning
Public Education: Liu Yuting, Su Yanjiao
Exhibition Arrangement: Li Yongge, Cao Ying, Zhou Yi, Zheng Yiyuan,
Zhang kaiXue, Zhai Changqing

China (Hainan) Museum of the South China Sea
Exhibition Coordination: Li Dongfeng
Exhibition Design: Zheng Ruiyu, Qi Tianqiao
Exhibition Promotion: Zhu Lei, Li Jingyu
Public Education: Chen Xiaobing, Sun Mengyuan, Yang Na
Exhibition Arrangement: Chen Zihan, Fu Xiaoyao, Li Jian, Li Qiren,
Tian Zhongyu

Tianyu Cultural Group Co., Ltd.
Exhibition Coordination: Tang Lei, Guo Zifeng, Xu Yalu
Editing of Text: Qi Fang

意大利

展览总策划

达尼埃拉·波罗（罗马国家博物馆馆长，罗马考古、艺术品和景观监管局局长）

法比奥·帕加诺（坎皮佛莱格瑞考古公园馆长）

西蒙·奎利奇（阿皮亚古道考古公园馆长）

弗拉维奥·埃尼（圣塞维拉航海博物馆馆长）

策展人

考古学部分：丽塔·奥列玛、雷纳托·塞巴斯蒂亚尼、米雷拉·塞洛伦齐、皮耶尔弗兰切斯科·达勒姆

钱币部分：加布里埃拉·安杰利·布法利尼

参展人员

意大利文化遗产与活动部博物馆司：安东尼奥·兰皮斯、安东尼奥·塔拉斯科、亚历山德拉·戈比

罗马国家博物馆：

文物修复部：M. 安杰利尼、G. 班迪尼、S. 博尔吉尼、F. 科佐利诺、D. 帕佩蒂、I. 拉皮内西、劳拉·鲁格瑞、G. 塞韦里尼

典藏部：M. 阿维诺、G. 德安吉丽斯、M. 罗吉

档案部：A. 佩尔戈拉、R. D’阿戈斯蒂诺、L. 曼达托

皮耶特拉 - 帕帕壁画室图像复原：西蒙·博尼

罗马考古、艺术品和景观监管局：

文物修复部：M. 米拉齐

土地保护部：保拉·弗拉耶加里

文化遗产和活动部—哈德良别墅和埃斯特别墅：卢西拉·D’亚历山德罗

策展委员会

罗马国家博物馆：

达尼埃拉·波罗（艺术史学家）、加布里埃拉·安杰利·布法利尼（钱币学家）、

萨拉·科兰托尼奥（考古学家、罗马国立博物馆展览办公室负责人）、

米雷拉·塞洛伦齐（考古学家）

罗马考古、艺术品和景观监管局：

弗朗西斯科·普洛斯佩雷蒂（建筑师）、雷纳托·塞巴斯蒂亚尼（考古学家）、

蒂齐亚纳·切卡里尼（考古学家，罗马考古、艺术品和景观监管局展览办公室负责人）

撰文

加布里埃拉·安杰利·布法利尼
丽塔·奥列玛
西莫内·博卡迪
萨拉·科兰托尼奥
K. 曼尼诺
保拉·米涅洛
雷纳托·塞巴斯蒂亚尼
米雷拉·塞洛伦齐
皮耶尔弗兰切斯科·达勒姆

展品说明作者

西莫内·博卡迪（No. 118-162）
安东内拉·贝尼尼（No. 10）
克劳迪奥·博尔戈尼奥尼（No. 11,66,113,116）
卡洛塔·卡鲁索（No. 13, 67,68）
萨拉·科兰托尼奥（No. 2,14,15,17-26,31,72,114）
阿莱西娅·康蒂诺（No. 52, 53, 54, 55, 56）
弗拉维奥·埃尼（No. 75）
保拉·弗拉耶加里（No. 45,78,97,98, 110, 111, 112）
S. 穆斯科（No. 1）
埃德维杰·帕泰拉（No. 43, 44）
米里亚·罗吉（No. 30,117,69,70,16,58-60,85-92）
雷纳托·塞巴斯蒂亚尼（No. 42,46-51, 57,76,77,79-84,93-96,99-109）
米雷拉·塞洛伦齐（No. 33-40, 73,74）
皮耶尔弗兰切斯科·达勒姆（No. 3-4-64-71-115）

ChinaMuseum International 有限公司

展览协调：埃莉奥诺拉·法莱塞迪

展览设计

主要设计机构：n!studio 工作室 - EaWe 项目公司
n!studio 工作室设计主创：盖特·迪杰苏、苏珊娜·费列尼
n!studio 工作室设计团队：弗兰切斯卡·科斯坦蒂尼、比安卡·戈梅利尼、费代里卡·罗马尼奥利；马泰奥·阿米卡雷拉（后期渲染）、焦万纳·狄西莫内（后期渲染）
平面设计及多媒体制作：
Archquadro 联合设计公司：劳拉 · 克罗尼亚莱、但丁 · 安东努奇

博物馆设计顾问

乔瓦尼·布赖恩

翻译

莱拉·米夫提亚

The Italian Committee

The Organizer of the Exhibition

Daniela Porro (Director of the National Roman Museum; the Special Superintendent of Archeology, Fine Arts, and Landscapes of Rome)

Fabio Pagano (Director of the Campi Flegrei Archaeological Park - Archaeological Museum of the Campi Flegrei in the Castle of Baia)

Simone Quilici (Director of the Appia Antica Archaeological Park - Antiquarium of Lucrezia Romana)

Flavio Enei (Director of the Santa Marinella Civic Museum - Museum of the Ancient Sea and Navigation)

Curators

Archeological section: Rita Auriemma, Renato Sebastiani, Mirella Serlorenzi, Pierfrancesco Talamo

Numismatics section: Gabriella Angeli Bufalini

The Exhibition Team

Directorate General of Museums: Antonio Lampis, Antonio Tarasco, Alessandra Gobbi

National Roman Museum:

Conservation (M. Angelini, G. Bandini, S. Borghini, F. Cozzolino, D. Papetti, I. Rapinesi, L. Ruggeri, G. Severini);

Registrars Office (M. Avino, G. De Angelis, M. Roghi);

Photography (A. Pergola, R. D'Agostino, L. Mandato)

Graphic reconstruction of Pietra Papa (Simone Boni)

Special Superintendence of Rome:

Conservation (M. Milazzi),

Safeguarding of Heritage Office (P. Fraiegari)

MiBAC – Villa Adriana and Villa d'Este: Lucilla D'Alessandro

Curator Committee:

National Roman Museum: Daniela Porro art historian, Gabriella Angeli Bufalini numismatic, Sara Colantonio archaeologist, Mirella Serlorenzi archaeologist

Special Superintendence of Rome: Francesco Prosperetti architect, Renato Sebastiani archaeologist

Managers of Exhibitions Office:

National Roman Museum: Sara Colantonio

Special Superintendence of Rome: Tiziana Ceccarini archaeologist

Authors of Catalogue Texts

Gabriella Angeli Bufalini

Rita Auriemma

Simone Boccardi

Sara Colantonio

K. Mannino

Paola Miniero

Renato Sebastiani

Mirella Serlorenzi

Pierfrancesco Talamo

Authors of Object Descriptions

Simone Boccardi (descriptions nos.118-162)

Antonella Bonini (descriptions nos. 10)

Claudio Borgognoni (descriptions nos. 11,66,113,116)

Carlotta Caruso (descriptions nos. 13, 67,68)

Sara Colantonio (descriptions nos. 2,14,15,17-26,31,72,114)

Alessia Contino (descriptions nos. 52, 53, 54, 55, 56)

Flavio Enei (descriptions nos. 75)

Paola Fraiegari (descriptions nos. 45,78,97,98, 110, 111, 112)

S. Musco (descriptions nos. 1)

Edvige Patella (descriptions nos. 43, 44)

Miria Roghi (descriptions nos. 30,117,69,70,16,58-60,85-92)

Renato Sebastiani (descriptions nos. 42,46-51, 57,76,77,79-84,93-96,99-109)

Mirella Serlorenzi (descriptions nos. 33-40, 73,74)

Pierfrancesco Talamo (descriptions nos. 3, 4, 64, 71, 115)

ChinaMuseum International S.r.l.

Exhibition coordination: Eleonora Falesiedi

Project Design:

Main contractor of project design: n!studio ASIA – EaWe Project

n!studio ASIA Main Project design: Gaetano di Gesu architect, Susanna Ferrini architect

n!Studio Asia Project design Team: Francesca Costantini architect, Bianca Gommellini architect, Federica Romagnoli architect

Render: Matteo Amicarella architect, Giovanna de Simone architect

Graphic And Multimedia Project:

Achquadro Associates: Laura Crognale architect, Dante Antonucci architect, project design team Archquadro

Museographic Consultant:

Giovanni Bulian architect

Translations:

Leila Myftija

目录 Contents

序言

PREFACE

序一

我很荣幸为“向海而生：古罗马海港的传说”展览图录作序。在意大利共和国与中华人民共和国的支持下成立的中意文化合作机制框架下，该展览由罗马国家博物馆与中国博物馆协会合作组织。展览依次在宁波、海南等地举办，讲述罗马与海洋之间的内在联系，彰显罗马在地中海（即拉丁语“我们的海”）上建立起的帝国的强大力量。

这是一个由罗马国家博物馆策划的科学质量与文化高度齐具的精良展览项目，所选文物涵盖绘画、马赛克、雕塑、青铜作品，反映了古代世界日常生活的方方面面。

特别值得注意的是在内米发现的卡利古拉船舶中的青铜器，以及皮耶特拉 - 帕帕别墅的装饰场景复原。该建筑复原坐落于台伯河岸的，专为此次展览而作，之后将在罗马展出。它从文化层面进一步证明了这些创举是如何惠及包括文化交流在内的众多领域的。

罗马国家博物馆马西莫宫钱币收藏中的一组 45 枚硬币意义非凡，因为它们体现了这些经典钱币收藏的价值。这部分馆藏见证了在地中海这个多元文化的摇篮里、在这个文化冲突与交流并存的舞台上所发生的近代和过去的故事。

展览最后一部分以一种激发想象的叙述方式，通过探索发现、科学方法和新的深度，向观众介绍了海洋考古学，或更准确的说法——水下考古学。

衷心感谢罗马国家博物馆馆长达尼埃拉 · 波罗，策展人丽塔 · 奥列玛、雷纳托 · 塞巴斯蒂亚尼、米雷拉 · 塞洛伦齐和加布里埃拉 · 安杰利 · 布法利尼，以及博物馆工作人员，感谢他们对此展览的无私奉献。它无疑是庆祝意中建交五十周年背景下最精彩的一页篇章。

乔瓦尼 · 帕内比安科

意大利文化遗产与活动部秘书长

PREFACE I

I am very pleased to introduce the catalogue for the "Portus - The sea of the ancient Romans" Exhibition organized by the National Roman Museum in the framework of the Italy-China Cultural Forum, established under the patronage of the Italian Republic and the People's Republic of China, and in collaboration with the *Chinese Museums Association*. The exhibition, first displayed in Ningbo, then in Hainan and, finally, in Shanghai, narrates the intrinsic relationship between Rome and the sea, bringing to light the magnitude of the great power on which it built its Empire: the Mediterranean, *mare nostrum*.

The National Roman Museum has created an exquisite project with a high scientific and cultural profile, selecting archeological materials that reflect the importance of pictorial, mosaic, sculptural, and bronze productions, which evoke aspects of daily life in the ancient world.

Of particular significance are the bronze artifacts originating from Caligula's ships discovered in Lake Nemi, or the reconstruction of a decorated room from the Pietra Papa complex, set on the suggestive bank of the Tiber River. This reconstruction, created especially for the exhibition, will subsequently be presented in Rome, further expanding the cultural proposal and proving how these initiatives are profitable, not only in terms of cultural exchanges.

A group of 45 coins from the "*Medagliere*" of Palazzo Massimo, National Roman Museum, are of extraordinary interest, since they further enhance the formidable numismatic collection. A testimony of recent and past stories of a Mediterranean that was the cradle of polymorphic civilizations, and a theatre of conflicts and exchanges between populations.

The final section of the exhibition focuses on *marine archeology*, namely, *underwatcr archcology*, through the suggestive narration of discoveries, scientific methodologies, and new frontiers in the deep sea.

I would like to give a heartfelt thank you to Daniela Porro, Director of the National Roman Museum, to the curators, Rita Auriemma, Renato Sebastiani, Mirella Serlorenzi, and Gabriella Bufalini Angeli, and to the museum staff for their profuse commitment in creating this project, which certainly constitutes one of the most interesting moments in the context of the fifty-year celebration of the bilateral relations between Italy and China.

Giovanni Panebianco

Secretary General of the Ministry of Cultural Heritage and Activities

序二

提到古罗马，大多数人能想象到的是历史课本里辉煌璀璨的罗马文明，或者是汉丝绸之路西边的终点罗马帝国。但真实的古罗马到底是什么样？其文明创建的基础是什么？其强大的实力来自哪里？这些问题的答案对于东方古国的我们，鲜有人清楚地知道。古罗马只是存在于国人心中的一个传说，一些存在于文学、影视、绘画作品里的碎片。

为了让观众直观清晰并富有兴致地了解这个依托海洋和河流崛起的地中海帝国——罗马，我们自意大利罗马国家博物馆、罗马考古、艺术品和景观监管局、坎皮佛莱格瑞考古公园、阿皮亚古道考古公园、圣塞维拉航海博物馆 130 余件珍贵文物，合作举办“向海而生：古罗马海港的传说”特展。

2019 年是中华人民共和国成立 70 周年，也是中意建立全面战略伙伴关系 15 周年，明年还将迎来中意两国建交 50 周年。今年 3 月，国家主席习近平对意大利共和国进行了国事访问。访问期间，习近平主席指出，中意都是拥有灿烂文化的文明古国，两国关系有着深厚的历史积淀。双方要密切人文交流，加强文化、教育、影视、媒体等领域交流合作，筑牢民心相通工程。此次展览的策划和成功举办正是中意两国深化文化交流推广的硕果之一，更是以博物馆展览为载体，对“一带一路”倡议的积极响应。

“国际港口名城，东方文明之都”宁波被称为“海丝活化石”，宁波中国港口博物馆有幸成为此展览进入中国的第一站，我们深感荣幸。作为国内唯一研究、展示和收藏中国港口历史的国家级博物馆，我们希望通过对比两个文明古国的港口与城市，以史鉴今；我们也希望在有限的展期内，把古罗马的航海故事告诉给尽可能多的观众，以小见大地了解世界文明史。

我们与意大利的策展人和博物馆同行共同开展了深入细致的工作，奉献给中国观众一个充满知识而又生动有趣的展览。展览叙述的主线是一番虚拟水上之旅。旅程沿台伯河水道行进，穿梭于罗马的各大港口之间，从大海之中到位于城市中心的提贝里诺港，观众如同安坐在船中观看风景一般欣赏展览。展览囊括了许多重要的文物和让人如临其境的数字化重现，观众身处其中，能真切地感受到古罗马人的理想与信仰、政治与生活、文化与技术。

摊开古代丝绸之路的地图，它的一端是东方都城长安，另一端是罗马帝国。在倡导“一带一路”建设的今日，这份长达 2 000 余年的羁绊弥足珍贵。罗马文明基于海洋而诞生、繁荣，给今天留下了一笔重要而珍贵的海洋文化遗产。此次展览是一次人类文化跨文明交流共享的盛宴，我们将继续相互学习、对比、合作，共同守望人类文明的过去和未来。

冯毅

宁波中国港口博物馆馆长

PREFACE II

When talking about ancient Rome, most people can recall the splendid Roman civilization presented in the history textbook and think of the Roman Empire, western end of the Silk Road. But what was the real ancient Rome like? What was the basis of the creation of its civilization? Where did its strong power come from? For us from the ancient civilization of the East, the answers to these questions are rarely well known. Ancient Rome is just a legend living in the mind of Chinese people, or some fragments existing in literature, films and paintings. In order to help the audience to understand Rome, the Mediterranean Empire rising from the oceans and the rivers, in a clear and interesting way, we organize this special exhibition "Portus - The sea of the ancient Romans" with the cooperation and over 130 precious cultural relics of the National Roman Museum,Special Superintendent of Archeology, Fine Arts, and Landscapes of Rome,Campi Flegrei Archaeological Park - Archaeological Museum of the Campi Flegrei in the Castle of Baia, Appia Antica Archaeological Park – Antiquarium of Lucrezia Romana, and Santa Marinella Civic Museum - Museum of the Ancient Sea and Navigation.

2019 marks the 70th anniversary of the founding of the People's Republic of China as well as the 15th anniversary of the establishment of a comprehensive strategic partnership between China and Italy. The two countries will also celebrate the 50th anniversary of their diplomatic relations next year. In the past March, during the state visit to the Republic of Italy, President Xi Jinping pointed out that both China and Italy are ancient civilizations with splendid culture, and Sino-Italian relations have a profound historical foundation. Both sides should boost people-to-people and cultural exchanges, and enhance exchanges and cooperation in such fields as culture, education, film and television and media, so as to consolidate the popular support for friendship between the two peoples. The planning and successful organization of this exhibition is one of the fruits of China and Italy's deepening cultural exchange and promotion, and also a positive response to the "One Belt, One Road" initiative through a museum exhibition as its carrier.

"International Port City, Capital of Eastern Civilization", Ningbo is known as the "living fossil" of the Maritime Silk Road. It is a great honor for China Port Museum in Ningbo to be the first venue of China to hold this exhibition. As the only national museum of China that studies, displays and collects the history of Chinese ports, we hope to compare the relationship between ports and cities of the two ancient civilizations, to make the history an experience for today; we also hope to tell the navigation story of ancient Rome to as many visitors as possible during the limited exhibition period, guiding them to a discovery of the history of world civilization through this exhibition.

In order to present to Chinese audience an exhibition with rich knowledge and full of interest, we have carried out intensive and meticulous work with Italian curators and museum colleagues. The main line of the storytelling of this exhibition is a virtual water tour. The journey goes along the Tiber waterway, passing through the major ports of Rome, from the sea to the port of Tiberino in the center of the city. When seeing the exhibition, the audience feel like sitting in the boat and enjoying the scenery. With many important cultural relics and the digital reproduction as vivid as the real scene, the audience here can genuinely perceive the ideals and the beliefs, the politics and the life, the culture and the technology of the ancient Romans.

Unfolding the map of the ancient Silk Road, we see the eastern capital of Chang'an at one end, and the Roman Empire at the other end. Today, in the context of the Belt and Road Initiative, this 2,000-year-old relation is especially precious. The birth and the prosperity of Roman civilization was based on the ocean, which left for today an important and precious marine cultural heritage. This exhibition is a feast of cross-civilization communication and sharing of human culture. With the continuing mutual learning, comparison and cooperation between us, we witness together the past and the future of human civilization.

Feng Yi
Director of China Port Museum

序三

2000 多年前，分处亚欧大陆东、西两端的秦汉帝国与罗马帝国交相辉映，对世界历史进程产生了深远影响。中国史籍称古罗马“其人民皆长大平正，有类中国，故谓之大秦”，而古罗马则通过来自东方的丝绸认识中国，称中国为“塞里斯”（Seres），意为丝国。

在当时的历史条件下，虽然双方相隔万里，商品贸易主要通过中亚、西亚地区国家作为中转点，但双方都曾试图与对方建立直接交流。《后汉书 · 西域传》记载：“和帝永元九年（公元 97 年），都护班超遣甘英使大秦。”汉使甘英途经条支、安息诸国抵达波斯湾，因渡海困难而折返，未能前往古罗马。“（大秦）与安息、天竺交市于海中，利有十倍……其王常欲通使于汉，而安息欲以汉缯彩与之交市，故遮阂不得自达。”直言古罗马意欲绕过安息、天竺等贸易中介，探索通往东方的海上通道，与中国进行直接贸易。“至桓帝延熹九年（公元 166 年），大秦王安敦遣使自日南徼外献象牙、犀角、玳瑁，始乃一通焉。”尽管学界对此使团的性质一直纠缠不清，但两国此时已有贸易往来，是不争的事实。

成书于公元 1 世纪末的《厄立特里亚海航行记》记录了希腊—罗马船队经红海、阿拉伯海到印度诸港的海上航线。同一时期的《汉书 · 地理志》记载了自徐闻、合浦等南海港口经中南半岛、南洋群岛到印度半岛东南海岸的黄支国、已程不国的海上航线。中国人和罗马人在印度、斯里兰卡地区出现了交集。稍晚的《魏略 · 西戎传》记载“大秦道既从海北陆通，又循海而南，与交趾七郡外夷比”，形象地描述了从大秦国到中国的两条路线：一条是沿陆路向东；另一条走海路，沿着红海，穿过亚丁湾及印度洋，抵达南海周边的“交趾七郡”。三国时期，一位名叫秦论的大秦商人即循此路来到建业，并与孙权进行了深入交流。“权问论方土风俗，论具以事对”。

古罗马从公元前 8 世纪在意大利半岛中部兴起，历罗马王政时代、罗马共和国，于公元前 1 世纪前后扩张成为横跨欧洲、亚洲、非洲的罗马帝国。它凭借自身实力发展海上贸易，建造技术先进的商船，发现并利用季风规律进行航海，使这些商船一度遍及地中海、黑海、红海、阿拉伯海，甚至远航至南海地区。通过繁荣的海上贸易，来自世界各地的物产源源不断地输往罗马。《后汉书 · 西域传》记载：“（大秦）土多金银奇宝，有夜光璧、明月珠、骇鸡犀、珊瑚、虎魄、琉璃、琅玕、朱丹、青碧。刺金缕绣，织成金缕罽、杂色绫。作黄金涂、火浣布。又有细布，或言水羊毳，野蚕茧所作也。合会诸香，煎其汁以为苏合。凡外国诸珍异皆出焉。”其中有产自埃及、叙利亚等地的琉璃（玻璃），开采自地中海的珊瑚，来自波罗的海沿岸的虎魄（琥珀），来自阿富汗的青金石，来自叙利亚的刺金缕绣，以及来自阿拉伯、印度地区的香料等。

中国（海南）南海博物馆按照中央有关指示精神，紧扣“一带一路”重大倡议，精准定位，重点做好文物研究展览、国际交流合作、水下文物保护等方面工作，积极打造“21 世纪海上丝绸之路”文化交流的重要平台。此次我们联合宁波中国港口博物馆引进意大利五家文博机构的 130 余件文物，举办“向海而生：古罗马海港的传说”特展，穿越历史长河，跨越浩瀚大海，不仅在于使参观者发思古之幽情，加深对古罗马航海文明历史价值的认识，而且在于启发我们面向世界，架起友谊的桥梁，努力开展文明间的交流和对话，发挥文博交流重要阵地作用，为中外文化交流与发展贡献力量。

辛礼学

中国（海南）南海博物馆书记、副馆长

PREFACE III

Over 2,000 years ago, interactions between Qin & Han dynasties at the eastern end of the Eurasia and the Roman Empire at the western end of the continent, not only brightened the civilization of each other, but also had a profound impact on the course of the world's history. Chinese historical records refer to ancient Rome as "Great Qin, whose people are tall and well-shaped like Chinese", while China, who came to be known by ancient Rome through eastern silk, was called "Seres", the country of silk.

Commodity trade between the two countries, thousands of miles apart, was achieved, under the conditions of that time, mainly through Central Asian and Western Asian countries as transit points. But both sides have tried to establish direct communication with each other. As recorded in *the Book of the Later Han - Treatise on the Western Regions*, "in the 9th year of Yongyuan (97 A.D.) during the reign of Emperor He, Protector General Ban Chao sent Gan Ying to the Great Qin." Gan Ying the envoy of Han dynasty, who probed as far as the Persian Gulf, through Seleucid Empire and Parthian Empire, discontinued his trip because of the difficulties in crossing the ocean and failed to reach ancient Rome. "(The Great Qin) trades with Parthia and Northwest India by sea, with a profit margin of ten times...The king of the country always wanted to send envoys to Han, but Parthia, wishing to control the trade in multi-colored Chinese silks, blocked the route." This reveals the fact that ancient Rome intended to bypass the intermediaries, such as Parthia and Northwest India, to explore the sea route to the East and to trade with China in a direct way. "In the 9th year of Yanxi (166 A.D.) during the reign of Emperor Huan, the envoy of the Emperor Antoninus passed the Vietnam sea to offer ivory, rhinoceros horn and hawksbill turtle shell, which marked the first communication between China and Europe". Although the academic circles still haven't figured out the nature of the mission, it is an indisputable fact that the two countries have already built trade relations at that time.

The Periplus of the Erythraean Sea, finished at the end of the 1st century A.D., recorded the sea routes of Greek-Roman fleets through the Red Sea and the Arabian Sea to reach the Indian ports. Of the same period, *the Book of Han - Treatise on Geography* recorded the sea routes from the South China Sea ports, such as Xuwen and Hepu, through the Indochinese Peninsula and the South Pacific Mandate, to Kanchipuram and Sri Lanka on the southeast coast of the Indian Peninsula. Chinese and Romans thus encountered in India and Sri Lanka. Later, *Weilüe - Xirong Biography* recorded that "compared to the seven prefectures of Jiao Zhi, the Great Qin can be reached both by land from the north and by sea from south". It vividly depicts the two routes from the Great Qin to China. One is eastward along the land, the other is along the Red Sea, through the Gulf of Aden and the Indian Ocean, to the "seven prefectures of Jiao Zhi" in the vicinity of the South China Sea. During the Three Kingdoms period, a Great Qin merchant named Qin Lun came to Jianye following this road and had a profound exchange with Sun Quan. "Sun Quan asked Qin Lun about customs in the Great Qin, Qin Lun responded with concrete examples".

Ancient Rome rose from the middle of the Italian Peninsula in the 8th century BC. After Roman Kingdom and the Roman Republic, it expanded into Roman Empire across Europe, Asia and Africa around the 1st century BC. It developed its maritime trade and built merchant ships with advanced technology, discovered and made use of the laws of the monsoon in the navigation, allowing the merchant ships spread to the Mediterranean Sea, the Black Sea, the Red Sea, the Arabian Sea and even to the South China Sea. Through prosperous maritime trade, products from all over the world were continuously exported to Rome. *The Book of the Later Han - Treatise on the Western Regions* recorded that "the ancient Rome is full of priceless treasures, including glowing jade, pearl, rhinoceros, coral, amber, colored glaze, white jade, ruby, sapphire. Cloth sewn with gold thread making colorful damask silk. Asbestos cloth covered with gold. Fine cloth made by natural silkworm cocoon. Storax made of juice of a mixture of perfume. All kinds of exotic treasures come from this place". Among them there are colored glaze (glass) from Egypt, Syria and other countries, corals from the Mediterranean Sea, amber from the Baltic coast, lapis lazuli from Afghanistan, gold embroideries from Syria, and spices from Arabia and India.

In accordance with the spirit of the relevant directives of the central government, and closely following the important initiative of "One Belt, One Road", China (Hainan) Museum of the South China Sea orientates itself precisely, focuses on the research and the display of cultural relics, on the international communication and cooperation, on the underwater preservation and other relevant work, to create actively a trans-cultural platform of "the 21st Century Maritime Silk Road". This time, together with China Port Museum, we introduce over 130 pieces of cultural relics from five Italian museums or cultural institutions for the special exhibition entitled "Portus - The sea of the ancient Romans". Crossing the long history and the vast ocean, this exhibition is not only to evoke deep emotions in the visitors towards the history, or to deepen their understanding of the historical value of ancient Roman maritime civilization, but also to inspire us to see the world, to build a bridge of friendship, to carry out trans-civilizational exchanges and dialogues, to enhance the role played by museums and cultural institutions in the cultural communication, and to make contributions to cultural exchange and development between China and the world.

Xin Lixue

Secretary and deputy director of China (Hainan) Museum of the South China Sea

序四

在意大利共和国和中华人民共和国政府的支持下，中意文化合作机制于 2016 年成立，目标是建立一个促进文化合作的平台，以增进两国文明历史的相互了解为重点，并通过临时展览促进博物馆之间的交流。

在这一重要背景下，罗马国家博物馆为能与中国博物馆合作举办“向海而生：古罗马海港的传说”展览感到荣幸并充满动力。作为馆长，我意识到这一伟大项目的重要性，罗马国家博物馆希望通过提供兼具历史和艺术价值的大量文物，为此展览慷慨献力。

我们两国地理距离虽远，但古老文明相近。将两国人民联系起来，是促进两国现代文化对比和交流的一条宝贵渠道。

此次将我们联系起来的主题是海洋。它的回响、无限、神圣，从古至今影响着无数诗人和艺术家。海洋无边无际，讲述着未知的世界、未知的人们、冒险的旅程，以及试图超越人类想象的发现。

此次展览所展出文物的特点在于其在绘画、马赛克、雕塑、青铜和日常艺术品制作方面突出的重要性，其中一部分是首次赴海外展览。

展览中一件非常重要的展品是尤利西斯大幅马赛克，它象征着受众神责难、游荡于地中海、克服无数危险回归家乡的希腊英雄。马赛克描绘的是神话中尤利西斯遇上塞壬那一刻发生的故事。这些迷人而邪恶的生物，长着鸟身或鱼身和美女面庞，以欺骗性的歌声迷惑水手，使他们陷入超现实的幻境，导致船只失控，发生海难，最终致死。

带来观展过程中一个重要时刻的，是在罗马绘画艺术史上有极其重要意义的一件物品——根据罗马城外台伯河边皮耶特拉 - 帕帕豪华别墅完整绘制的、对两个地下房间的场景复原，这是它们首次公开展出。最初这两个房间覆盖着一个可从上层浴室进入的桶形拱顶天花板，其建成年代约为公元 2 世纪中叶。

在拱顶蓝绿色的背景上，可以看到各种鱼在游弋，在彩绘墙壁上，画着节日船只驶过台伯河。这些绘画展示了一系列精心创作的、使画面更生动更新颖的图案。这些古代绘画中汇集了静物、神话、日常生活场景等不同类型的元素。

来自内米船舶上的青铜器同样具有很高的艺术水平。这是一种独特的游船，是真正的漂浮在水上的宫殿，由卡利古拉皇帝以奢华的东方住宅为蓝本建造。这两艘巨大船舶，一艘长 71 米、宽 20 米，另一艘长 75 米、宽 29 米，作为他在距罗马约 30 公里内米湖边的豪华住宅的附属建筑。

两端有青铜狮头或狼头的横梁装饰，来自第一艘船。四个船舵的横梁手柄装饰，来自第二艘船。

45 枚高质量、高价值的硬币见证了在地中海这个多文明摇篮中，在人与物交汇的剧场里，昨天和今天上演的故事：物品虽小，却渗透于每个生活角落，触及各个社会阶层，跨越各种边界，快速传达理念和文化。

最后，同样具有极高考古意义的，是那些与日常生活息息相关的海洋主题艺术品（青铜、油灯、石棺等），它们见证了海洋对罗马人的重要性。这些自然主义和神话性质的海洋主题，甚至是对亡者最后旅程的隐喻，都给予艺术家和工匠诸多启发。

海洋迷人和矛盾的性质以各式各样的体验形式在展览中得以有效呈现，仿佛邀请观众踏上一次旅程。

我们的机构之间的合作有效而愉快，也正是这种合作，造就了今天这个美好的展览，希望将来彼此的合作能够更进一步，让我们可以在同样有效和有趣的文化之旅上扬帆远航。

达尼埃拉 · 波罗

罗马国家博物馆馆长，罗马考古、艺术品和景观监管局局长

PREFACE IV

The Italy-China Cultural Forum, established under the patronage of the Italian Republic and the People's Republic of China in 2016, has the objective of creating a platform to promote collaborations in the cultural sector, with particular focus on the reciprocal knowledge of each civilization and the history of both countries, as well as to promote exchanges between museums through temporary exhibitions.

Following this important institutional agreement, the National Roman Museum is greatly satisfied for the collaboration established with the Chinese museums that will be hosting the "Portus - The sea of the ancient Romans" Exhibition. As director of the Museum, and acknowledging the importance of this ambitious project, the National Roman Museum wanted to generously collaborate by providing numerous artifacts of very high historical and artistic value.

To be able to compare populations that are geographically distant from one another, yet close in many cultural aspects of their ancient civilizations, represents a privileged channel for promoting a dialogue and an exchange between the modern cultures of our countries.

On this occasion, the unifying theme is represented by the sea: a resounding, infinite, divine, element that has influenced poets and artists since the beginning of time. The endless expanses of the sea tells of unknown worlds and people, adventurous journeys, and discoveries that try to surpass the imagination of man.

The artifacts displayed in the exhibition are characterized by their importance with regard to their pictorial, mosaic, sculptural, and bronze productions, as well as through objects used in daily life, some of which sailed across the waters of the sea for the very first time.

Of remarkable importance is the large mosaic of Ulysses, representing the Greek hero who was condemned by the gods to wander the Mediterranean Sea, overcoming numerous perils and adventures before returning home. The mosaic depicts an important moment in the narration of the myth, when Ulysses meets the Sirens - fascinating creatures with the body of a bird or fish and with the beautiful face of a woman. These evil monsters enticed sailors with their deceptive songs, taking them to a surreal and fantastical dimension, where they would lose control of their ships, run aground, and meet their inevitable death.

A core part of the exhibition is represented by an object of exceptional importance in pictorial Roman art: the reconstruction of two completely painted underground rooms from the luxurious villa of Pietra Papa - constructed just outside Rome along the Tiber River - will be presented to the public for the very first time. The two rooms were originally covered with a barrel vault ceiling, with access from the rooms containing the thermal baths on the upper level, and probably date back to approximately mid-2nd century A.D.

A variety of swimming fish were depicted on the green-blue background of the vault along with festive ships sailing on the waters of the Tiber. These paintings represent a summa of the figurative repertoire that was re-elaborated to give life to a vivid and original representation. Different genres such as still-lifes, mythological repertoires, and scenes from daily life all come together in these ancient paintings.

The bronzes originating from the Nemi ships are of a very high artistic level. The ships were a unique example of ceremonial vessels. Veritable floating palaces, created by Emperor Caligula, in the image of luxurious oriental abodes. The ships he built were two - the first (prima nave) measured 71 meters in length and 20 meters in width, while the second (seconda nave) measured 75 meters in length and 29 in width, and they were used as a sort of guesthouse for the Emperor's lavish imperial residence on Lake Nemi, located about 30 kilometers from Rome.

The decorations of the wooden beams, which were crowned with bronze heads of lions and wolves, originate from the first ship, while the hands that decorated the beams near the four rudders were part of the second ship.

A group of 45 coins of extraordinary quality and interest are proof of recent and past stories of a Mediterranean that was the cradle of many civilizations, and a theatre of conflicts and exchanges not only among populations but also of goods: small objects capable of penetrating into every earthly and social status, crossing borders and rapidly conveying ideas and cultures.

And, finally, the artifacts related to daily life (bronzes, oil lamps, sarcophagi, and so on), are also of great archeological importance. These were created following a marine theme, which demonstrates how important the sea was to the Romans. Artists and craftsmen were inspired by marine subjects, of both naturalistic and mythological nature, and even used them as a metaphor for the last journey of the deceased.

The fascinating and ambivalent nature of the sea, therefore, travels across all different forms of life experiences, efficiently represented throughout the exhibition, which was conceived as the allegory of a journey that visitors are invited to take.

I truly hope that the fruitful and delightful collaboration between our institutions, here to present and speak of this beautiful exhibition, may further grow in the future, allowing us to navigate in equally valid and interesting common cultural endeavours.

Daniela Porro

Director of the National Roman Museum

展览

EXHIBITION

背景介绍（代前言）

INTRODUCTION TO THE EXHIBITION

本展览讲述了罗马与海洋之间的紧密关系：一个依托海洋和河流而崛起的地中海帝国。展览共分为五个部分，向观众展示了变幻莫测的水上景观：从海上生命和海洋神话传说（第一单元），到在罗马地缘政治历史上具有举足轻重作用的半岛沿岸码头以及陆上航线和水路间的重要港口，其中包括内陆港口（第二单元）。展览内容丰富，包罗万象。

展览叙述的主线是一番理想的、虚拟的、充满乐趣的水上之旅。旅程沿台伯河水道轴线行进，囊括了克劳迪乌斯港口和图拉真港口等海洋港口及位于城市中心的提贝里诺港（罗马历史最为悠久的港口）等各大港口。而我们就宛如安坐在一艘从河岸上牵引前行的船（河驳船）上，切身体验。

大河上游，游客可通过实体展示和数字技术欣赏河畔教皇皮耶特拉宫殿的详细重建过程。维苏威地区的城市中心和港口与罗马形成鲜明对比，三维重建技术和考古发现让我们能更深入地认识这里蜚声在外的古迹：著名的波佐利纪念碑、巴亚温泉浴场、艾比达菲奥海岬的皇宫和狄俄尼索斯神像，等等。

当然，展览主角当属船舶，正如意大利小说家兼记者迪诺·布扎蒂描述“安德烈亚·多里亚”号时所写：“……一个国家最完美的融合之一，就是其最高贵品质的集中体现，是不断的探索精神，这是我们真正的文明，是最令人信服的见证之一……”（第三单元）。本部分通过铭文、肖像和纪念物等对军船进行了展示，尤其介绍了内米湖卡利古拉战

The narration proposed through the exhibition tells of the intense relationship between Rome and the sea: the maritime aspect of the great power that built its Mediterranean Empire along the sea and along rivers. The 5 sections of the exhibition present visitors with several variations of these water landscapes, starting from the life and mythography of the sea (Section 1) to the description of the waterfronts of the peninsula and of those protagonists of the geopolitical history of Rome that were its ports: junctions between land routes and waterways, also inland (Section 2).

One main narrative focal point is the story of an ideal, virtual, and virtuous journey along the waterway axis of the Tiber river, among the ports of Rome, starting from the sea (the Ports of Claudius and Trajan) and reaching the Portus Tiberinus (the earliest port in Rome) in the heart of the city, as if we were aboard a navis caudicaria (river barge) towed from the banks.

In ascending the great river, visitors will be able to enjoy a detailed reconstruction - both physical and digital - of the Villa Papa Pietra, set in the suggestive wings of the river bank.The city centers and ports of the Vesuvian area will act as a counterattraction to Rome - Pozzuoli, with its famous monuments, and Baia, with its thermal baths and the nymphaeum of Punta Epitaffio - thanks to 3D reconstructions and original findings, such as the statue of Dionysus in the nymphaeum.

A major role is reserved to ships. Dino Buzzati (Italian novelist and journalist) once wrote when speaking of the Andrea Doria: "...one of the most perfect confluences of a country, a synthesis of its most noble qualities, one of the most convincing testimonies of our true civilization..." (Section 3). Thanks to epigraphs, iconographic images, and monuments, the exhibition puts emphasis on military ships, several highly representative elements of the ships of Caligula from Lake Nemi, and merchant ships, also narrating life aboard these

船和商船一些极具代表性的元素，同时还讲述了船员在战船上的生活。展览展示了船舶从地中海各地运输的各种货物，从基本必需品到奢侈品一应俱全（第四单元）。本部分展示了不寻常的路线、优惠的价格、丰厚的回报、大胆的商业运作、精湛的工艺和艺术技巧，并通过罗马国家博物馆收藏的各类硬币和奖章，讲述了地中海航行及许多商业、军事、“民间”传说和神话故事。这一枚枚小小的圆形金属承载着历史的记忆影像，是文明的宝贵见证，在过去与现在的历史交替中见证了同一个主题：海洋。在教皇统治时期，奇维塔韦基亚港口、安齐奥港口和特拉奇纳港口的新设施，以及作为海洋主角的船舶，是权力和财富的象征，将游客带入了战争与和平时期的各种场景——与罗马硬币上描绘的克劳迪乌斯和图拉真的古老码头正相呼应。通过三维重建和多媒体装置，将丰富的图像结构作为钱币展示的背景，带领游客穿越地中海，开启一段富有启发意义的历史旅程。

展览的最后一部分（第五单元）讲述了水下考古情况。此外，展览通过播放意大利广播电视公司（RAI）电视档案馆的一系列视频和电影，介绍了科学研究方法和深海前沿技术。

R. 奥列玛

vessels. The exhibition illustrates the variety of goods - from basic necessities to luxury goods - that were transported in the holds of ships from one point to another of the Mediterranean (Section 4). The displays are extraordinary stills of routes, of preferential circuits, of lucrative investments, of daring trade transactions, and of excellent artisanal and artistic skills, and dedicated to navigation in the Mediterranean and to its multiple trade, military, “civilian”, and mythological aspects, displaying a selection of coins and medals from the very rich numismatic collection of the Medagliere in the National Roman Museum. Images of memories impressed in that small, round piece of metal. Precious testimonies of a civilization where past and present alternated, in pursuit of a single leitmotiv: the sea. During the time of the papacy, the new structures of the ports of Civitavecchia, Anzio, and Terracina, as well as ships - the true protagonists of the sea, symbols of power and wealth, able to evoke tales of war and peaceful scenarios of peace - echoed the ancient Ports of Claudius and Trajan depicted on Roman coins. A rich iconographic structure poses as a background for the numismatic images, emphasized by 3D reconstructions and by multimedia installations that will take visitors on a suggestive journey into the past, through the waters of the Mediterranean.

The final part of the exhibition (Section 5) recounts underwater archeology. Discoveries, but also the methodology of scientific research and new frontiers of the deep sea, with a series of videos and films from the RAI television archives.

R. Auriemma

UNIT 1

THE CHARM OF THE SEA

LIFE AND MYTH

第一单元

海洋的魅力

生命与神话

回声、无限、神圣——在古人的诗歌创作中，海洋的定义常常伴随着这些符号。海是神圣的生命之源，水的流动和变化的元素中映射着女性的繁殖力：维纳斯，爱的女神和自然的生命力量，从波涛汹涌的大海中诞生。在“荷马史诗”所描述的大海里，白胡子的海神被海怪缠绕，代表了环绕地球的海洋，地球上所有的水都是由他创造的，这是男性具有创造力的一种表现。海洋也是神圣的，它是神的居所，是尼普顿的王国。海神用他的三叉戟可以造成致命的风暴。新娘安菲特里忒·尼普顿在一群活泼的海神（提阿索斯）的陪伴下穿过广阔的海洋：海神特里同长着鱼形身体，在涅柔斯的五十个骑着海鳗般生物（皮斯瑞克斯）的美丽女儿涅瑞伊得斯的环绕下乘风破浪；其中最著名的是泰提·阿喀琉斯的母亲和不幸被波吕斐摩斯所爱的加拉提。

无边无际的大海向我们诉说着未知的世界、未知的人，以及充满冒险和探索的旅程。尤利西斯的神话展现了人类跨越国界和对新知识的不断探索、离开和返回故土的艰辛旅程，以及赋予“大海所哺育的不屈不挠的想象力”以形状和具象的必要性。这里展示的黑白镶嵌图案代表了尤利西斯从特洛伊战争返回家园一路所遭遇的各种磨难中的一个片段。它描绘了尤利西斯和塞壬相遇的故事——塞壬是一种有着鸟或鱼的身体和美丽脸庞的怪物，这些怪物用美妙的歌声吸引水手，使他们忘却自己的职责，离开船舵、放下船桨，直到船只失事。镶嵌画描绘了这个神话传说中的一个场景，尤利西斯用蜡封住同伴们的耳朵，使他们不被蛊惑，并让他们把自己紧紧绑在桅杆上，倾听这美妙的歌声。

海洋是生命的摇篮，也是死亡的源泉：无法居住、充满危险，残酷的风暴会给航海家带来致

The echoing, infinite, divine sea. These are just some of the epithets that frequently accompany the definition of the sea in the poetic compositions of the ancients. The sea is divine, since it is a source of life. The fluid and changeable element of water contains in itself the fertilizing feminine element: Venus, goddess of love and the generating force of nature, wasborn from the foam of the rough sea; in Homer’s Oceanus, the great old bearded god of the waters, accompanied by sea monsters and identified as the sea that surrounds the earth, is the principle masculine creator who generated all the waters of the world. But the sea is divine also as a dwelling place for gods. It is the kingdom of Neptune, god of the sea who would upset it with the power of his trident, causing deadly storms. With his bride, Amphitrite, Neptune crossed the wide expanses of the sea accompanied by a lively marine procession (thiasos) of gods:Triton, with his fish-shaped body, traveled the waves surrounded by the fifty beautiful daughters of Nereo, the Nereids, riding eel-like animals (pistrixes); among the most famous are Thetis - mother of Achilles - and Galatea, who was unhappily loved by Polyphemus.

The endless expanses of the sea speak to us of unknown worlds and people, adventurous journeys and discoveries. The myth of Ulysses represents the idea of travel aimed at overcoming borders and new forms of knowledge, of departures and returns to dear places, of the need to give shape and tangibility to the indomitable fantasy that the sea fosters. The mosaic in white and black tesserae presented depicts one of the many difficulties to which the gods condemned Ulysses during his journey home from the Trojan war. The scene represents Ulysses and the Sirens, fascinating beings with the body of a bird or a fish, and with a beautiful woman’s face. These creatures would lure sailors with their deceptive songs, causing them to forget their duties, to leave their rudders and oars, until they became shipwrecked. The mosaic presents the scene of the myth in which Ulysses protects his shipmates by having them plug their ears with wax so that they would not become bewitched, while he asks to be tied to the mast of the ship, eager to listen to the prodigious song of the Sirens.

The sea as a source of life and of death, all in one: unlivable, dangerous, its fatal storms condemning voyages

尤利西斯与塞壬马赛克
公元2世纪—3世纪
大理石

命的海难。海洋的矛盾性尤其体现在能够引起航行危险的各种海洋怪物身上，特别是其中最可怕的海妖——可怕而贪婪的斯库拉，它专门袭击海上往来船只。斯库拉腰身以上为美女，腰身以下缠绕着一条由恶狗围成的腰环，腰环上的恶狗总是伸长脖子。连塞壬美妙的歌喉都是死亡和毁灭的先兆，更不用说那些凶猛的掠食者了，它们在古代频繁地破坏海上通行安全、掠夺财富。在狄俄尼索斯的冒险之旅中，他曾看到神在海盗船上蹒跚而行，后来变成了海豚。

海洋是神的家，也是各种商业活动的交通纽带，因此与财富和繁荣紧密相关。海洋的魅力和矛盾性

to mortal shipwrecks. The ambivalent nature of the sea is underlined by a whole series of monstrous creatures that, originally, would evoke the very dangers of navigation, especially in its most frightening and difficult courses. These included the terrifying and voracious Scylla - that would attack ships - depicted with a woman's head and bust on a fish-shaped body from which protruded the heads of dogs, as well as the Sirens with their very sweet songs, which were harbingers of death and destruction, not to mention the ferocious pirates who undermined the safety of sea traffic and their riches, so frequent in antiquity that one of Dionisius' adventures describes how the god stumbled upon a ship of pirates who were then transformed into dolphins.

The fascinating and ambivalent nature of the sea, home

在罗马艺术和工匠的作品中得到了充分的体现。在这个展区，展出的是日常生活用品，如油灯、喷泉元素、盘子和装饰性家具贴花，而创造上述展品的艺术家和工匠的灵感，来自于海洋主题：既有自然元素（鱼、贝壳、渔民、船只），也有神话元素（神灵、巨大的动物、海上游行的人物），甚至有隐喻逝者最后旅程的元素。这些展品上常见的元素是海豚，单独出现或与普蒂（裸体且有翅膀的孩子，作为丘比特的化身）结伴。海豚在古代是一种很受喜爱的动物，因为它能加快海船的航行速度，并与神话（总是出现在尼普顿和安菲特里忒的海洋游行中）、变形（海盗被酒神狄俄尼索斯变成海豚）和救援沉船（在神话中，遇险的年轻人被一群海豚救了出来）有各种各样的联系。同样值得注意的是，古人讲述的许多故事都涉及海豚对人类的友谊和忠诚，尤其是对儿童的忠诚。事实上，儿童经常被设计成骑在马背及其他动物背上的形象。

特别值得一提的是马赛克地板装饰，突出了海洋主题的审美，展示了海洋的魅力，与该区域的功能相得益彰。而且这些装饰的主题大多与水相关，与“马赛克故事中的海洋”部分的 MNR 地板马赛

to gods but also concretely linked to commercial activities and, therefore, to the wealth and prosperity that derived from them, finds ample space in Roman artistic and artisanal productions, where the marine repertoire is found in its multiple aspects. This section displays objects from daily life, such as oil lamps, fountain elements, plates and decorative furniture sconces, where artists and artisans were inspired by marine subjects, both naturalistic (fish, shells, fishermen, ships), as well as mythological (gods, monstrous creatures, and figures from marine processions), also as a metaphor for the last journey of the deceased (tn. The thiasus or thiasos in Greek is a congregation or a retinue that gathers to celebrate a god, or a procession of aquatic beings). A recurring theme was the dolphin, alone or with putti (naked, winged children - the personifications of the god Cupid). The dolphin was much loved in the ancient world because it evoked the speed of navigation and was widely connected to myths (always present in Neptune and Amphitrite's marine procession), to the theme of metamorphosis (pirates transformed into dolphins by the god Dionysus), and of rescues from shipwrecks. (In fact, in the myth of Airon, the young man was saved by dolphins). Noteworthy, finally, are the numerous stories reported by the ancients centered on the friendship and loyalty of dolphins towards men and, above all, children, often represented riding on the backs of dolphins.

The mosaic floor decorations deserve a special mention, where the aesthetic and evocative charm of the marine theme

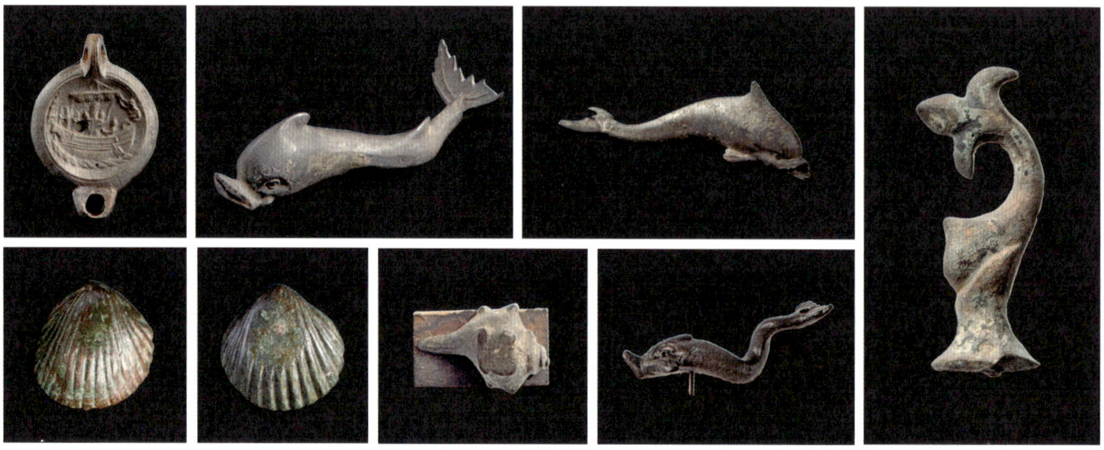

人鱼石棺立面
公元3世纪下半叶
大理石

克画主题类似。马赛克画地板从公元前 1 世纪开始在罗马世界传播开来，在铺设马赛克画地板之前，需要铺设好几个垫层。在意大利的不同地区发现了相同的图像主题，这表明图像和马赛克画作品都有参考模型。这里展示的诸多以海洋为主题的马赛克画，原本可能放置于温泉浴场的环境中，或是在公、私环境中与水相关联。因此，画作的艺术主题通常与这个地方的功能直接相关。在一幅以海洋为主题的马赛克画中，中心场景是涅瑞伊得斯躺在一头海牛的鱼状尾巴上，两侧是两名年幼的鱼人特里同（右边人物的尾巴已经不见了），还描绘有在海浪中嬉戏的一只章鱼和两条鱼。这幅绘有骑在海洋动物身上的维纳斯和涅瑞伊得斯的马赛克画，其四边环绕着装饰性元素；在水中还绘有海豚、海鳗、鲻鱼、章鱼和其他鱼类。维纳斯占据了中心场景，她是从大海中诞生的爱与美的女神，她的左手拨弄着头发。

conforms to the function of the place they were located - often linked to the presence of water - as is the case of the MNR floor mosaics presented in the section, "The Sea in the Stories of Mosaics." The mosaic floors, which required several preparatory layers before the tiles were set, became popular in the Roman world starting from the 1st century B.C. The presence of the same iconographic themes found in different places in Italy suggests that models of reference existed for both pictorial and mosaic works. Many of the mosaics with marine themes presented here can be collocated originally in thermal baths or connected to the presence of water, both in public and private contexts, so that the aesthetic appeal of the subject often directly refers to the function of the location. In the mosaic with a Marine Thiasos, the central scene is occupied by a Nereid resting on the fish-shaped tail of a sea bull . Two young tritons (the tail of the right figure was lost) stand on each side of the group, while an octopus and two fish are depicted among stylized sea waves. Along its edges, the mosaic with Venus and Nereids on marine animals has four promotes (tn. decorative elements with heads) of winds. The aquatic figures include dolphins, morays, mullets, octopuses, and fishes. All these creatures frame the central scene occupied

以海洋为主题的马赛克画

海洋主题的大型马赛克图像投影：维纳斯和涅瑞伊得斯的马赛克

海洋主题的大型马赛克图像投影；
海洋和鱼的马赛克

鱼类图谱
公元2世纪末—3世纪初
白色和彩色石灰石、橙色玻璃石、灰色大理石

俄刻阿诺斯——大洋河流之神，是两幅马赛克画作的主角。这两幅马赛克画描绘了长有胡须的神灵头像，四周围绕着海怪、长有鱼形尾巴的生物以及水生植物和波浪。

六种颜色鲜亮的鱼组成的小马赛克画是一种象征，带有微小的彩色镶嵌图案，并采用了复杂的表现形式，这是一种更为朴素的马赛克画地板的核心元素。根据其海洋动物的主题，以及画中所包含的丰富的食物元素，我们推断此作品的位置可能是在宴会厅。

S. 科兰托尼奥

by Venus - the goddess of love and beauty born from the foam of the sea - who is tousling her hair with her left hand.

Oceanus, god of the waters, is the protagonist of two mosaics in which the scene develops around the bearded head of the god surrounded by monsters and animals with fish-shaped tails, aquatic plants, and waves .

The small, colorful mosaic with six fish represents an emblem - a mosaic work with minute polychrome tesserae (tiles) in a complex representation - which was the central element of a mosaic floor that was more modest in quality . The theme of marine fauna and, therefore, of the richness and abundance of food, leads us to believe that the work might have been located in a banquet hall.

S. Colantonio

尤利西斯与塞壬马赛克

公元 2 世纪—3 世纪
大理石
高 420 厘米，宽 373 厘米
意大利罗马国家博物馆 - 戴克里先浴场，编号 519957

Mosaic with Ulysses and the Sirens
2nd - 3rd century A.D.
height 420 cm, width 373 cm
National Roman Museum, Baths of Diocletian Inv. 519957

帝国时代，道路边驿站里温暖的浴池多采用马赛克装饰。由于非法挖掘，部分马赛克被破坏了。植物图案装饰的边框环绕着由尤利西斯和塞壬构成的核心画面。图案中，英雄戴着颇具特色的圆锥形帽子，身靠主桅杆，风帆卷起，护卫队——三个同伴——分散在他周围。这艘海船是典型的货船（由船尾装饰中的火炬形状、圆形的龙骨以及大舵可以看出这一点）。唯一保留完好的塞壬形象位于尤利西斯的左边。她身着短上衣，弹着七弦竖琴。在她头上，有两行希腊铭文，是希腊题字 ERMIWNH（赫尔迈厄尼，希腊神话中墨涅拉俄斯与海伦之女、俄瑞斯忒斯之妻）。马赛克中还有一行铭文 LEONTIC（利昂蒂斯）在尤利西斯头部旁边。水手们的头上还有清晰可读的名字 FHLI（费利克斯）和 BIKTWR（比克特罗）；相同的名字 BIKTWR（比克特罗）出现在左边一位水手的头上。这些名字可能指驿站的所有者，更可能是指与所描绘场景相关的角色。马赛克下缘有三块带有几何棋盘装饰和拉丁文铭文的格子图案框架。它们被进行了相关处理，将马赛克向浴池方向延展。这样，进入其中的人便可以看到这些文字。在中央的格子图案框架中，有拉丁文题词，也许可以解释为：“将为你提供更多食品和财富（DOME PERRECIONE FECIS TIBI FAORE RENOBASTI NOBIS FORTUNA）以及给你更多（QUAE TIBI DABIT PLURIA）。”

鱼类图谱

公元 2 世纪末—公元 3 世纪初
白色和彩色石灰石，橙色玻璃石，灰色大理石
高 56.5 厘米，宽 52 厘米
重 30 千克
意大利罗马国家博物馆 - 马西莫宫，展品编号 1030

Mosaic with Fish

late-2nd - early-3rd century A.D.
height 56.5 cm, width 52 cm
weight 30 kilograms
National Roman Museum, Palazzo Massimo Inv. 1030

这件作品描绘了一个黑色边框中的六条鱼，分别是鳟鱼，黄花鱼和鲻鱼。鱼身那鲜艳的色彩在白色背景下分外突出。海洋中有多种色彩，因而画面中的其他色块可以解释为藻类或波浪。这件作品构成了一种特色——用精细的彩色马赛克将带有希腊传统风格的场景嵌入宽阔的地板中心。作品中海洋动物的主题表现得极为成功，这种主题寓意丰盛的食物，被广泛用于宴会厅的装饰。

宙斯 - 阿蒙头像浮雕石板

公元 2 世纪
大理石
高 64 厘米，宽 86 厘米，厚 14 厘米
坎皮佛莱格瑞考古公园 - 巴亚城堡中的坎皮佛莱格瑞考古博物馆，展品编号 317752

Bas-Relief Plate with Head of Zeus Amon

2nd century A.D.
height 64 cm, width 86 cm, thickness 14 cm
Phlegraean Fields Archeological Park - Archeological Museum of the Phlegraean Fields in the Castle of Baia Inv. 317752

宙斯 - 阿蒙头像浮雕石板，制作材质为普罗康尼西奥大理石，出土自波佐利策勒路。宙斯 - 阿蒙这位埃及神明有着人类和动物的双重特征：胡须和刚直的鬓毛，额头上有一根挂在公羊角上的带子；他的耳朵被置于画面中心位置——这与所有的透视规则相违背；两棵（现仅存一棵）果实累累的果树（丰饶角）环绕着他的脸庞。这块石板的一侧是火炬，因此它很可能是某块墓碑的一部分。宙斯 - 阿蒙在托勒密时代（公元前 3 世纪—公元前 1 世纪）成为狄俄尼索斯的扈从队的一员。

骨灰瓮

公元前 1 世纪下半叶
雪花石膏
整体高 34 厘米，直径 40 厘米；瓮口直径 31.4 厘米（瓮）；盖子高 7.5 厘米，直径 18.4 厘米
坎皮佛莱格瑞考古公园 - 巴亚城堡中的坎皮佛莱格瑞考古博物馆，展品编号 2001.06-07

Cinerary Urn with Lid

second half of the 1st century B.C.
height 34 cm, diameter 40 cm; diameter of opening 31.4 cm (for the urn); height 7.5 cm, diameter 18.4 cm (for the lid)
Phlegraean Fields Archeological Park - Archeological Museum of the Phlegraean Fields in the Castle of Baia Inv.2001.06-07

这件雪花石膏材质的有盖骨灰瓮出土自位于库迈中门的古罗马墓地的陵墓。骨灰瓮（手柄）和盖子（塞子）的小部件并不是单独加工而成的，里面可能有一位年龄在 30 岁以上的女性的烧焦骨骼。罗马共和时代晚期后，我们可以发现罗马人对这类特殊手工制作器物极富兴趣：先是从古埃及进口，然后是专门制作。逝者的名字一般刻在骨灰瓮的口上。

海洋主题的大型马赛克图像投影：维纳斯和涅瑞伊得斯的马赛克

罗马国家博物馆，展品编号 108376

Mosaic with Venus and Neridi

National Roman Museum Inv. 108376

通过多媒体数字技术，重现海洋主题马赛克图像的细节。

海洋主题的大型马赛克图像投影：马赛克与海洋

罗马国家博物馆，展品编号 124729

Mosaic with Ocean
National Roman Museum Inv. 124729

通过多媒体数字技术，重现海洋主题马赛克图像的细节。

海洋主题的大型马赛克图像投影：海洋和鱼的马赛克

罗马国家博物馆，展品编号 571835

Mosaic with Ocean and Fish
National Roman Museum Inv. 571835

通过多媒体数字技术，重现海洋主题马赛克图像的细节。

法尔内西纳别墅 F-G 走廊中的海洋主题壁画

罗马国家博物馆，展品编号 124729

Projections of Pictures with Marine Scenes in the F -G Corridor of Villa Farnesina
National Roman Museum Inv.124729

通过多媒体数字技术，重现海洋主题马赛克图像的细节。

骑海兽的海仙女涅瑞伊得斯

公元前 1 世纪中期
大理石
长 110 厘米，宽 110 厘米，厚 93 厘米
重 1500 千克
阿皮亚古道考古公园 - 卢克雷齐娅罗马文物馆，展品编号 393005

Nereid on Sea Monster

mid-1st century B.C.
height 110 cm, width110cm, depth 93 cm
weight 1,500 kilograms
Appia Antica Archeological Park - Antiquarium of Lucrezia Romana Inv. 393005

涅瑞伊得斯是海神内雷奥和水仙女多里斯的女儿，是仁慈的神，其信奉者遍及整个地中海地区。她们的名字代表了海洋现象和海洋各方面的无限变化。这些居住在海洋深处的海仙女经常骑着半人半鱼的海神、海豚和海马来到海面玩耍。在艺术作品中，她们一般表现为优雅的女性和所骑怪物的力量相结合的形象。海仙女涅瑞伊得斯的雕像并不常见，这类主题更多地出现在马赛克镶嵌画、绘画和石棺上，通常用于装饰水池和喷泉。

几何马赛克装饰

公元 2 世纪后半叶— 4 世纪
马赛克
高 76 厘米；宽 105 厘米；厚 / 深 6 厘米
重约 125 千克
罗马国家博物馆 - 戴克里先浴场，展品编号 121507

Threshold with Mosaic

2nd - 4th century A.D.
height 76 cm, width 105 cm, thickness 6 cm
National Roman Museum, Baths of Diocletian Inv. 121507

复合建筑物房间 D 和房间 E 之间通道的门槛采用了这种马赛克装饰。它由白色石灰石和玄武岩镶嵌而成，相对于房间中和壁画上的马赛克而言，它虽不引人瞩目，却也不失为优雅的几何图案艺术品。

骑海豚的爱神喷泉

公元 2 世纪中期
白色大理石
高 31 厘米，宽 28.8 厘米，厚 13 厘米
重 25 ～ 28 千克
罗马国家博物馆 - 戴克里先浴场，展品编号 2003226

Fountain with Sea God

mid-2nd century A.D.
height 31 cm, width 28.8cm, depth 13 cm
weight 25-28 kilograms
National Roman Museum, Baths of Diocletian Inv. 2003226

这座小雕塑呈现了一个骑着海豚、长着翅膀的儿童形象。他被认为是丘比特，或者是朱诺女神之子帕拉蒙 - 波图努斯——他奇迹般地被海豚从水中救了出来。事实上，他名字的意思是“驱赶暴力与死亡的人”。随着时间的推移，他成了航海的守护神。同样的形象也出现在皮耶特拉 - 帕帕房间 E 的一幅壁画中。

人鱼石棺

公元 3 世纪下半叶
大理石
高 25 厘米，宽 155 厘米，厚 4.5 厘米
重 40 ～ 45 千克
罗马国家博物馆 - 戴克里先浴场，展品编号 9183+9167

Sarcophagus Base

second half of the 3rd century A.D.
height 25 cm, width 155 cm, thickness 4.5 cm
weight approx.40-45 kilograms
National Roman Museum, Baths of Diocletian Inv.9183+9167

在立视图的中央，由海洋半人马举起的布围起来的位置，是死者的肖像。死者的面部几乎无法辨识。肖像面向左侧，发型非常有特色。在海洋半人马的两侧，分别有两对帆张得极满的船。每艘船上有两名船员，一名在划桨，另一名在船边拉网。通常情况下，石棺上描绘的都是与肖像画中的死者生前相关的场景，暗指死者在通往九泉之路上的最后一次旅行。

骑海兽的爱神喷泉

帝国时代
铜
高 24 厘米，宽 21 厘米，厚 7 厘米
重 1.8 千克
罗马国家博物馆 - 马西莫宫，展品编号 65845

Bronze Fountain Element with Amore on Sea Monster

Imperial Age
height 24 cm, width 21 cm, depth 7 cm
weight 1.8 kilograms
National Roman Museum, Palazzo Massimo Inv. 65845

带有爱神形象（带翅膀的赤裸孩童形象，通常用于表示神之爱）的喷泉。爱神骑着一头长满鳞片的海怪，海怪有龙的头、鳍状的前爪、鱼骨样的下身。喷泉构件的一些细节是雕刻而成的——例如海怪口中的牙齿和胸部的鳞片。在海怪的前爪之间，是一条有椭圆形和扁平部分的管状物，用于排水。

海洋场景玻璃盘

公元 4 世纪
玻璃板
重建直径 28 厘米
最长 22 厘米，最宽 13.5 厘米，高 3.5 厘米
罗马国家博物馆 - 马西莫宫，展品编号 62849

Glass Plate

4th century A.D.
reconstructed diameter 28 cm
length max, 22 cm, width max, 13.5cm; height 3.5 cm
National Roman Museum, Palazzo Massimo Inv. 62849

这是雕刻而成的盘子的碎片，装饰和构图非常复杂，并且可能占据了盘子的整个表面，图案交叉排列在不同尺寸的矩形和圆形框架中。在大的拼花和长方形的图案中，出现了与海洋有关的场景：一名或多名渔民正在捕鱼，他们有的在收网，有的在撒网；各种各样的海洋动物嬉戏其间，非常生动。专注于海洋场景的装饰主题在公元 4 世纪至 5 世纪的艺术品中极为常见，使用者包括异教徒和基督徒（有的装饰中明确引用了《圣经》中的章节），在玻璃和金属品的制作中也有大量对比性的海洋场景装饰。

海洋场景油灯

公元 2 世纪末—3 世纪中叶
陶
高 5.5 厘米，宽 15 厘米，盘状部分直径 10.5 厘米
罗马国家博物馆 - 马西莫宫，展品编号 62349

Oil Lamp

late-2nd - mid-3rd century A.D.
height 5.5 cm, width 15 cm,diameter 10.5cm(for the plate)
National Roman Museum, Palazzo Massimo Inv. 62349

圆盘由两个同心的切口连接而成，上面装饰着一艘海船，船员们正在降低船帆，也许是因为他们即将抵达画面左侧小灯塔所指示的港口。在波浪之间，有一个小的通风孔。油灯的灯脚是环形的。在油灯的底部印着弗洛伦特（FLORENT）字样。

海豚壁饰

帝国时代
铜
长 33 厘米，高 10 厘米
罗马国家博物馆 - 马西莫宫，展品编号 65859

Bronze Sconce
Imperial Age
length 33 cm, height 10 cm
National Roman Museum, Palazzo Massimo Inv. 65859

青铜贴花采用完全融合的技术制成，主题是一只扭动的海豚。海豚是古罗马人装饰中经常出现的主题：这种动物能够唤起航行的速度，并且与神话有着千丝万缕的联系（总是出现在海神尼普顿和安菲特里忒的海洋航行中），比如神话《幻变》（狄俄尼索斯神将海盗变成了海豚）、《救助沉船》（在苍鹭的神话中，那位年轻人正是被一群海豚救活了）中都出现过海豚的形象。值得注意的是，在众多古代故事中，海豚对人类，特别是儿童表现出了友谊和忠诚——孩子们经常像骑马一样跨在这种动物的背上。

海豚壁饰

帝国时代
铜
长 32 厘米，宽 10 厘米，高 10 厘米
罗马国家博物馆 - 马西莫宫，展品编号 8047

Fountain Element
Imperial Age
length 32 cm, width 10 cm, height 10 cm
National Roman Museum, Palazzo Massimo Inv.8047

呈现出伸展姿势的海豚形象。它内部挖空，腹部下方有一个用于水管安装的洞，水从海豚的嘴中排出。雕塑中用小圆圈所表现的鳍和眼睛等细节，制作得非常细致。

贝壳壁饰

帝国时代
铜
长 4.5 厘米，宽 4 厘米，高 2 厘米
罗马国家博物馆 - 马西莫宫，展品编号 65868/1

Sconce

Imperial Age
length 4.5 cm, width 4 cm, height 2 cm
National Roman Museum, Palazzo Massimo Inv. 65868/1

绘有贝壳图案的青铜装饰壁灯。扁平的表面让人误以为它是浅杯的杯脚——65868/2 号文物就属于这种情况。

贝壳壁饰

帝国时代
铜
长 3 厘米，宽 4 厘米，高 2 厘米
罗马国家博物馆 - 马西莫宫，展品编号 65868/2

Sconce

Imperial Age
length 3 cm, width 4 cm, height 2 cm
National Roman Museum, Palazzo Massimo Inv. 65868/2

绘有贝壳图案的青铜装饰壁灯。扁平的表面让人误解它是浅杯的杯脚——65868/1 号文物就属于这种情况。

法螺壁饰

帝国时代
铜
高 2.6 厘米，长 4.3 厘米
罗马国家博物馆 - 马西莫宫，展品编号 65869

Sconce

Imperial Age
height 2.6 cm, length 4.3 cm
National Roman Museum, Palazzo Massimo Inv. 65869

绘有“曲拉通（tritone）”图案的青铜装饰壁灯。曲拉通是一种锥形海螺，也被称为“布罗尼亚（brogna）”，常被水神们用作号角。

海豚壁饰

帝国时代
铜 青铜贴花
高 2 厘米，宽 3 厘米，长 6.7 厘米
罗马国家博物馆 - 马西莫宫，展品编号 65860

Bronze Sconces

Imperial Age
length 2 cm, width 3 cm, height 6.7 cm
National Roman Museum, Palazzo Massimo Inv. 65860

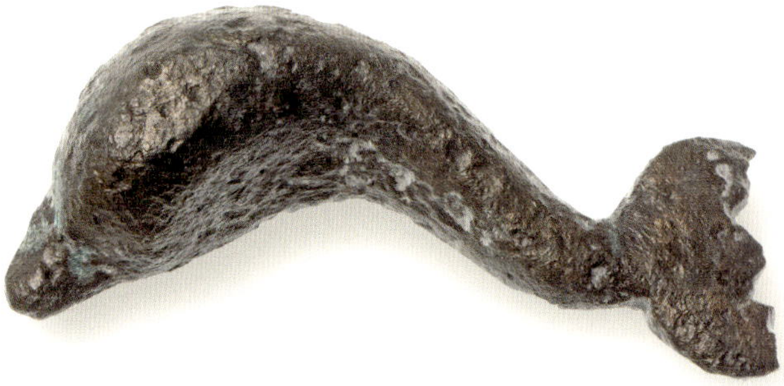

海豚壁饰

帝国时代
铜
高 2 厘米，宽 3.5 厘米，长 8 厘米
罗马国家博物馆 - 马西莫宫，展品编号 65862

Bronze Sconces

Imperial Age
length 2 cm, width 3.5 cm, height 8 cm
National Roman Museum, Palazzo Massimo Inv. 65862

海豚壁饰

帝国时代
铜
高 5 厘米（含金属棍），宽 1.2 厘米，长 5.5 厘米
罗马国家博物馆 - 马西莫宫，展品编号 65863

Bronze Sconces

Imperial Age
height（including pin）5 cm, width 1.2 cm, length 5.5 cm
National Roman Museum, Palazzo Massimo Inv. 65863

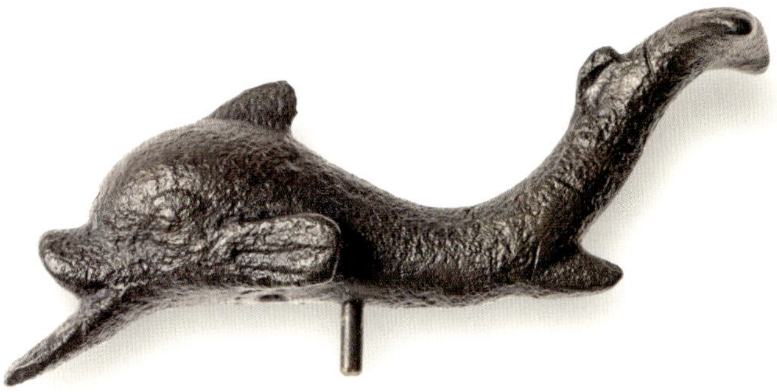

海豚壁饰

帝国时代
铜
长 7 厘米，高 2.5 厘米（高度含金属棍长在内），宽 1.5 厘米
罗马国家博物馆 - 马西莫宫，展品编号 65864

Bronze Sconces

Imperial Age
height（including pin）2.5 cm，width 1.5 cm, length 7 cm,
National Roman Museum, Palazzo Massimo Inv. 65864

海豚壁饰

帝国时代
铜
高 6 厘米（包含底座），宽 2.5 厘米
罗马国家博物馆 - 马西莫宫，展品编号 65866

Bronze Sconces

Imperial Age
height（including base）6 cm，width 2.5 cm
National Roman Museum, Palazzo Massimo Inv. 65866

青铜贴花采用完全融合的技术制成，主题是一只扭动的海豚。这些海豚壁饰和 65859 号文物类似：抬起宽阔的尾鳍，吻部非常发达，眼睛清晰突出，鳞片上有轻微的切口。海豚的腹部有一个小孔，用于安装销钉。这类装饰用于家具上。

海豚壁饰

帝国时代
青铜
高 6.2 厘米（包含底座），长 3.5 厘米，宽 1.9 厘米
罗马国家博物馆 - 马西莫宫，展品编号 4766

Bronze Handle

Imperial Age
height（including base）6.2 cm，width 1.9 cm, length 3.5 cm
National Roman Museum, Palazzo Massimo Inv. 4766

有海豚尾巴的青铜手柄，末端是百合花装饰图案。

UNIT II

WHERE LAND AND SEA ROUTES MEET

PORTS OF ROMAN ITALY

第二单元

海陆交汇

意大利古罗马海港

第一部分

从海洋到城市，追溯台伯河

2A. THE PORTS OF ROME - FROM THE SEA TO THE CITY, SAILING UP THE TIBER

过去数个世纪中，罗马扮演的都是大都会与政治中心的角色，用现在的话来说，在当时罗马是推动全球化市场发展的引擎，其影响力超越了罗马帝国政治与军事的界限。位于这片辽阔领域腹心的地中海，堪称其商业交通中心。

罗马居民逾百万，要使这座大都市保持繁荣发展，需要大量商品来满足城市人口的粮食需求，以及与城市生活息息相关的其他需求。在当时，城市建筑无止境地扩建，同时兴建了众多规模宏大、装潢精美的公共建筑。

在旧大陆（欧、亚、非三洲），海洋和内陆水域（湖泊和河流）运输历来是最经济有效的货物运输方式。然而，罗马并非一座海滨城市，它距离海岸约 30 公里。自其建立城市以来，台伯河一直是它与海洋联系的主要通道，也是人们和货物往返罗马城的基本运输轴线。台伯河宛如一条大型高速公路，每天都承载着运输特殊物品的重任，如大理石、大型方尖碑、巨柱、珍贵的织物、熏香、象牙，以及专为弗拉维圆形露天剧场和罗马斗兽场诸项比赛准备的凶猛动物等。

罗马与海洋的连接，始于奥斯蒂亚港口，终于台伯河口。从 200 公里外那不勒斯海湾的波佐利出发，船队将抵达阿文提诺山脚下的河港——那是罗马的主要内陆港口。

公元 1 世纪初，这种基于港口基础设施体系的海运系统，远不足以养活这样一座庞大的城市。

克劳迪乌斯皇帝时期，罗马附近港口面积不足。

In the past and for centuries, Rome was a very large city, a megalopolis. It was the political and driving heart of a market that today we would call "global"; one that extended beyond the political-military boundaries of the Roman Empire. The Mediterranean basin was at the center of this immense territory and its commercial traffic.

To supply this metropolis - that reached its maximum splendor with over one million inhabitants - enormous quantities of goods were needed, which had to satisfy both the basic food necessities of the population, as well as other needs that were linked to the life of a city where the expansion of constructions had no limits and lavish public buildings, extraordinary in size and decorations, were built.

Transportation by water, sea, and inland waterways (lakes and rivers), was the most efficient and economic way of transporting goods. However, at more than 30 kilometers from the coast, Rome was not, and is still not, a seaside city. Since the beginning of its urban history, the Tiber river has been its main link with the sea; the fundamental axis on which people and goods traveled to and from the city. The river was a large highway on which, on a daily basis, exceptional loads of marble, large obelisks, monumental columns, precious fabrics, incense, ivory, ferocious animals for competitions in the Flavian Amphitheater (the Colosseum), and much more traveled.

Maritime connections with Rome were guaranteed from the port of Ostia at the mouth of the Tiber, and from Puteoli (Pozzuoli), in the Gulf of Naples, 200 kilometers away. The river port at the foot of the Aventine Hill, was the city's main internal port.

At the beginning of the 1st century B.C., this system of port infrastructures was dramatically insufficient to supply a city of one million inhabitants.

In 46 A.D., Emperor Claudius dealt with the problem of the inadequately sized sea port near Rome by beginning the

公元 46 年，皇帝开始在奥斯蒂亚以北几公里处建造另一座巨大的人工港口（占地约 200 公顷）。新港口名为波尔图斯 · 奥古斯都港，简称波尔图斯。公元 64 年，港口竣工，尼禄皇帝为其举行了揭幕仪式。公元 110 年至 117 年间，为进一步丰富此前港口的一些功能，图拉真皇帝在一个占地 34 公顷的新六边形流域周围对这些港口进行了扩建和重构，将其建设为商业港口的中心枢纽。

在奥斯蒂亚港口和台伯河港口范围内，广阔的运河与道路网络交错，最终解决了帝国首都的物资供应问题。在此后大约一千年的时间里，波尔图斯港持续不断地为这座城市服务。直至今天，倘若您乘坐飞机抵达罗马，那座巨大的六边形港口仍能跃入眼前。

R. 塞巴斯蒂亚尼，M. 塞洛伦齐

construction of a large artificial port (about 200 hectares) just a few kilometers north of Ostia. The new port, Portus Augusti, or more simply, Portus, was completed in its first layout and inaugurated by Emperor Nero in 64 A.D. But it was Trajan, between 110 and 117 A.D., who overcame the functional limits of the layout of the previous port, enlarging and reorganizing it around a new hexagonal basin measuring 34 hectares, which became the nerve center of the commercial port.

The proximity of Ostia and of Portus to the Tiber, joined by a vast network of canals and roads, definitively resolved the import and supply system for the capital of the Empire and, for about a millennium, Portus continued to serve the city. Today, its large hexagonal shape can still be seen when arriving to Rome by plane.

R. Sebastiani, M. Serlorenzi

第一节 克劳迪乌斯和图拉真的港口

2A.1. THE PORTS OF CLAUDIUS AND TRAJAN

波尔图斯

波尔图斯港位于奥斯蒂亚以北约 2 公里处，囊括了以南北两侧两座大型人工码头为界限的一部分流域。两座码头的入口向西开放，一座大型灯塔矗立其间。这一流域向南，是第二流域，流域南侧是一个占地约 1.07 公顷的小型长方形码头，再往南则是由图拉真建造的六边形流域。三个流域共同形成了这片超过 235 公顷的水域，相邻而建的仓库容纳了往返罗马的大部分货物。

宽约 40 米的图拉真洼地和北运河使台伯河和这些流域及外海相连。图拉真洼地是船只在河流和罗马间往返的要道，同时充当了台伯河的泄洪区，让罗马免受洪水侵扰。北运河的使用时间似乎很短，这或许与港口的建设有关。

克劳迪乌斯流域，深约 8 米，用于锚定货船和大型海上商船，同时也是船只停靠并等待通过大运河、进入图拉真港的要地。船只可以在六边形流域停靠和卸载货物。达森纳码头深约 6 米，规模则要小得多，很有可能是河上驳船的停靠区域，例如通过图拉真洼地和台伯河驶往罗马的“克劳迪卡里艾”号船。

图拉真的六边形流域深约 7 米，铺有斜坡墙，是港口系统的核心，其极有可能由大马士革伟大的工程师和建筑师阿波罗多罗斯设计。六边形便于建造直线型码头，有助于船只到达、装载、卸载、离港等有序进行，同时可以容纳更多船舶。因此，如果从克劳迪乌斯港出发并通过运河进入六边形流域的货船在流域中央位置抛锚，可以在码头免费停泊。

PORTUS

The Portus Augusti was constructed approximately 2 kilometers north of Ostia and included a portion of the sea delimited to the north and south by two large artificial piers, with its entrance that opened towards the west marked by a large lighthouse in a central position. The second basin, further south, was a small rectangular Darsena, or moor, measuring approximately 1.07 hectares, while the third was the hexagonal basin built by Trajan. Together, the three basins formed more than 235 hectares of water and the adjacent warehouses would have contained most of the goods to and from Rome.

Two canals connected the basins to the Tiber and to the sea: the so-called Fossa Traiana and the Northern Canal, both approximately 40 meters wide. The former made it possible for boats to be transported to the river and to Rome, and also constituted a catchment area for the Tiber, which was used to reduce the risk of flooding in the city; the second seems to have been used only for a short period of time, perhaps linked to the construction of the port.

The Claudius Basin, with a depth of approximately 8 meters, must have been created for anchoring the onerariae (onerarias) - large maritime merchant ships - and became the area where the ships would stop and wait to cross the large entrance canal of the Port of Trajan, to then dock and be unloaded in the hexagonal basin.The Darsena, which was much smaller in size and approximately 6 meters deep, could have been the docking area for river barges, the naves caudicariae, which entered the Fossa Traiana and reached the Tiber to then arrive in Rome.

Trajan's hexagonal basin, probably designed by the great engineer and architect, Apollodorus of Damascus, was 7 meters deep, with flagstone scarp walls, and it constituted the heart of the port system. The hexagonal shape offered rectilinear docks and allowed for a more efficient sequence of arrivals, loading and unloading procedures, and departures, giving way to the passage of a much larger number of ships

环形的规则序列和编有号码的系缆桩，很好地体现了锚定船舶和管理装载操作的严格顺序和程序。

在图拉真的推行下，港口基础设施的重组也涉及了内陆码头。实际上，克劳迪乌斯港的内部核心分别受南北和东西方向的两个大型直线型码头保护。

东西码头长 150 米、宽约 8 米，由于其顶端有一座灯塔，所以在传统意义上被称为“灯塔的一部分”。码头将克劳迪乌斯流域最内部部分限制在南部，以对大型仓库建筑区域和由图拉真建造、通往新六边形港口的运河提供保护，使其免受密史脱拉风的侵害。该码头位于港口设施的中心位置，并处在克劳迪乌斯流域和通往内陆的运河之间。

长长的南北码头同样具备保护克劳迪乌斯流域最内部、引导船只入港的功能。同时，码头以及巨大的纪念柱廊被用作布景，以颂扬帝国首都港口的宏伟和壮丽。

几个世纪以来，这些码头历经多次修复和扩建，并在其上修筑了很多“服务建筑”。对于货物装卸工人及数以千计的港口服务人员而言，这些建筑必不可少。

灯塔码头上还修建了一个大型温泉设施，一直沿用至古罗马帝国末期，甚至在公元 6 世纪末建造城墙时仍能正常使用。

六边形流域北侧的两座建筑物与新流域和码头体系构成了图拉真时期波尔图斯港最重要的元素之一：皇宫和军火库。这些建筑位于整个港口系统的中心，处于克劳迪乌斯流域和图拉真流域之间。

皇宫占地超过 3.5 公顷，高约 20 米，是一座三层楼的大型综合建筑。建筑西侧是一个设计有宏伟柱廊的大型纪念性建筑立面，北侧是住宅区，内设豪华房间，内饰彩色镶嵌画和彩绘石膏制品。同

than in the past. The onerarias that entered the hexagon from the Port of Claudius through the connecting canal could cast their anchors in the central area while they waited to moor at the docks. The regular sequence of mooring loops and bitts, formed by numbered columns, suggests that a strict order and procedure was used for anchoring ships and managing the loading procedures.

The reorganization of the port infrastructure carried out under Trajan also affected the internal piers. The inner part of the Port of Claudius was, in fact, protected by two large straight jetties arranged respectively in a north-south and east-west direction.

The east-west pier, 150 meters long and approximately 8 meters wide, is traditionally referred to as “della Lanterna” because of the lighthouse that stands on it. The jetty circumscribed the innermost part of the large Claudius Basin to the south, in order to protect from storm surges - caused by the mistral - the area where the large warehouse buildings stood and the canal used to access the new hexagonal port built by Trajan. This jetty was, therefore, located in a central position in the port facility, between the Claudius Basin and the canal used to access the inner basins.

The long north-south jetty was also used to protect the innermost part of the Claudius Basin and direct the flow of ships that entered the port, while also functioning as a scenic backdrop created by a large monumental colonnade that enhanced the grandeur and magnificence of the port of the imperial capital.

These jetties were restored and widened many times over the centuries and numerous structures and service buildings were built on them. These were used for loading and unloading goods and for the daily life of the thousands of people who worked at the ports.

A large thermal bath complex was also part of the “della Lanterna” pier, which was active until late antiquity and was certainly still functioning at the time the walls were constructed in the 6th century A.D.

Two buildings were located on the north side of the hexagonal basin that, along with the new system of basins and piers, constituted one of the most significant elements of Portus during Trajan’s times: the Imperial Palace and the

时，设立了通往克劳迪乌斯流域南侧的服务区。房间环绕着一个带柱廊的庭院，形成柱廊式内院，内院中央的水池是一楼矩形水池的一部分，储藏室与之毗邻。

由于皇宫结构和位置的特殊性，必须由主管当局集中管理港口和检查货物，包括协调克劳迪乌斯和图拉真两个流域之间海上运输船只的活动、系泊顺序、装卸、货物定性和定量验证、相关费用、仓库分配和场所租赁等事宜。实际上，皇宫是港口的行政中心，也可能是负责城市供应系统运作等重要官员的居所。又或许，皇宫也是帝国军队指挥中心所在地，由那不勒斯海湾（西部）的米塞诺和亚得里亚海（东部）的克拉赛（拉文纳）调遣兵力。

相关资料显示，图拉真离世后，皇宫在公元117年左右竣工，但不断被侵占挪作他用，直至公元6世纪中叶。

帝国军火库是一座整体约240米×58米的建筑群，与皇宫建造于同一时期。最后一个军火库位于东部，由三座建筑物组成，每座建筑物按照以下顺序划分：一条走廊、三个狭窄的海湾、一条走廊和一个宽阔深槽区段。这些区段用于商船和军舰的制造或大修。考古发掘数据显示，这些区段深达27米。有可能是供军火库接待商船和军队，以保护台伯河口和进入罗马的入河口所用。

六边形流域的四面修建有许多大型加长建筑物，传统上被认为是仓库。在流域入口的另一侧有一座寺庙，与六边形流域入口对齐，专门供奉皇帝，用以祭祀。

运河沿线设置仓库，是为了满足快速转运货物往返台伯河的需要。截至目前，尽管小麦通常被认为是仓库储存的主要货物，但关于储存在波尔图斯仓库中的货物种类的数据非常稀少。不过，六边形

Arsenals. These structures were located in the center of the port complex, between the Claudius and Trajan Basins.

The Imperial Palace was a large complex extending over more than 3.5 hectares, built on three floors, for a total of approximately 20 meters in height.The western side of the building had a large monumental façade with a magnificent colonnade, while the north side consisted in luxurious rooms, belonging to the residential part of the complex, with polychrome mosaics and painted plasterwork, as well as service areas that opened onto the southern side of the Claudius Basin. These rooms were arranged around a colonnaded courtyard - the peristyle - with a central tub, which was part of a large rectangular cistern located on the ground floor. Service rooms used for storage were organized around it.

The Imperial Palace was probably the central point for several specific activities regarding port management and the control of goods by the competent authorities, which might have included: coordinating the transport ships that sailed between the Claudius and Trajan Basins, mooring sequences, loading and unloading procedures, relevant expenses, assignment to warehouses, and rental of spaces in the warehouses. It was practically the administrative heart of the port. Probably the most important officials in charge of the city's import and supply system resided in the Palace. It was also perhaps the seat of the central command of the imperial fleet, deployed in Misenum in the Gulf of Naples (the western one), and in Classe (Ravenna), on the Adriatic Sea (the eastern one).

The excavation data show that the Imperial Palace was completed around 117 A.D., upon Trajan's death, and was occupied on a continuous basis until the mid-6th century A.D.

The Imperial Arsenals, a complex of approximately 240 x 58 meters, were built in the same period as the Imperial Palace. Located to the east of the Palace, the arsenals were structured in sections formed by three buildings, each of which was divided in the following sequence: a corridor, three narrow bays, a corridor, and a wide bay. The bays were probably used during the construction of commercial and military ships or for major repairs of the same. From the excavation data, it seems as if the bays reached a height of 27 meters. The arsenals might have housed trade ships but also a detachment of the

流域东南侧和码头沿线的仓库似乎为此观点提供了一些依据。事实上，即使仓库内容纳的东西尚不可知，但仍有一些特别措施值得注意，例如仓库中有用来缓解温度和湿度变化的高架地板（悬吊）——高架地板多半用于储存小麦，尽管“仓库在一年中的不同季节用于存放不同货物”这一说法显得更合理。

公元 2 世纪初，埃及亚历山大港出发的粮食船队已经可以航行至波尔图斯，而从 2 世纪末期开始，从利比亚港口和突尼斯港口出发的非洲粮食船队也加入了这一行列。已经确定，亚历山大商人与粮食船队、来自意大利罗马和整个地中海地区的商业活动的有关人员姓名的丧葬铭文直接相关。

总而言之，波尔图斯是罗马帝国的主要交通枢纽，与帝国首都罗马的内河港口直接相连。

直至当代，整个欧洲和地中海地区都从未再出现过如此庞大和运营有序的港口。

R. 塞巴斯蒂亚尼

military fleet, positioned to protect the mouth of the Tiber and the entrance to Rome.

Large, elongated buildings, traditionally identified as warehouses, rose along four of the six sides of the hexagon. A temple - dedicated to the cult of the Emperor - aligned with the entrance to the hexagon and flanked on both sides by a pair of long storage buildings, was located on the opposite side of the entrance to the basin.

The arrangement of the warehouses along the canals had to accelerate the transfer and handling of the goods to and from the Tiber. Only a few data exist so far regarding the nature of the goods stored in the Portus warehouses, although wheat is commonly considered to be the main goods that were preserved in these buildings. The warehouses on the south-eastern side of the hexagon and along the dock seem to provide some support to this idea. In fact, even if their content is not known, the constant presence of suspensurae (tn. pavements suspended over a cavity that created a space, which allowed for changes in temperature and moisture to be mitigated), suggests that they were used for grain storage, even if it is more credible to think that various goods were stored there during different seasons of the year.

At the beginning of the 2nd century A.D., Portus was probably reached by the grain fleet that departed from Alexandria and the same probably occurred for the African grain fleet, in the late 2nd century, which departed from the ports of Libya and Tunisia. Merchants from Alexandria were identified in direct relation with the grain fleet, along with funerary inscriptions bearing the names of individuals linked to trade activities deriving from Rome, Italy, and the entire Mediterranean.

In conclusion, Portus served as the main hub of the Roman Empire, in direct tandem with the inner river port of Rome, the capital of the Empire.

All of Europe and the Mediterranean would no longer be witness to such a large and well-organized port until the Modern Age.

R. Sebastiani

图拉真肖像

公元 2 世纪初
玄武岩
带底座高 40 厘米，头高 26 厘米，宽 18 厘米，厚 21 厘米
罗马国家博物馆 - 马西莫宫，展品编号 61160

Portrait

early-2nd century A.D.
height with 40 cm base, head height 26 cm, width 18 cm, depth 21 cm
National Roman Museum, Palazzo Massimo Inv.61160

图拉真大帝于公元 98 年至公元 117 年在位执政。这尊肖像展示了图拉真大帝的外貌特征，例如，头发向前梳理盖住部分额头的发型，大鼻子，抿紧的嘴和突出的下巴，这些细节加在一起不仅重现了这位大帝的外貌和年龄，而且展示出了他坚定和独断的性格。这尊图拉真大帝头像被置于一系列官方肖像中。这些肖像是图拉真大帝立柱带状装饰中的“祭祀肖像”，描写的是皇帝站在祭坛旁边主持相关宗教仪式的景象。

君士坦斯一世粮食供给长官题词祭坛

公元 2 世纪—公元 4 世纪
大理石
高 101 厘米，宽 64 厘米，厚 50 厘米
重 680 千克
罗马国家博物馆 - 马西莫宫，展品编号 106

Altar
2nd - 4th century A.D.
height 101 cm, length 64 cm, depth 50 cm
weight 680 kilograms
National Roman Museum, Palazzo Massimo Inv.106

这个祭坛（或称为“名誉祭坛”）保存了两段铭文，一个在正面，一个在左侧，而右侧则装饰有浅浮雕。

正面铭文经过精心雕琢，磨平了之前的铭文，叙述了康斯坦斯（Costante）大帝（公元 337 年—350 年在位执政）统治期间奥雷利乌斯 · 阿维尼乌斯 · 辛马库（L.AURELIUS AVIANIUS SYMMACHUS）的卓越贡献。文中说明，皇恩浩荡，皇帝为功绩显著的官员举行庆祝仪式，这位官员是一位杰出人物，官居多职，包括“安纳那”——负责当时粮食、食用油和酒料的供应和分配。由题词中提到的酒判断，这段铭文制作的时间约为公元 340 年至 350 年。

在祭坛的右侧，刻画了一艘用于运输食品的纪念性海船，上面清楚地写着“安纳那”奥雷利乌斯 · 阿维尼乌斯 · 辛马库的题词；船尾的舵手，船头还有一个人物，船中心载荷的是装有食用油和葡萄酒的双耳瓦罐，都可以清晰地辨认出来。祭坛左侧是一篇简短的铭文。参考当时的执政官任期，可以确定铭文的日期为公元 284 年 5 月 2 日，因此，这一时间大约是在正面铭文“安纳那”题词的 60 年前。“安纳那”的职位由奥古斯都皇帝设立，负责管理国家的财政收入和实物收入。

正面铭文：

“祝福通过（他的）仁慈和美德增加公益的人，他是我们的主人，弗拉维 · 朱利叶斯 · 康斯坦丘斯（Flavius Iullius Constantius），虔诚，幸运，成功，胜利，奥古斯都。奥雷利乌斯 · 阿维尼乌斯 · 辛马库，克拉西缪斯头衔，主管粮食供给的长官，向他的神圣精神和威严致敬，（特此撰文）。”

左侧铭文：

“在我们的领主卡里努斯 · 奥古斯都（CARINUS AUGUSTUS）和努美瑞阿努斯 · 奥古斯都（NUMERIANUS AUGUSTUS）执政的那一年，在六月布日之前的第六天，特此撰文。”

第二节 皮耶特拉－帕帕流域靠岸处

2A.2. THE PIETRA PAPA RIVER DOCK

台伯河两岸的景观受到台伯河的影响巨大。台伯河是一条商业动脉，它将罗马和临近的港口连接起来，每天都有各类货物途经此处，这些货物来自帝国的各个地方，但也有来自远东市场的货物，其中最远的来自中国。很快，河两岸成为建设商业中心、仓储中心的重要区域，此外还有利用河道水源、房屋，尤其是住宅进行作业的手工工厂，以及能够欣赏到令人心旷神怡的河岸风景的生产性建筑。沿着台伯河流经之处，还可以发现很多墓葬建筑。

在城墙外不远的地方就曾发现了一片上述建筑群，它正好对应现在的台伯河岸的皮耶特拉－帕帕街区位置。对这片建筑遗迹的初次发掘是在1915

The landscape along the banks of the Tiber could not but be conditioned by the river and its function. A commercial artery that connected Rome to its Ports and through which all sorts of goods from every part of the Empire, but also from far eastern markets, transited daily, even to China. Soon, the banks of the river became strategic places for building emporiums and warehouses, but also artisanal structures that could benefit from the presence of water, homes and, above all, residential as well as production buildings that enjoyed the relaxing view of the river. Funerary buildings and sepulchers were also located along the Tiber river, which could be seen by those who crossed it.

This scenario was discovered in an area outside, but not far from, the city walls near the current Lungotevere di Pietra Papa. The first excavations were conducted in 1915 when, following an imposing flood of the Tiber, the remains of thermal baths were uncovered, characterized by black

年。当时台伯河在经历一次巨大的洪水之后，一些温泉浴场遗迹重见天日，其地板特色鲜明，由黑白马赛克瓷片构成，描绘了体育场的画面。在第一次世界大战期间，政府迅速开展调查并进行了文献记录，然后又重新把它覆盖了起来。此后，1939—1940 年间，在清理和扩宽河滩地区的工程中又发现了一批重要的建筑物遗迹：一幢大型郊区别墅，建于公元前 1 世纪到公元 2 世纪之间，建筑周围墙壁绘有精美的图案；一处公元 2 世纪中叶的温泉场所；以及一处可能用于寺庙或同样形状的墓葬建筑的混凝土地基。

遗憾的是，缓慢的发掘速度、河水的持续泛滥以及第二次世界大战的爆发，都使得详细并精准的记录工作难以继续下去，因此也就无法准确地对其背景进行复原。但是，多亏了进行挖掘工作的 G. 亚科皮所留下的有关建筑种类的记录和描述，使得一些建筑主体的功能得以确认。

尽管构建的平面图不是特别精确，但我们可大致识别出在河岸靠河处有一个以圆形造型为特征的小温泉。它所处的位置并不是随机挑选的，事实上，除了可以欣赏到河流的全景之外，房间里也可以享受到阳光的照射。这处小型设施极其简陋，面积也不大，大致推断当时它是供在这段河道上中转和歇息的工人和小商人使用。

皮耶特拉－帕帕建筑遗迹照片

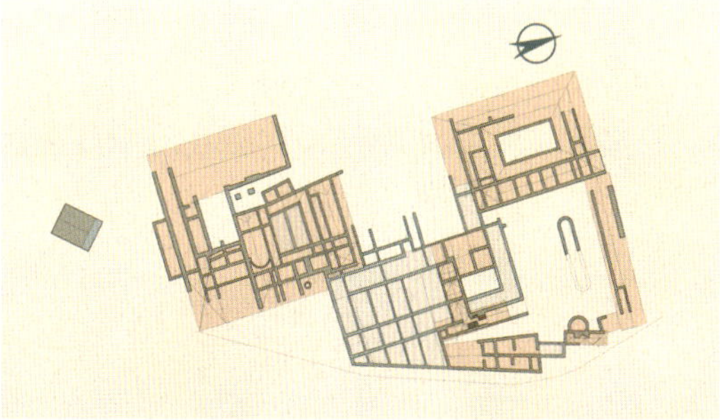

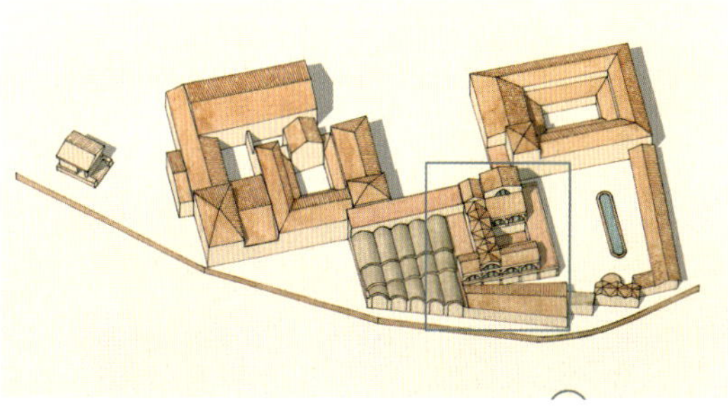

皮耶特拉－帕帕发掘平面图 D–E 区域的局部平面图和 3D 重建

and white mosaic floors depicting gymnasium scenes. The execution of the investigations during World War imposed that the documentation be compiled rapidly and the site be covered up again. Later, between 1939-1940, works dedicated to cleaning and widening the river floodplains brought to light an important complex of buildings: a large suburban villa dating back between the 1st century B.C. and the 2nd century A.D., with finely painted rooms; thermal building from the mid-2nd century A.D.; a cement base perhaps attributable to a small temple or a funerary building.

Unfortunately, the speed of the excavations and the continuous flooding of the river, as well as having to work during World War II, did not allow to complete precise and detailed documents that would have allowed for an accurate reconstruction of the context. However, thanks to the type of buildings and the descriptions left by G. Iacopi, who conducted the excavations, it was possible to identify the function of several of these buildings.

The floor plans designed, although not particularly exact, allow to recognize, in the bottom portion, right on the banks of the river, a small thermal bath characterized by a circular room. Its position is anything but casual. In fact, the building could benefit from the water, from the exposure of the rooms to sunlight, as well as from the panoramic view of the river.

在北岸的更高处，坐落着一栋大型别墅，保留了非常精细的规划布局。这栋住宅不属于一个单一的建筑时间段，而是经历了从公元前 1 世纪到公元 2 世纪长达三个世纪的一系列修复、修改和扩建。建筑最后完工时，拥有两个门廊，其中最大的坐落在北侧，而东面是一个带拱廊的大花园；花园中心有一个长长的水池，水池的短面是曲线状池壁。水池用来饲养鱼类，它的位置也是这座别墅的核心。小厅的东侧有 A、B、C 三个房间，用于温泉疗养，较低处则是 D、E、F 三处房间，也是这座建筑物最古老的设施。

由于最后三个房间位于地下，使得屋顶得以保存下来，特别是墙壁上和拱顶上一系列特殊图案的壁画。从两个房间的装饰上还可以看到复杂几何元素形状的马赛克地板，一个是黑白色，另一个是彩色（保存在马西莫宫中）。地板是在壁画创作一个世纪后铺设的，其技术和风格特征可以追溯到公元 3 世纪至 4 世纪。

在平面图中，这些房间的西面是一系列长长的平行设施，看起来像是仓库。

如果推测正确，这座别墅可能和鱼类养殖有关，由于还出现了和该河道港口直接相连的仓库，也可能具有商业用途。在发掘工作中，还发现了一个长长的拥有石灰质护堤石的河堤，河堤上建有阶梯，很可能是为了保护堤岸后的重要建筑设施而建造的。

建筑物主人的奢华和社会地位体现在马赛克的使用、图案装饰、客厅或地下会议室的质量等方面。炎炎夏日，清凉的客厅和地下会议厅供温泉主人招待客人们使用，这些画描绘出河岸生活和为了积累财富而饲养多种动物的鲜活景象。同时，考虑到此处物产面积大约有 10 000 平方米，这些绘画的生产和销售商可能是一位靠着沿岸业务而发达的亚历山港的大商人，这点或许可以从墙壁装饰物上由希腊

Due to its simplicity and small size, the bath was thought to be used by patrons of the river port, therefore, substantially by workers and less important merchants.

To the north, higher up, at least one large villa was located, which preserved a very articulate layout. It does not belong to a single phase of construction but was the result of a series of restorations, modifications, and extensions carried out over three centuries, from the 1st century B.C. to the 2nd century A.D. In the last period of its life, it was comprised of two porches, the largest located on the north side, and also a large garden with arcades to the east. At the center of the latter was a long basin with a curvilinear wall on its short sides, used for fish farming and which was also the villa's source of production. Rooms A, B, and C, which were clearly used as thermal baths, opened up onto the east side of the small atrium while, on a lower level, there were rooms D, E, and F, obtained from the oldest substructions of the building.

The underground condition of these last rooms has allowed to preserve the height and the ceilings but, above all, the exceptional pictorial cycle on the walls and on the vaults. The decoration of the two rooms also included mosaic floors with complex geometric patterns, one in black and white and the other polychrome (the latter preserved in Palazzo Massimo), which were created more than a century after the paintings and that, due to their technical and stylistic characteristics, date back between the 3rd and 4th centuries A.D..

To the west of these rooms, a series of characteristic long, parallel rooms are represented in the layout, which can

皮耶特拉－帕帕 D 房间的马赛克

发掘地照片

文字组成的花饰和埃及神明画像那里得到佐证。

西北边看起来是第二个居所，它围绕着一个大拱廊，并有配有仓库和一个大水池，这部分建筑物占地面积足有 6 500 平方米，也属于上述同一住宅。

沿着河流继续向西，住宅建筑逐渐被一些丧葬建筑景观所取代。例如一座建筑是由方形矮墙构成，应该是一座寺庙，但也很可能是一处形似寺庙的墓葬。

本世纪初，考古人员对匆忙收集到的考古资料进行分析，清晰勾勒出一个古罗马商人眼中地地道道的河岸生活图景。台伯河上有很多活动：那里曾是一条嘈杂的商业要道，其河岸多处地点建有仓库和商业设施，其间进行着繁忙而密集的劳作；也曾是一条水道，滋养了贵族住宅里的树木和花园，

be assimilated to warehouses.

If the interpretation presented is correct, this villa was probably used for production purposes tied to fish farming, but also for trade, given the presence of the warehouses that are directly connected to the river dock. In fact, the excavations uncovered a long embankment with travertine mooring stones and stairs, probably built to protect the important complex of structures behind it.

The luxury, wealth, and social level of the owner is reflected by the quality of the mosaics and the pictorial decorations, also found in underground living rooms or meeting rooms, which were used during the summer months and to entertain clients of the thermal baths or the owner's guests with lively scenes alluding to river life and the variegated fauna that could have been bred in the fish farm. A reason for ostentatious wealth, also considering the size of the property, which measured 10,000 square meters. Perhaps the individual who commissioned the paintings was a wealthy merchant from Alexandria who became rich through the activities that took place along the river, as would seem to be confirmed by the Egyptian divinities and the cartouches written in Greek that were present on the boats depicted on the wall paintings .

To the north-west there seems to be the presence of a second dwelling, around an atrium, equipped with warehouses and a large cistern for water, unless this portion of buildings measuring approximately 6,500 square meters also pertained to the same villa described above.

Continuing west along the river, residential buildings gave way to a more natural landscape where several funerary buildings were located, the first of which consists of a square podium that was interpreted as being a temple, but which more likely can be attributed to a sepulcher in the shape of a temple.

The interpretation of the archeological data that was hastily collected at the beginning of the century clearly outlines a slice of river life as it would have appeared to the eyes of a Roman merchant. The Tiber hosted many activities: it was a chaotic and noisy commercial artery and, in many places, its banks housed warehouses and commercial facilities where intense and hectic work activities took place. It was a course of water lined with trees and gardens of noble residences and also river parties, such as those depicted in the paintings of Pietra Papa, where parade boats set up for festivities hosted

像是皮耶特拉 - 帕帕街区发现的绘画中所描绘的那些——贵族们经常在河边聚会，游船在此徜徉，聚会上有乐队和舞蹈。自然条件优越的居民区是一片精神慰藉之地，更是怀念和凭吊祖先们的好地方。

房间 E—F 的重建

对皮耶特拉 - 帕帕街区综合建筑群内两个房间的重建是以绘画的形式呈现的。这是两处地下建筑，我们现在仍然可以看到拱顶的装饰，可以从视觉和情感上感受到室内的冲击。

这是两个分别被命名为 D 和 E 的长方形房间，最初被半圆拱顶所覆盖，从房间里通过一个作为通光井用的小厅，可以进入到地面上的温泉设施内。D 房间大小为 4.20 米 ×2.50 米，最大高度为 2.60 米；它通过东侧的门和房间 E 相通，通过南侧的门和房间 F 相通。此外，D 房间北侧有一个天窗将其和地面的一个区域连通。地板是黑白色马赛克，装饰为几何形状花纹。墙壁下部的墙基是高为 0.45 米的黑色大理石，大理石上方（包括拱顶）全部有复杂的装饰，装饰以海洋为背景，海底有许多鱼类，两边是一对长船，船舷上站着几个人。此次展览仅展示了这个房间的一个侧面复原，装饰的剩余部分正在进行修复。在拱顶的砖上有一个公元 123 年的

choirs and dances and, in less residential areas, where nature excelled, it was a place for the spirit and for welcoming and remembering the deceased.

RECONSTRUCTION OF ROOMS E-F

For the first time, the complete reconstruction of two rooms in the architectural complex of Pietra Papa is presented through paintings. Since they were underground, the decorations on the vaults were also preserved, allowing us to perceive the visual and emotional impact inside these rooms.

These are basically two rectangular Rooms, D and E, both originally covered with a barrel vault and that could be accessed from the thermal rooms of the upper floor through a small staircase that also served as a light well to allow light to enter from outside. Room D measured 4.20 x 2.50 meters with a maximum height of 2.60 meters. It communicated with Room E through a door on the east side and with room F through a door on the south side. In addition, Room D had an opening in the northern side that connected it to a room above. The floor of the room was made of black and white mosaics with geometric patterns. A dark marble plinth, which measured 0.45 meters in height, ran along the lower part of the walls. The rich decoration of a seabed with numerous fish extended above it, also including the vault. On the longer sides, pairs of boats were depicted with various figures on board. Only one panel of this room is on display, while the rest of the decoration was entrusted to reproductions. The presence of a stamp on a brick of the vault with “123 A.D.” impressed on it allowed to accurately date the pictorial decoration.

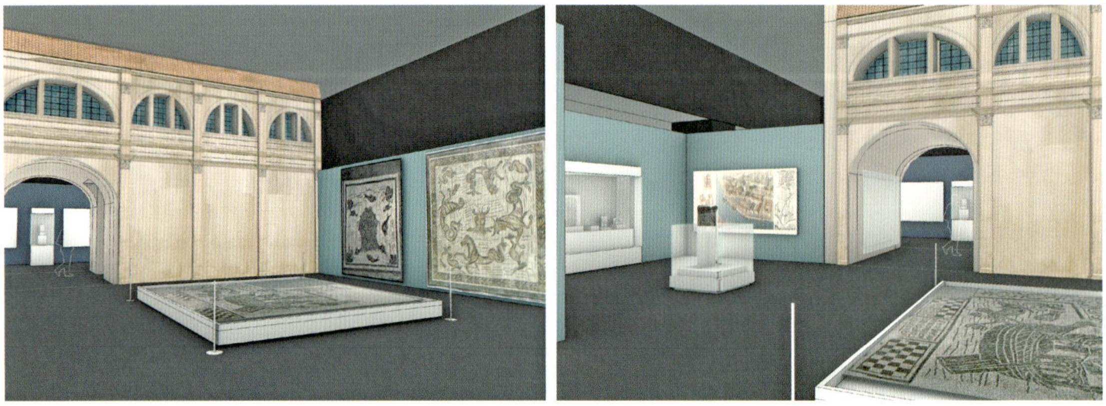

D房间的3D重建

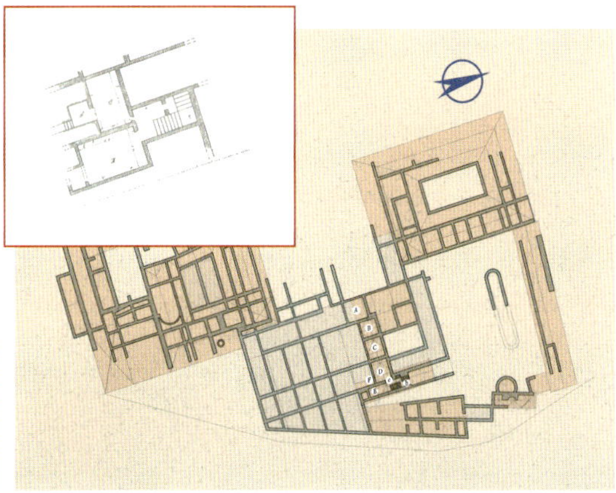

地下区域平面图

皮耶特拉－帕帕，入口处马赛克地板

印痕，因此我们能确认绘画装饰建造的确切时间。

房间 E 大小为 4.50 米 ×3.00 米，通过一个小型黑白马赛克门槛和 D 房间连通。房间内的绘画展现了几条以海洋和鱼类为背景的船只。

鉴于位于地下且与温泉设施紧密连接，这个房间可能是供人休息的场所，让人在炎炎夏日享受清凉，或许还可以为部分客人提供餐饮。

在此停留会让人身心愉悦，感觉就像坐在或躺在海底：抬头向上看，拱顶满是在海洋中自由遨游的鱼类的装饰；向侧面看是许多游船出游的景象，描绘出前面提到的节日期间在贵族花园露天处看到的景色。这些绘画同时还展现了河岸生活的细节和别墅水池内养殖的多种鱼类，别墅主人——可能是一个靠养鱼和贩售来自埃及的异域商品而发家致富的商人——靠它们积累了财富，他喜爱炫耀自己的社会地位和奢华生活。

绘画装饰

蓝绿相间的背景上描绘了装饰华丽的帆船，船上有不同的人物形象：有的准备划船，有的正在泊船靠岸，有的在船尾摆舵激励船员奋力工作。引人注目的是船体两端关于彩色花卉和镜子的图案装饰；在船体中央，可辨认出是一些神灵的形象画：

Room E measured 4.50 x 3.00 meters and, except for the rich colored mosaic floor with geometric patterns (reproduced here), it was entirely reconstructed. It communicated with Room D through a small threshold in black and white mosaic. In this case as well, the paintings represent various boats that sail across a seabed with fish.

Given their underground position and their close connection to the thermal complex, these rooms were probably used for resting, where one could keep cool on hot summer days, or perhaps as sitting rooms for conversation or for serving meals to a limited number of guests.

They were probably pleasant to stay in, and the sensation might have been that of sitting or lying at the bottom of the sea. In fact, looking up, the vault appeared entirely covered with fish swimming in the sea while, on the sides, a series of festive boats sailed up the river, reproducing the view that one might have seen outdoors, from the gardens of the residence, on a feast day. At the same time, the paintings allude to river life and the variegated fauna that could have been bred in the fish farm of the villa, which probably contributed to the wealth of the owner - perhaps, as was specified, a merchant who became rich through fishing farming activities and the trade of exotic products from Egypt – and who loved to flaunt his social and economic status.

PICTORIAL DECORATION

Richly decorated boats were represented on the blue-green background of the water with figures on board who were intent on rowing, or carrying out mooring procedures, or

塞拉皮斯、手握权杖或酒神杖的伊西斯，或许还有得墨忒耳，以及衣服呈褶状的胜利女神。这些绘画的边沿处装饰有很多不同的元素：面具、半人半鱼人、鲸鱼、鸭子、公鸡、两条鱼；在一个较大的镜子图案里，镜子中出现了男性和女性欢聚的场面，他们手握高脚杯和鲜花花环。

这些没有桅杆和帆的船与沿河运送货物或乘客的船只相似（斯卡菲、雷努恩科利或林恩特雷），但是船身上刻有的神话人物图像及其尺寸多变、内容复杂的装饰，使它们看起来像是在台伯河上节日期间用于比赛的船只。船的周围是鲜活的鱼类动物，虽然鱼和船只大小比例并不协调，但是因为描绘得很写实，仍然可以辨认出来。另外还可以看到一条乌贼、一只贻贝、一条礁梭鱼、一片海、一条针鱼、一条形似领航鱼的鱼、一只鲑鱼、一条金鲷鱼和一条三文鱼。

这些绘画再现了原始的生活场景，并赋予其生

even helmsmen at the stern while they incited their shipmates. The pictorial decorations of the hulls are remarkable with their floral motifs and polychrome mirrors on the ends, and gods and goddesses depicted in the center: Serapis, Isis, a figure with a scepter or thyrsus, perhaps Demeter, and draped Victories. Various elements alternated in the polychrome panels along the edges: masks, tritons, dolphins, a duck, a rooster, two fish, and a patera (tn. a circular ornament in architecture worked in relief on friezes). The larger mirrors were decorated with festive male and female figures holding plates, wine glasses, or wreaths in their hands.

The small boats, without a mast and sails, resemble those used for transporting goods or passengers along the river (scaphae, lenuncoli or lintres), but because of their rich decorative apparatus with mythological figures and oriental divinities, and their size, they tended to look more like gala boats used for parties on the Tiber. Lively fish fauna can be seen all around and, even if there is no coherence in the proportions between the various fish and boats, it can still be recognized thanks to the realism with which it was depicted. The fauna includes a cuttlefish (sepia elegans), a mussel, a striped red mullet (mullus surmuletus), a sea urchin

皮耶特拉－帕帕绘画装饰：小船

皮耶特拉-帕帕绘画装饰：鱼

命。绘画种类多样，包括静物、鱼类养殖场景，源自古希腊的角斗、神话故事、河岸生活场景。有些不协调的画面尤为醒目，比如一些河船和丰富的海洋生物之间的联系，像是一部科普目录。填充于画面各个部分的鱼类之间的大小比例也不准确，鱼类和船只之间的比例也不协调。画者对细节的渲染格外引人注目并具有独创性，然而，在表现形式的选择上，不能从全景角度和尺寸上准确地描绘各类物品。从壁画的风格和附带的公元 123 年的印痕来看，壁画应该是公元 2 世纪中叶的作品。

M. 塞洛伦齐

(paracentrortus lividus), a needle fish (belone agus), perhaps a pilot fish (naucrates ductor), a rock fish (scarpena scrofa), a two-banded sea bream (diplodus vulgaris), and a skipjack (euthyunnus alletteratus) .

These paintings represent a summa of the figurative repertoire that was re-elaborated to give life to an original representation. Different genres were combined in it, such as still-lifes, fish farming scenes, images of groups in battle deriving from Hellenistic models, mythological repertoires, and also scenes of river life. Some inconsistencies are evident, like the association of river boats with a rich marine fauna - detailed as if they were in a scientific catalog - or the lack of realistic dimensional relationships both between the fish that fill each space and between the fish and boats. The rendering of the details is remarkable, and the choice of images is original. However, the ability to reproduce the various subjects in the correct perspective and size is lacking. The frescoes date back to about the mid-2nd century A.D., both from a stylistic aspect, as well as from the presence of stamps dated 123 A.D.

M. Serlorenzi

皮耶特拉 – 帕帕房间 D 的南墙，海洋场景壁画

公元 2 世纪上半叶
彩绘灰泥层
高 112 厘米，长 232 厘米
重 120 千克
罗马国家博物馆 - 马西莫宫，展品编号 121460 A

Painted Plaster from Pietra Papa
first half of the 2nd century A.D.
height 112 cm, length 232 cm
weight 120 kilograms
National Roman Museum, Palazzo Massimo Inv. 121460 A

在房间 D 的南墙上，装饰着以海洋场景为内容的壁画，画中小船的船头装饰着狼头和天鹅颈状的雕饰。

该船船身被涂成黄色，其边缘有蓝色和黄色条纹，船尾和船头的镶板被涂成红色、蓝色和黄色，彩色背景上有白色的发光小雕像。右上方有两个装饰板，其中一个带有建筑画，稍微向下一点是一种彩绘卷轴，上面写着“ΛAKENA”。船头是弯曲的，向上抬起。

船上有三个赤身裸体的长发划船者。

这幅画的底部均由“海水”组成，六种不同种类的大鱼在水中游动。

皮耶特拉 – 帕帕房间 D 的南墙，海洋场景壁画

公元 123 年
彩绘灰泥层
高 162 厘米，长 276 厘米
罗马国家博物馆 - 马西莫宫，展品编号 121460 B

Painted Plaster from Pietra Papa
123 A.D.
height 162 cm, length 276 cm
National Roman Museum, Palazzo Massimo Inv. 121460 B

房间 D 的南墙上的石膏与拱顶部分装饰着游在海底的不同鱼类。我们可以从中识别出金枪鱼、红鲷鱼、鲷鱼和红鱼。

皮耶特拉－帕帕房间 D 的南墙，海洋场景壁画

公元 123 年
彩绘灰泥层
高度 141.5 厘米，宽 250 厘米
重 150 千克
罗马国家博物馆 - 马西莫宫，展品编号 121460C

Painted Plaster from Pietra Papa

123 A.D.
height 141.5 cm, width 250 cm
weight 150 kilograms
National Roman Museum, Palazzo Massimo Inv. 121460 C

这块壁画位于出入口左侧的垂直墙壁上。在蓝绿色的水中，有几条鱼在游动，在水里可以看见鱼的影子，画面底部是海豚和墨鱼。

皮耶特拉－帕帕房间 D 的北墙，海洋场景壁画

公元 123 年
彩绘灰泥层
高 109 厘米，长 330 厘米
重约 150 千克
罗马国家博物馆 - 马西莫宫，展品编号 121461A

Painted Plaster from Pietra Papa

123 A.D
height 109 cm, length 330 cm
weight approx.150 kilograms
National Roman Museum, Palazzo Massimo Inv. 121461 A

这幅画中间绘有一条装饰精美的红色小船，该船包括一个“羽毛状”的船头和直形的船尾；船尾有弯曲的、呈天鹅颈形状的装饰；朝向船头的小舱由一个开放式的小凉亭组成。在船尾有两个桨手，第三名桨手位于船头。船体装饰有大型彩绘版；在红色的背景上是白色的人物小雕像：右边是一个躺着的人，左边是一个拿着盾牌的战士。用于装饰船边缘的颜色有蓝色、绿色、黄色、红色和紫色。在画面右侧，一条巨大的海鱼正从上面俯冲下来；在船下面的海洋中，可以看到其他三种鱼类。船的中心缺少了一块画面。

皮耶特拉－帕帕房间 D 的北墙，海洋场景壁画

公元 123 年
彩绘灰泥层
高 165 厘米，长 195 厘米
重 130 千克
罗马国家博物馆 - 马西莫宫，展品编号 121461B

Painted Plaster from Pietra Papa
123 A.D.
height 165 cm, length 195 cm
weight 130 kilograms
National Roman Museum, Palazzo Massimo Inv. 121461 B

房间 D 的北墙上有一个拱顶，上面绘有在海底游泳的鱼，包括红鲷鱼、金头鲷、金枪鱼和蝎子鱼。

皮耶特拉－帕帕房间 D 的北墙，海洋场景壁画

公元 123 年
彩绘灰泥层
高 167 厘米，长 221 厘米
罗马国家博物馆 - 马西莫宫，展品编号 121461C

Painted Plaster from Pietra Papa
123 A.D.
height 167 cm, length 221 cm
National Roman Museum, Palazzo Massimo Inv. 121461 C

皮耶特拉 - 帕帕房间 D 北墙上的一部分拱顶和通往房间 E 的通道的壁画中，描绘了一条鲻鱼、一条鲷鱼和一条梭鱼在已经严重褪色的海底游泳。

皮耶特拉－帕帕房间 D 的西墙，海洋场景壁画

公元 123 年
高 202 厘米，宽 271 厘米
重 150 千克
罗马国家博物馆 - 马西莫宫，展品编号 121461D

Painted Plaster from Pietra Papa
123 A.D.
height 202 cm, width 271 cm
weight 150 kilograms
National Roman Museum, Palazzo Massimo Inv. 121461 D

皮耶特拉 - 帕帕房间 D 的西墙上装饰着海洋场景的壁画，可以从中辨认出虾、海蛇和梭鱼。

皮耶特拉－帕帕房间 E 的东墙，海洋场景壁画

公元 123 年
彩绘灰泥层
高 171 厘米，长 300 厘米
重 150 千克
罗马国家博物馆 - 马西莫宫，展品编号 121463

Painted Plaster from Pietra Papa
123 A.D.
height 171 cm, length 300 cm
weight 150 kilograms
National Roman Museum, Palazzo Massimo Inv. 121463

位于房间 E 的东墙。两条小船被一只攻击章鱼的大海豚分开的场景，占据了画面大部分空间。右边的第一条小船是弯曲的，船头和船尾都非常高，两个桨手面对面坐着，画面已模糊到几乎完全看不清。船体采用铰接式的装饰：以三个红色和黄色的方形连接起来，还有框架和彩色线条；船尾和船头两个模板也装饰有几何图案。第二艘船的形状与第一艘类似，但显得又长又薄。它的装饰分为五组，带有框架和线条。两个相对而坐的人物手持船桨，其中一个坐在船头。两艘船的中央部分都涂成了黄色，船尾和船头都有红色背景的正方形图案。

第三节　城市中的河岸港口

2A.3. THE RIVER PORT IN THE CITY

城市中的第伯里努斯港是古罗马时期台伯河上最古老的港口，它位于波亚里奥广场和提贝里纳岛之间。

随着时代的发展，第伯里努斯港已逐渐无法满足城市的需求，因此需要另建一个新的港口。人们选中了城墙外阿文提诺山脚下的台伯河河岸处，从这里可以一直通向大海。共和国时期，也就是公元前 1 世纪和公元前 2 世纪之间，港口后方广阔的平原发展成为商业区，人们在此处建立了多个用于存储、交易的建筑设施（商场、艾米莉亚港、加尔巴拿仓库、洛里安那、锡耶纳，等等）。

古罗马历史学家蒂托 · 李维证实，在公元前 193 年，地方行政官员马尔克 · 艾米利奥 · 雷皮多和卢齐奥 · 艾米利奥 · 保罗开始投资建设新的台伯河港口和商场设施，这是一个用于装卸和货物交易的场所。在这次政府公共工程建设中，一个专门用于港口服务的矩形建筑拔地而起，它就是艾米莉亚港。据李维记录，公元前 174 年，商场铺设了石板路并建造了围栏。考古发现，艾米莉亚港还建造了向下通往河中的阶梯。

1919 年至 1920 年，在建造现代河堤的过程中，考古人员发现了一段古罗马共和国时期的码头，它设有通往河中的阶梯和石灰质的泊船石。码头后面是一条从城墙三个门洞城门延伸出的道路，道路沿着河岸前进，连接着古老的奥斯蒂亚路，通往奥斯蒂亚和台伯河入海港口。

公元 1 世纪初奥古斯都时代，码头被彻底改造，码头前扩建了一排由矩形房屋组成的建筑，房顶有

The portus tiberinus, the most ancient river dock of Rome, located near the Forum Boarium and Tiberina Island, was located inside the city.

Over time, this space became insufficient for the needs of the citizens and a new port had to be built. The part of the bank of the Tiber was chosen, at the foot of the Aventine Hill, outside the walls, towards the sea. During the Republican Age, between the 2nd and 1st centuries B.C., the vast plain behind the port turned into a commercial and trading district, with the construction of buildings used for preserving and storing goods, (Emporium, Porticus Aemilia, Horrea Galbana, Lolliana, Seiana, and so on).

The Roman historian, Livy (LIV. 35.10.11-12), testified that, in 193 B.C., the city magistrates, Marcus Aemilius Lepidus and Lucius Aemilius Paullus, ...with money from fines... began the construction of the new river port and the Emporium, an area equipped for unloading, trade, and transactions related to goods. At the same time, within the same intervention on public works, the construction began for a large rectangular building closely linked to port services, which took on the name of Porticus Aemilia. Livy also wrote that, in 174 B.C., the Emporium was paved and fenced, the Porticus Aemilia was restored, and steps to the river were created (LIV. 40.51.6-8).

During the construction of the modern river embankment between 1919 and 1920, a section of the quay from the Republican Age, with access ladders from the river and travertine mooring stones, was discovered. A road was located behind the new port structure, which exited the city walls, from the Porta Trigemina and, along the quay, it connected to the ancient Via Ostiensis, which led to Ostia and to the seaport at the mouth of the Tiber.

With Augustus, at the beginning of the 1st century A.D., the quay was greatly modified, and a building was constructed in front of it consisting of a double series of large, rectangular rooms with vaults, aligned along the axis of the river,

拱顶，它们沿着河流的轴线排列，面积是之前的两倍，带有朝向台伯河的玻璃天窗，另一侧是方便货运马车出入的宽阔的大门。

此后，公元 1 世纪末期到 2 世纪初期，这里建造了一个地面用石灰质地砖铺成的码头，上面装有像展览中展示的狮头那样的镂空石头，码头被用来作为河道繁忙期装货和卸货的小广场。

接着，一系列带有穹窿的新房屋拔地而起，其中一部分是通过翻新旧仓库得来的，并且房屋前面沿河配备了斜面墙体结构（现在已经消失了），以保护它免受洪水的侵袭。在其旁边，建造了一个所谓的沉箱防波堤：采用填土浇筑混凝土技术，建造了一系列圆筒形穹窿；穹窿的平屋顶由石灰华板铺成，充当广场和防洪码头。原有仓库被夷为平地，这使可利用空间增加了一倍；在防洪码头的高度，人们建造了新的大门。沉箱防波堤的上层被人们用作办公室。一个砖砌楼梯将仓库和办公室层连接了起来。这幢建筑物还有一条长长的有顶走廊，也可称其为地道，其中有一段约 250 米的建筑完好无损。事实上，港口此处的结构为三层。最高的一层（现在已经几乎完全消失）有一些铺着黑白瓷砖的马赛克痕迹，它有一条长长的露天走廊连接着办公室。在这条通道的地板上开有天窗，可以照亮下部的地道；在地道的地板上与这些天窗对应的位置，有主下水道的开口，用来处理雨水。在地道中，天窗开口正对着的是河对面的其他仓库，这些仓库顶部的窗户开口很宽，漏斗窗像狼的嘴一样，从外部的上层走道采光。根据印压在砖头上的印章信息可知，这些工程应该始建于公元 105 年到 118 年之间，即图拉真皇帝统治时期和哈德良皇帝统治初期。这些设施应该是货物在通往城市大型仓库之前进行前期装货、检查和分配的场所。

illuminated by skylights facing the Tiber and that was also equipped with large entrance doors for transportation carts found on the opposite side.

Later on, between the end of the 1st and the beginning of the 2nd centuries A.D., a quay was built - paved with large travertine slabs, equipped with perforated mooring stones, such as the lion head displayed in the exhibition - that was presumably used as an unloading and loading yard when the river overflowed.

A subsequent intervention created a series of new rooms with vaulted roofs, partly obtained by restoring the older warehouses. A scarp wall (of which nothing is left today) had been built in front of the structure along the river, created to protect it from floods. Behind this, a so-called caisson dock was constructed: a series of barrel vaults were built using a concrete casting technique poured against an earth fill. The flat covering of the vaults - paved with travertine slabs - was used as a square and as a flood quay. The warehouses of the original building were lofted, in order to double the space, and new doors were created at the same level of the flood quay. On the level above these, other spaces of the same size were located, which were thought to have been offices. The discovery of a brick staircase demonstrated that warehouse floor and the office floor were connected. A long, covered corridor, the cryptoporticus - of which a portion of about 250 meters is still intact - was built adjacent to this building. At this point, the port structure was divided into three levels. The highest level (now almost entirely non-existent), was paved with a mosaic of black and white tiles of which very few fragments remain, and the upper level also had a long open corridor that connected the offices to each other. The skylights opened up on the floor of this corridor and were used to direct light into the underlying cryptoporticus. In correspondence with the skylights, in the beaten earth floor of the cryptoporticus, a junction pit connected with the main sewer, which was used to dispose of rainwater. Other warehouses faced the cryptoporticus, opposite the previous ones. These had wide openings, placed on the opposite side of the river, with hopper windows from which light shined through from the upper external walkway. According to the information provided by the stamps impressed on the bricks, these interventions began

1868—1870年期间，在教皇庇护九世的授意下，路易吉·布鲁扎神父在港口设施最下游进行挖掘，他发现了一长段防波堤和斜坡墙、双卸货斜坡、根据各种不同时期河水能够到达的高度而定的石块停泊处，以及停泊和卸货的出入口。这段工程建于图拉真皇帝和哈德良皇帝统治期间。

河岸港口的扩建和整修工程，以及码头和仓储的重建，是一项连贯有序的工程，由图拉真皇帝发起，旨在让罗马附近的整个商业贸易交流更加便捷、安全和有效。但是在其统治期内未能完成，工程断断续续的维护和重建工作一直持续到公元3世纪初期。

河岸港口的建设和发展促进了其身后平原地带的逐步城市化。对仓储区域、商业区域和连接奥斯蒂亚路的道路的建设，让现代城区内部保留下无数的痕迹。在这片区域内发现的碑文材料证明了无数港口区域贸易手工业者和建设者的存在。五个世纪以来，阿文提诺山脚下的平原成为这座城市最重要的物流区，也是罗马的经济中心。

这里有运往帝国各省及境外的各种各样的货物商品。其中包括小麦、油、酒（也就是所谓的地中海三大特产），也有来自东方的鱼酱、香料和其他奢侈品、原材料、石头、木料、金属、颜料、各类手工制品，这些统统可以从港口的发掘和港口附近河道水域的打捞物品中找到证据。

大理石贸易是当时最重要和最复杂的商品贸易之一。大理石种类繁多，且多半来自远方（非洲、希腊、近东）。在古罗马帝国首都这样一座充满壮观建筑物的城市里，大理石是一种需求量极大的珍贵材料。皇家及贵族的需求促进了这项贸易的发展:大理石以达到半加工程度的石块或半成品圆柱的形式通过大河驳船运达罗马，此后再由城市的工匠们

in a period between 105 and 118 A.D., during Trajan's rule and at the beginning of Hadrian's. These rooms were probably used as an area where goods were first unloaded, inspected, then distributed to large city warehouses.

Between 1868-70, under the commission of Pope Pius IX, Father Luigi Bruzza performed several excavations in the downstream portion of the port, where he discovered a long stretch of pier with a scarp wall, double unloading ramps, moorings in large blocks of travertine placed at various heights - according to the level that the river reached each time - and access openings for docking boats and unloading goods. This is a work that can be attributed to the years of the Trajan and Hadrian principalities.

The project for expanding and adapting the river port system - with the restructuring of the docks and warehouses commissioned by Trajan, in order to make the intense commercial traffic that developed around Rome faster, safer, and more efficient - therefore, appeared unitary, coherent, and homogeneous, although it was not completed under Trajan's reign but continued uninterrupted, with maintenance and restructuring works, until the beginning of the 3rd century A.D.

The construction and growth of the river port led to the gradual urbanization of the plain behind it, with the construction of warehouses, commercial areas, and roads that connected to the Via Ostiense, of which many traces remain within the modern day neighborhood. The epigraphic material found in this area proves the existence of numerous guilds of craftsmen and traders in the port areas. For more than five centuries, the plain at the foot of the Aventine Hill became the main logistics area of the city, the economic heart of Rome.

All types of goods transited through here to and from the provinces of the Empire and beyond its borders: foodstuffs, wheat, oil, wine (the so-called "Mediterranean triad"), but also fish sauce, spices, other luxury goods from the East; raw materials, stone, wood, metals, dyes; manufactured goods of all kinds, proven by the variety of materials found in the excavations performed in the port area and the recoveries in water in the portion of the river in front of the port.

One of the most important and most complex trade of goods to manage was quarry marble. Various types of marble, often from far away (Africa, Greece, Near East),

加工成成品。这种特殊货物的尺寸和重量常会造成城市内交通堵塞，且容易破碎，因此港口内部专用场所的组织管理就显得极其重要。众所周知，必须要有很宽阔的自由码头才方便卸载和运移大理石。布鲁扎神父挖掘发现了大量的大理石，因此可以推断：直到哈德良统治时期，这段码头都是用于卸载大理石的，后期这段码头被整改，用于装卸其他货物。在一段斜坡的初始段墙体中镶嵌的砖块上绘制有一个双耳瓶，似乎能说明这种变化。该港口另一个卸载和搬运大理石的区域位于朝向城市的港口上游。奥斯蒂亚路是城市前的一段路，如今，它被命名为马尔莫拉塔路（“大理石路”）并不偶然。

公元 4 世纪到 5 世纪之间，由于古罗马帝国面临巨大危机，贸易急剧减少，许多地下设施和地道被遗弃，里面填满了陶器碎片（主要是双耳瓶）和泥土。

随着帝国的衰落，从公元 6 世纪开始，哥特和拜占庭之间的战争爆发（希腊—哥特战争，公元 535 年—553 年），台伯河左侧河岸港口设施被废弃，越来越多的船只集中停泊在另一侧岸边，并逐渐发展成为现代的河岸港口。

R. 塞巴斯蒂亚尼

were a highly sought after precious material for a city full of monumental buildings, as was the capital of the Roman Empire. Commissions from the Empire, but also those of rich patrician families, supported this trade. Blocks of marble and semi-finished columns arrived in Rome on large river barges. The marble was then worked or finished by artisans in the city. The size and weight of this particular type of goods, the need to make the blocks - that were often huge and very fragile - easily transportable within the city, made it very important to properly organize the spaces inside the port. We know that there had to be vast sections of docks available for unloading and handling the marble. A great quantity of marble was found during Father Buzza's excavations. This part of the quay was used as a statio marmorum up until Hadrian's era, when the reorganization works of the quay for other types of goods were started - as the image of an amphora on a panel inserted in the wall at the beginning of one of the ramps seems to indicate. Another area of the port used for unloading and handling marble was located in the most upstream part of the port, towards the city, in front of the urban section of Via Ostiense which, by no coincidence, today bears the name of Via Marmorata (tn. a name that alludes to "marmo", marble in Italian).

Between the 4th and 5th centuries A.D., with the decrease in trade caused by the overall crisis of the Roman Empire, most of the hypogeum structures and the cryptoporticus were abandoned and closed. They were then filled with debris, which were mostly remains of amphorae.

With the fall of the Empire, starting from the 6th century A.D., and the war between the Goths and the Byzantines (Greek-Gothic War, 535-553 A.D.), the ports on the left bank of the Tiber were abandoned, while the moorings were concentrated on the other bank, which would then become the river port in modern times.

R. Sebastiani

阿波罗头像

公元 1 至 2 世纪前后—4 世纪
大理石
高 16 厘米，宽 12 厘米，厚 12 厘米
重 2.3 千克
罗马考古、艺术品和景观监管局，展品编号 600083

Head of Apollo

1st/2nd - 4th century A.D.
height 16 cm, width 12 cm, thickness 12 cm
weight 2.3 kilograms
Special Superintendence of Archeology, Fine Arts, and Landscapes of Rome Inv. 600083

2018 年，在罗马特拉斯提维尔（Trastevere）的特拉斯提维尔历史区贾尼科洛山（Gianicolo Hill）的山坡上，在希里亚科圣所（Siriaco Sanctuary）进行的发掘中，人们发现了这件阿波罗头像。这尊雕像的头部由大理石雕刻而成，可以追溯到公元前 1 世纪。它原本是一座雕像的一部分，该雕像现已失传。

头像是和其他大理石雕像一起被发现的。目前这个遗址中的雕像只有部分被挖掘出来，墙壁的遗迹显示出红色和黄色的绘画痕迹。目前还不清楚放置的时间，以及为什么这组雕像会被放置在这种环境中。从地层学、地形朝向和墙体结构来看，雕塑所处的环境似乎是附属于所谓希里亚科圣所建筑的一部分。

圣殿建于公元 1 世纪，位于森林及泉水附近，泉水供奉着仙女芙丽娜，她是与水有关的女神。圣殿是在东地中海被征服之后，罗马引进东方异教的一个重要证据，这是罗马帝国的多民族特性、人口流动及其边界内活跃交流所形成的产物。它的位置与台伯河右岸古城部分的商业和生产作用相关，直接与河港和仓库区接壤。这是古城的一部分，不同文化和民族的人群在此混居。

命运女神福尔图娜雕像

约公元 1 世纪
大理石
高 92 厘米，宽 24 厘米，厚 32 厘米
重约 90 千克
罗马考古、艺术品和景观监管局，展品编号 566906

Statue of Fortuna

Possibly 1st century A.D.
height 92 cm, width 24 cm, thickness 32 cm
weight approx.90 kilograms
Special Superintendence of Archeology, Fine Arts, and Landscapes of Rome Inv. 566906

这尊在古罗马河港地道的填土中发现的古希腊大理石无头雕像展示了一个站立的女性形象。她是命运女神福尔图娜的造型，身着女式大披肩——这种披肩是古希腊时代的衣着样式，通常为白色。该雕像底座为圆形，除了头部，部分手臂和双手也有缺失。她的左臂抱着一件象征财富的经典物品：丰饶角。大理石无头雕像的历史可以追溯到罗马帝国时代。

海豚雕像

公元 1 世纪—2 世纪
大理石
长 21 厘米，宽 13 厘米，厚 34 厘米
重 13 千克
罗马考古、艺术品和景观监管局，展品编号 566905

Dolphin Statuette

1st - 2nd century A.D.
length 21 cm, width 13 cm, depth 34 cm
weight 13 kilograms
Special Superintendence of Archeology, Fine Arts, and Landscapes of Rome Inv. 566905

白色大理石海豚，无嘴，由细长的下颌骨、背鳍和尾鳍组成。海豚身体的左侧有一个扣钉孔。雕塑外表处理细致，眼球轮廓清晰，眼睑非常明显。海豚雕塑的身体末端呈拱形，呈现出运动时的形态。扣钉孔打在身体左侧下方，表明这只雕塑属于一个以海洋为主题的雕塑组，或者是喷泉或水道口的装饰。这件雕塑发现于台伯河上的古河港地道的废弃物层中。

饰有赫拉克勒斯形象的油灯

公元 1 世纪—2 世纪（公元 90—130 年）
大理石
陶
生产地区：意大利中部
高 3.3 厘米，长 11.8 厘米，直径 9.5 厘米
重 116.7 克
罗马考古、艺术品和景观监管局，展品编号 600057

Decorated Oil Lamp

1st - 2nd century A.D. (90-130 A.D.)
Area of production: Central Italy
height 3.3 cm, length 11.8 cm, diameter 9.5 cm
weight 116.7 grams
Special Superintendence of Archeology, Fine Arts, and Landscapes of Rome Inv. 600057

圆嘴赤陶油灯，浅米色，缺失环形耳柄。灯身圆形，深度较浅，灯喙圆直，灯身两侧有两个长方形装饰。大圆盘为一个带凹槽的圆形物，带有赫拉克勒斯的浮雕装饰。这位半人半神的英雄被描绘成赤身裸体站着的样子，肩上披着狮子皮（尼米亚猛狮的皮，这是他第一次努力得来的战利品）。他右手拿着棍棒，左手拿着双耳大饮杯——这是一种古希腊杯子，有两个把手。在灯的底部，可以看到一个扁平的圆环，那是一个纹样模糊的刻印章：IYL // RT。

青铜饰针

公元 1 世纪
青铜
高 1.9 厘米，长 5.3 厘米，宽 3 厘米
重 12.2 克
罗马考古、艺术品和景观监管局，展品编号 600064

Bronze Fibula

1st century A.D.
height 1.9 cm, length 5.3 cm, width 3 cm
weight 12.2 grams
Special Superintendence of Archeology, Fine Arts, and Landscapes of Rome Inv. 600064

扣衣针用青铜制成，为简单的弧形，带有一个小球体的搭扣装饰被固定在针上。镫形部分是镂空的，并且以一个圆形元素收尾。这些扣衣针在公元 1 世纪的意大利很常见。扣衣针是一种较大的安全饰针，由一根针构成，也被称为鞋钎针，一端为弹簧，另一端是尖的，与一个弧形末端相连。作为服饰的功能配件，用于扣紧衣服。古罗马服装通常由长方形大块布料构成，披在身体上，由扣衣针固定，装饰得很繁复。

发簪

公元 1 世纪—2 世纪
骨
直径 0.4 厘米；长 10.8 厘米
重 3.1 克
罗马考古、艺术品和景观监管局，展品编号 600047

Hair Pin

1st - 2nd century A.D.
diameter 0.4 cm, length 10.8 cm
weight 3.1 grams
Special Superintendence of Archeology, Fine Arts, and Landscapes of Rome Inv. 600047

这枚骨质发簪的外形为一只缠绕着蛇的手，呈锥形向尖端逐渐收缩。这件发簪发现自罗马泰斯塔西奥区。泰斯塔西奥区是古代城市的主要物流区，在台伯河港口两侧建有仓库。在古罗马，发簪常用于打理造型和固定头发。其质地包含多种材料，造型多样。当时，骨质发簪乃至更珍贵的象牙发簪遍布罗马帝国。

装饰骨板

公元 1 世纪—2 世纪
骨
宽 2.5 厘米，长 2.8 厘米，厚 0.6 厘米
重约 5.7 克
罗马考古、艺术品和景观监管局，展品编号 600045

Decorated Plate (Bone)

1st -2nd century A.D.
width 2.5 cm, length 2.8 cm, thickness 0.6 cm
weight ca. 5.7 grams
Special Superintendence of Archeology, Fine Arts, and Landscapes of Rome Inv. 600045

用拟人面具装饰的长方形骨板。在罗马世界，骨头和珍贵的象牙被广泛用于制作装饰元素，用来装饰桌子、置于餐桌旁的躺椅、床，以及盒子和容器等。

骨质家具饰板

公元 1 世纪—2 世纪
骨
宽 5.5 厘米，长 8 厘米，总厚度 2.5 厘米
重 49.6 克
罗马考古、艺术品和景观监管局，展品编号 600044

Plate (Bone)
1st - 2nd century A.D.
width 5.5 cm, length 8 cm, overall thickness 2.5 cm
weight 49.6 grams
Special Superintendence of Archeology, Fine Arts, and Landscapes of Rome Inv. 600044

羊蹄形骨板，可能是家具的装饰部件。

瓦檐饰

公元 2 世纪上半叶
陶
高 22 厘米，宽 16 厘米，厚 5 厘米
重 2 千克
罗马考古、艺术品和景观监管局，展品编号 583777

Antefix
first half of the 2nd century A.D.
height 22 cm, width 16 cm, thickness 5 cm
weight 2 kilograms
Special Superintendence of Archeology, Fine Arts, and Landscapes of Rome Inv. 583777

这件瓦檐饰是由来自罗马台伯岛的粉色黏土制成，饰有七瓣开槽的棕榈、三叶草簇和两朵垂花饰的边饰。样品缺少右上角，部分瓦片缺失。在希腊、伊特鲁里亚和罗马的世界中，神庙和公共建筑屋顶上的瓦檐饰是一种建筑装饰元素。这些瓦檐饰一般由赤陶制成，但也有用石头和大理石制成的。棕叶饰是最常见的装饰图案之一。

带戳记的陶砖

公元 1 世纪
陶
长 57 厘米，宽 57 厘米，厚 4 厘米
重约 4 千克
罗马考古、艺术品和景观监管局，展品编号 600091

Bipedal Brick

1st century A.D.
length 57 cm, width 57 cm, thickness 4 cm
weight 4 kilograms
Special Superintendence of Archeology, Fine Arts, and Landscapes of Rome Inv. 600091

这件双面砖来自罗马古河港，并加盖生产商印章：CALLISTI DVOR（UM） DOMITIO（RUM）。它来自多米提奥家族的砖窑，砖窑位于罗马上游的台伯河畔的特韦里纳的穆尼亚诺领土上。双面砖是典型的罗马建筑用砖，呈正方形，侧面长 2 罗马尺（59.4 厘米），用于建造拱门和水平面。

2 个釉面陶瓷墨水瓶残片

公元 1 世纪
陶
高 2.8 ～ 3.4 厘米，宽 2.8 ～ 3.1 厘米，长 6.6 ～ 7.3 厘米
罗马考古、艺术品和景观监管局，展品编号 599838

Inkwell

1st century A.D.
height 2.8 - 3.4 cm, width 2.8 - 3.1 cm, length 6.6 - 7.3 cm
Special Superintendence of Archeology, Fine Arts, and Landscapes of Rome Inv. 599838

两块釉面陶瓷墨水瓶残片分别是一块壁片与一部分上部圆盘装饰。赤陶墨水瓶是用模具和陶车制作而成的。残片主体上的釉面涂层是绿色的，带孔的部位为黄色（即所谓的“浅黄褐色”的黄色），孔用于引入着色剂。盘形装饰为植物纹样矩阵，由心形叶片和玫瑰花结构成。这两个残片发现于 2005—2009 年对罗马新泰斯特卡乔市场区域内与河港相连的古代仓库展开的挖掘中。

釉面陶瓷墨水瓶残片

公元 1 世纪
釉面陶瓷
高 3.7 厘米，长 4.8 厘米，厚 1.1 厘米
罗马考古、艺术品和景观监管局，展品编号 599842

Inkwell

1st century A.D.
width 3.7 cm, length 4.8 cm, thickness 1.1 cm
Special Superintendence of Archeology, Fine Arts, and Landscapes of Rome Inv. 599842

釉面陶瓷墨水瓶碎片，陶车注模成型，外釉面为绿色。墨水瓶壁为植物纹样的矩阵装饰，由披针形的叶子和浆果组成。这件残片发现于 2005—2009 年对罗马新泰斯特卡乔市场区域内与河港相连的古代仓库展开的挖掘中。

釉面陶瓷墨水瓶残片

公元 1 世纪
釉面陶瓷
高 2.5 厘米，宽 7.5 厘米，直径（底）6 厘米
罗马考古、艺术品和景观监管局，展品编号 599839

Inkwell

1st century A.D.
height 2.5 cm, width 7.5 cm, diameter (bottom) 6 cm
Special Superintendence of Archeology, Fine Arts, and Landscapes of Rome Inv. 599839

釉面陶瓷墨水瓶碎片。圈底与附着在陶车上制作的赤陶壁形似，内外表面为釉面，呈黄色（所谓“黄褐色”）。这件残片发现于 2005—2009 年对罗马新泰斯特卡乔市场区域内与河港相连的古代仓库展开的挖掘中。

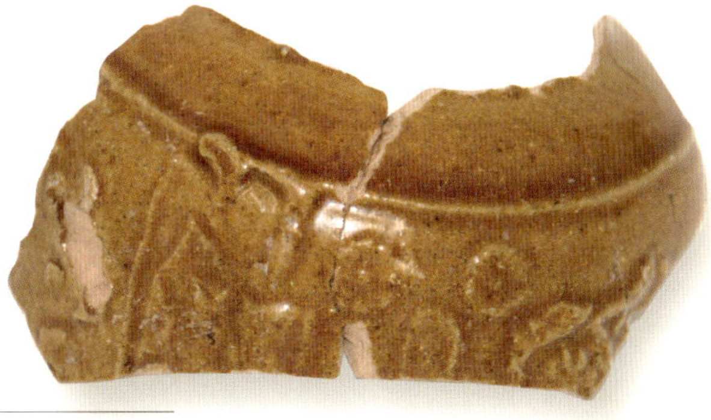

釉面陶瓷墨水瓶残片

公元 1 世纪
釉面陶瓷
最大高度 5.5 厘米，最大宽度 8.2 厘米
罗马考古、艺术品和景观监管局，展品编号 599840

Inkwell
1st century A.D.
max. height 5.5 cm, max. width 8.2 cm
Special Superintendence of Archeology, Fine Arts, and Landscapes of Rome Inv. 599840

用模具和陶车模压法制成的釉面陶瓷墨水瓶的残片。它有黄色釉面涂层（所谓“黄褐色”）；内部有滴状釉面。这两块瓷片用植物元素和人体图形作为基体装饰，它们与前一件釉面陶瓷墨水瓶碎片（展品编号 599839）是三块可以参照同一样品的墨水瓶壁的碎片。这几件残片于 2005—2009 年对罗马新泰斯特卡乔市场区域内与河港相连的古代仓库展开的挖掘中被发现。

釉面陶瓷墨水瓶残片

公元 1 世纪
釉面陶瓷
高 3.3 厘米，宽 6.3 厘米，长 4 厘米，直径（底）5 厘米
罗马考古、艺术品和景观监管局，展品编号 599841

Inkwell
1st century A.D.
height 3.3 cm, width 6.3 cm, length 4 cm, diameter (bottom) 5 cm
Special Superintendence of Archeology, Fine Arts, and Landscapes of Rome Inv. 599841

用模具和陶车模压法制成的釉面陶瓷墨水瓶的残片。它有绿色釉面（外部）；圈底由四块碎片和部分壁面重新组合而成，饰有“装饰用料浆”。该物品于 2005—2009 年对罗马新泰斯特卡乔市场区域内与河港相连的古代仓库展开的挖掘中发现。料浆装饰技术自古以来就被用于陶瓷装饰，例如米诺斯文化的陶瓷制品就曾使用这一技术。它是将半液体状黏土施用在仍然潮湿的陶坯上，以形成浮雕装饰。料浆的装饰类型多样，从凸出的小圆点再到波浪，都有。这个术语定义的是技术，而不是特定的装饰主题。

窑烧陶瓷废片

马帝国时代，约公元 1 世纪—公元 2 世纪
陶瓷
高 8 厘米，宽 25 厘米，长 20 厘米
重 0.40 克
罗马考古、艺术品和景观监管局，展品编号 600093

Pottery Furnace Scrap

Imperial Age, possibly 1st - 2nd century A.D.
height 8 cm, width 25 cm, length 20 cm
weight 0.40 grams
Special Superintendence of Archeology, Fine Arts, and Landscapes of Rome Inv. 600093

由具有明显施釉工艺的陶瓷制品留下的陶瓷废片。产生这类废片的原因有很多：器皿内出现错误的混合物成分，例如黏土过多，使器皿在烧制时不能承受高温；或是烧制过程中的温度误差或烧制过程中出现事故，例如在堆叠的烧制器皿中，放置在一个罐体和另一个罐体之间的间隔物断裂。这一废料发现于 2018—2019 年在罗马的特拉斯提维尔区进行的考古发掘活动中，地点在贾尼科洛山山坡上的科西尼宫花园。该地区因在 19 世纪末发现有一座豪华别墅遗迹而闻名（别墅后来被毁），该别墅的历史可以追溯到公元前 1 世纪末，别墅的主人是奥古斯都皇帝的女婿阿格里帕，它是工匠技术和生产区的物证。这个靠近台伯河和内河港口的生产区使用了贾尼科洛山的泉水。

搬运工小雕像

公元 1 世纪—2 世纪
陶土
高 4.9 厘米，宽 3.5 厘米
重 500 克
罗马国家博物馆 - 戴克里先浴场，展品编号 14904

Statuette of a Sack Bearer

1st - 2nd century A.D.
height 4.9 cm, width 3.5 cm
weight 500 grams
National Roman Museum, Baths of Diocletian Inv. 14904

搬运工雕像的上半身尚存，他的左肩上带着一个袋子，可能是用左臂抱着，而右臂则放下了。他似乎穿着一条无袖短上衣，绑在肩膀上，紧紧地贴着胸部下面。

搬运工小雕像

公元 2 世纪
陶土
高 13.3 厘米，宽 5.6 厘米，厚 3.8 厘米
重 700 克
罗马国家博物馆 - 戴克里先浴场，展品编号 51154

Statuette of a Sack Bearer
2nd century A.D.
height 13.3 cm, width 5.6 cm, depth 3.8 cm
weight 700 grams
National Roman Museum, Baths of Diocletian Inv. 51154

这名男性搬运工身穿短袖短上衣，胸部下方有窄扎带。他的双臂抱着一个袋子，肩膀上的重量使他的腿部弯曲。小雕像人物扛着口袋——从奥斯蒂亚和庞贝的登记册中可知，这是一名货物搬运奴隶。当时有城市河段，这些负责货物搬运的奴隶出现在台伯河水域，也就不足为奇了。

搬运工小雕像

公元 1 世纪—2 世纪
陶土
高 10.9 厘米，宽 4.6 厘米，厚 3.6 厘米
重 600 克
罗马国家博物馆 - 戴克里先浴场，展品编号 54010

Statuette of a Sack Bearer
1st - 2nd century A.D.
height 10.9 cm, width 4.6 cm, depth 3.6 cm
weight 600 grams
National Roman Museum, Baths of Diocletian Inv. 54010

这名男性搬运工小雕像的上半部分与前一个搬运工小雕像相似。

第二部分
维苏威火山脚下的那不勒斯海湾：佛莱格瑞海岸的港口
2B. THE GULF OF NAPLES BEYOND THE VESUVIUS: THE PORTS OF THE PHLEGRAEAN COAST

坎皮佛莱格瑞，位于那不勒斯的西北部，是一小片由火山岩组成的地区，它起源于 39 000 年前的火山大喷发，由此形成了佛莱格瑞火山口。这次火山活动催生出 40 多座火山，而其中一座名为索尔法塔拉的火山目前仍在活跃中。这一地区存在着丰富的历史文化资源，这使坎皮佛莱格瑞对我们来说具有重要意义。自公元前 9 世纪以来，便于船只停靠的小海湾、来自火山地下层的温泉和热蒸汽、肥沃的土壤以及面朝海洋的茂密树林的存在，不断吸引人们来此定居。彼时，奥比奇人定居在库迈山地和山下的平原上，之后他们又因埃乌贝亚和伊罗利亚的希腊殖民者的到来而被驱逐，而这些殖民者在公元前约 750 年就建立了库迈殖民地。

继罗马之后，古意大利最重要的一些城市在坎皮佛莱格瑞蓬勃发展：库迈，意大利南部的第一个希腊殖民地；波佐利，奥斯蒂亚前的国际大都市和罗马的主要商业港口；米塞努姆，帝国军队的大本营；巴亚，共和国晚期帝国社会名流的温泉浴场和住宅区。

F. 达勒姆

The Phlegraean Fields, north-west of Naples, is a small volcanic area that originated from an eruption 39,000 years ago, which formed the Phlegraean caldera. This volcanic activity resulted in the creation of over 40 volcanoes. One of these, the Solfatara, is still active. The geomorphological characteristics of the territory resulted in the natural resources that made the Phlegraean Fields a historical and cultural site of enormous importance for our civilization. The presence of inlets favorable for docking, thermal waters and hot vapors from the volcanic subsoil, the fertility of the soil, and also the presence of modest wooded hills overlooking the coast, favored the settlement of populations since the 4th century B.C.. At that time, the Opici had settled on the rock of Cumae and on the plain below. They were then driven out by the arrival of Greek colonists from Euboea and Aeolis, who founded the colony of Cumae around 750 B.C. .

The most important cities of ancient Italy, after Rome, flourished in the Phlegraean Fields. These included Cumae, the first ancient Greek colony in Southern Italy and the origin of the Fates of Roman mythology; Puteoli, a cosmopolitan city and the main commercial port of Rome before Ostia's; Misenum, seat of the imperial military fleet; Baia, thermal bath complex and residential area of the Late-Republican and Imperial elite.

F. Talamo

第一节 大型商用军事港口综合系统

2B.1. THE VAST INTEGRATED MERCHANT AND MILITARY PORT SYSTEM

公元前 1 世纪，罗马意识到佛莱格瑞海岸对控制地中海的重要性——拥有它是确保罗马军团在即将展开的大型海战中源源不断获得新生力量的必要条件。这将保证屋大维在那乌洛克对抗塞斯托·庞培（公元前 36 年）和在亚克兴对抗安东尼（公元前 31 年）的战争中成为胜利者。

事实上，罗马急需一个位于坎皮佛莱格瑞的军事港口，特别是在波佐利海湾，屋大维的海军上将、女婿马可·维普撒尼欧·阿格里帕在此找到了对建设军事港口所需的后勤基础设施最有利的地理条件：尤利乌斯港。

事实上，当时阿韦尔诺和卢克利诺沿海湖泊要比现在大得多，它们非常适合被建造成一个双港港池，而且佛莱格瑞地区凝灰岩层的厚度也有利于挖掘隧道。

建造尤利乌斯港的准备工作始于公元前37年，也就是屋大维耗费大量人力物力战胜庞培的前一年。卢克利诺和阿韦尔诺湖（c）之间的山脊被切断，形成一条连接两个港池的大型通航运河，外部的卢克利诺用于航行，内部的阿韦尔诺则用于船只的停泊和为船舶提供维护工作。人们开掘卢克利诺（d）沿海地带创建航道入口，与克奇奥山洞隧道对齐（e）——该隧道用于连接阿韦尔诺湖西北岸与广场东南部的库迈城，并且在最紧急的危险情况下，方便部队在库迈城内快速转移。另一条笔直的隧道——西比拉山洞（i），将阿韦尔诺的东南岸与卢克利诺的北岸相连。此外，根据原始资料记载，阿格里帕筑高了卢克利诺与海洋间（l）的堤坝，以

In the 1st century A.D., Rome recognized how strategically important the Phlegraean coast was for controlling the Mediterranean, which was necessary to affirm Rome's growing power in the imminent great naval battles that led to celebrating Octavian as the winner of these battles against Sextus Pompey in Naulochus (36 B.C.) and against Antony in Actium (31 B.C.).

In fact, Rome urgently needed a military port and, it was in the Phlegraean Fields, in particular in the Gulf of Pozzuoli, that Marcus Vipsanius Agrippa, Octavian's admiral and son-in-law, found the most favorable environmental conditions for creating the logistic infrastructures necessary for a military port: Portus Iulius.

In fact, the coastal lakes of Avernus and Lucrinus (the latter which was much larger at the time than today) lent themselves very well to creating a double harbor basin, and the consistency of the tuff bank, which makes up the Phlegraean territory, allowed to carry out tunnel excavations.

The preparatory procedures for the construction of Portus Iulius began in 37 B.C., just a year before the victory over Pompey, with the use of numerous men and vehicles. The ridge between the lakes of Lucrinus and Avernus(c)was cut, in order to create a large navigable canal that connected the two basins, where the external one, Lucrinus, was used for navigation and the internal one, Avernus, for storing ships and for maintenance. The coastal strip of Lucrinus was also cut(d), in order to build an entrance canal, aligned with another tunnel known as the "Grotta di Cocceio"(e) , which allowed to connect the north-west bank of Lake Avernus with the city of Cumae in the south-east sector of the forum. This was useful, in the event of imminent danger, to quickly move the troops into the city walls of Cumae. Another straight tunnel, the so-called "Grotta della Sibilla" (i), connected the south-east shore of Avernus with the north shore of Lucrinus. According to sources, Agrippa also raised an embankment that separated the Lucrinus from the sea(l), in order to guarantee the safety of

尤利乌斯港建造步骤示意图

确保湖泊及其堤坝上方的道路安全，根据斯特拉博的描述，堤坝长度为 8 个体育场（约 1480 米的长度总和）。

位于库迈卫城底部的区域被称为“罗马地穴”（f），隧道挖掘完工后，从城堡南部出海变成了现实（g）。

史料将这个强大的、贯穿凝灰岩的军事隧道体系归功于建筑师卢修斯 · 克奇奥 · 阿乌克托。遇到危险情况时，隧道群可快速转移部队以及造船厂的物资和劳动力，无须绕过将库迈与波佐利分开的米塞诺海角。

总的来说，这个基础设施网络是一套强大的战争体系，实现了在北部通过库迈港口控制沿海地带及在南部通过尤利乌斯港控制波佐利海湾的目的。

the lake and of the road above it, the legendary Via Herculea that, according to Strabo, was the length of 8 stadia (approx. 1,480 meters).

The tunnel cut at the base of the Acropolis of Cumae, known as the Crypta Roman(f), completed the work. This allowed to exit into sea, south of the stronghold(g) .

Ancient sources attribute to the architect, Lucius Cocceius Auctus, this formidable system of military tunnels cut in the tuff, used to rapidly move troops, in the event of imminent danger, and for supplies and labor in the shipyards, without having to circumnavigate the promontory of Misenum, which separated Cumae from Pozzuoli.

Overall, this network of infrastructures, a powerful war machine, allowed to monitor the coast through the port of Cumae to the north and the Gulf of Pozzuoli through Portus Iulius to the south.

Portus Iulius is now submerged due to a phenomenon called “bradyseism” (tn. the gradual rise and fall of the Earth’s

尤利乌斯港现在已被淹没，原因是诺沃山前方海岸线的海陆升降现象。诺沃山是于1538年在坎皮佛莱格瑞出现的最后一座火山。从航空照片及最近水下调查获得的平面图可以看出，该港口是从一条可通航的运河进入的。运河的长度约为350米，宽度为45米。 运河的西侧更容易受到风的侵袭，现在由一个已被淹没的巨石群所保护，巨石群由六根大柱子组成，柱子是平均大小为11米×10米的巨石，保存高度为5~6米，彼此相距约5米。它们是由内部核心为水泥的木制模板制成的，表层的残余部分保存在凝灰岩块中（凝灰岩砖块按菱形堆砌）。

沿着航道向北，在其东侧的半腰发现有一个小鱼塘。鱼塘通过两个进水口与大海相连，进水口上还留有用于给鱼塘换水的可滑动舱壁的凹槽石元件的残骸。

在港口船坞内部（鲁克林努斯湖），航拍照片显示有一个码头（95米×11米）和一个长长的柱廊。在附近的码头上，有两排同样的小房间，由凝灰岩砖块按菱形堆砌而成，被标识为货物仓库。

crust) along the stretch of coastline in front of Monte Nuovo, the last of the Phlegraean volcanoes, which emerged in 1538. What results from aerial photos and from plans obtained through these photos and through recent underwater surveys, the port was accessed from a navigable canal that measured approximately 350 meters in length (including the pilae) and 45 meters in width. The western side of the canal, which was more exposed to winds, was protected by a now submerged cliff, consisting of six large pilaes - stacked with an average size of 11x10 meters - that currently measure 5-6 meters in height, with a distance of 5 meters between the two. These were created through a wooden formwork system that had an internal cement core. Remains of the cube covering (reticulated work) were also preserved.

Following the canal to the north, at half of the height of its east side, a small fish farming pond was identified. This was connected to the sea by two water inlets. The remains of these include grooved stone elements that were used for sliding the bulkheads that aided in the exchange of water.

Inside the port basin (the lacus lucrinus), aerial photos show a pier (95x11 meters) and the presence of a long portico. Another quay was situated to the south of the pier, with two rows of warehouses, all of the same size.

The surveys carried out during the dive provided data that could not be collected from aerial photos alone. They

尤利乌斯港鸟瞰图

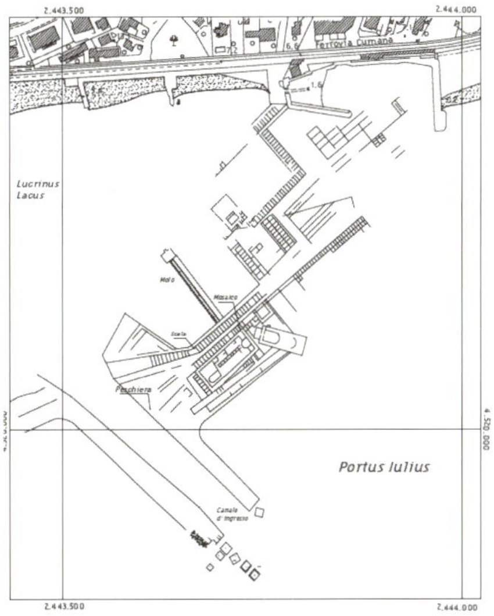

尤利乌斯港平面图

潜水调查提供了无法仅靠航拍照片推断出的细节。调查显示，货物仓库内配备有将易腐烂的货物与湿气隔离开的装置，以便让货物可以被完好地运送至罗马的大部分地区。这些隔离装置包括一种木质夹层——我们可以通过用于容纳垂直杆的孔（在好几个房间的地板上都能看到它们）以及用于架搁板的墙壁来识别它们。

其中一间房间保留了有白色、黑色和红色镶嵌物的彩色马赛克地板。中央的白色区域由具有“流动的波浪”花纹的条状带构成，黑色镶嵌物则沿着房间的外墙展开。

从航拍照片中可以看到另外一排房间，不过这些房间已经逐渐被沙子覆盖，只能让人们看到现在的海岸线。在尤利乌斯港这片区域曾有过很多的装卸活动，并且该区域在没有切断波佐利港口其他地理结构的情况下和波佐利港口进行了连接。1967年，成千上万的黏土油灯（制作于公元1世纪中叶）被发现并被复原，就证实了这一点。黏土油灯也许是在一个隔间——一个位于建筑群东部的最外部仓库——被发现的。不幸的是，发现的具体位置今已不明。这些灯可能是在晚上存放货物时使用的，正如它们变黑的喙所证明的那样。

也许是因为受到海陆升降造成的深水处沙土淤塞的影响，尤利乌斯港逐渐不再适合军舰通行，后来它重新变为商业港口，成了一个大型港口综合体。在大约3个世纪的时间里，它一直是罗马的补给港，在将埃及的粮食运到这座城市的过程中，发挥着至关重要的作用。

尤利乌斯港丧失军事功能可能发生在公元前12年左右。也许是听从了已成为尤利乌斯港建造者的阿格里帕的建议，屋大维（公元前27年成为奥古斯都）后来选择将坎皮佛莱格瑞和米塞诺小海湾作

documented that the warehouses were equipped with systems used to isolate the most perishable goods from moisture, while they were stored to be transferred in large part to Rome. These included wooden mezzanines, identified by the presence of holes for housing vertical poles - which could be seen in the floor of several rooms - and in the walls for shelves.

The polychrome mosaic floor with white, black, and red tiles was preserved in one of these rooms. The central white portion is framed by a band with a “flowing wave” motif using black tesserae, which runs along the perimeter of the room.

From the aerial photos, other rows of rooms were visible, which were progressively covered with sand, up to the current coastline. The intense loading and unloading activities carried out in this part of Portus Iulius, which was connected without significant interruptions to the rest of the structures of the Port of Puteoli, is confirmed by the recovery of several of thousands of clay oil lamps (mid-1st century A.D.) found in 1967, perhaps in a compartment of the horrea - the most external warehouses located in the eastern part of the complex - for which the exact topographical location was unfortunately lost. The lamps were probably used during the storage of goods at night, as demonstrated by their blackened beaks.

This was, therefore, a large port complex - created when Portus Iulius was no longer suitable for the transit of warships, probably after the seabed became covered with sand because of the phenomenon of bradyseism - which was then converted into a commercial port. For about three centuries, this port was used for the import and supply of goods for Rome, of vital importance for feeding the population with grain from Egypt.

Portus Iulius probably lost its military function around 12 B.C., when Octavian (who became Augustus in 27 B.C.) probably after being advised by Agrippa (who built Portus Iulius), again chose the Phlegraean Fields and the inlet of Misenum as the naval base of the imperial fleet, the classis Misenensium.

The same favorable conditions were found in Misenum, as in Portus Iulius, with its double basin, where the external one was used for navigation and the internal one for storage. These communicated with each other through a pons ligneus (tn. wooden bridge), which rose for the passage of ships, mainly small and fast liburnae.

米塞诺小海湾考古地图

坎皮佛莱格瑞考古公园藏浮雕石板

为帝国舰队的海军基地。

与尤利乌斯港的情况一样，米塞诺有着同样有利的环境条件：双港池，外部的港池可用于航行，内部的港池用于停泊船只。内外港池通过一个木质桥梁实现相互交流，往来船只主要是小而快的利布尼船。

2006 年进行的一项水下考古调查提供了关于海陆升降和米塞诺港外部港池构造的新数据。罗马时代与现今的海平面之间有 4 米之差，这个高度也与泰伦尼海岬罗马码头根部的差异是一样的。在港口的外部港池、距离彭纳塔海岬山脊约 50 米的地方，古人们使用水泥建造了一个装备有大型系缆桩的港口码头。这个码头总长约 550 米，可以停泊由 90 艘船组成的舰队，这反映出米塞诺军事港口的规模十分庞大。此外，现在我们已经知道，罗马港外部港池的构造分外特殊。事实上，外部港池是通过

An underwater archeological survey carried out in 2006 provided new data on the phenomenon of bradyseism and on the configuration of the external basin of the Port of Misenum. The difference in sea level between the Roman era and today reaches 4 meters, a height which is also compatible with the only mooring ring still situated at the base of the Roman pier at Punta Terone. A port quay - built in cement work and equipped with large mooring bollards - was identified at about 50 meters from the coastal ridge of Punta Pennata, which closed it to the north. This quay measured 550 meters in length, indicating the size of the military Port of Misenum. Its fleet was made up of 90 ships. Furthermore, a different conformation of the external basin of the Roman port was documented, with respect to what has been known so far. In fact, it is, in turn, divided into two bodies of water through opposing pilae, suggesting a more complex layout of the external body of water.

In conclusion, in the second half of the 1st century B.C., Octavian-Augustus built a formidable military port system in the Phlegraean Fields: first Portus Iulius, then Misenum. These military infrastructures, and the subsequent transformation of

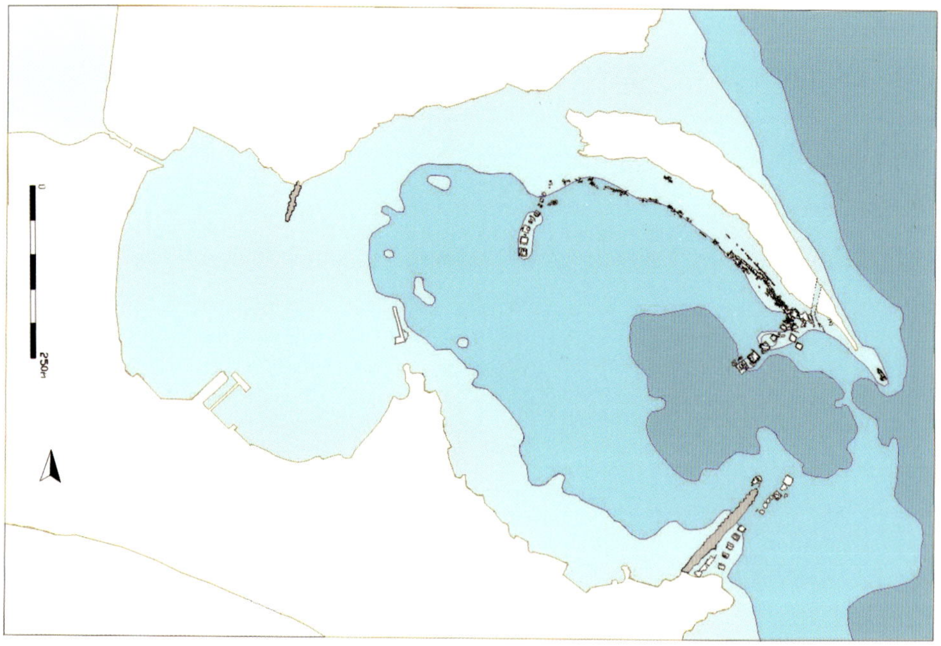

米塞诺港外部港池俯瞰图

相对的立柱细分为两个水域的，这表明外部港池更为复杂。

总而言之，在公元前 1 世纪下半叶，屋大维 · 奥古斯都在坎皮佛莱格瑞建造了一个强大的军事港口体系，首先是尤利乌斯港，然后是米塞诺港。有了这些基础设施，再加上将尤利乌斯港改造成罗马的主要商业港口，这些措施都有利于将佛莱格瑞这座城市纳入奥古斯都的政治和意识形态圈，并最终促进了该地区城市建设的巨大发展。在公元前 1 世纪上半叶，参议院的杰出代表们就已经在这里建造出了极具规格的住宅。

F. 达勒姆

Portus Iulius into the main commercial port of Rome, favored the inclusion of the Phlegraean cities into Augustus' political and ideological program. The result was a very large building and residential development in the Phlegraean area where, already in the first half of the 1st century B.C., prominent members of the senatorial class had built their prestigious homes.

F. Talamo

第二节 巴亚：皇宫、水下宫殿和艾比达菲奥海岬的温泉浴场

2B.2. BAIA: THE IMPERIAL PALACE, THE NYMPHAEUM, AND THE BATHS OF PUNTA EPITAFFIO

古老的巴亚俯瞰着一个小型的湖形海湾——巴亚湖，人们可以通过一条宽阔的运河从海上进入这个湖（但如今因为海陆升降，这个湖已经被淹没了。巴亚曾经是罗马时代最知名的温泉小镇。为了提高自己在沿海地带的优势，阿格里帕和屋大维在这里建造了一个安全的双港池港口，即尤利乌斯港。他们将卢克利诺的一侧朝向海洋开放，另一侧则向阿韦尔诺方向开放，并从该地区的森林中采伐木材建造船队。

此外，这里还有地下火山资源，含硫蒸汽（水蒸气）和温泉水（热水）从地下流出，公元1世纪（《自然史》第二卷，第17章）的拉丁文作家老普林尼曾赞美这些水对健康的益处。这里有许多向大海倾

Ancient Baiae (Baia), which overlooked a small lake-shaped inlet (Baianus lacus) and was accessible from the sea through a wide canal (now submerged due to the phenomenon of bradyseism - fig. 1), was the most famous and renowned thermal bath complex during the Roman era. Agrippa's and Octavian's decision to build a safe double-basin port, Portus Iulius, promoted the popularity of its coastline, opening up to Lucrinus on one side towards the sea and, on the other, towards Avernus, while also building a fleet using wood from the forests in the area.

Added to this were the volcanic resources of the subsoil, from which sulphurous vapors (vapor) and hot spring waters (calentes aquae) sprang. The health benefits of these were even celebrated by the Latin writer and philosopher, Pliny the Elder, in the 1st century A.D. (Nat. Hist. II, 17), and the salubrity of the location, with its blueberry-covered hills that sloped down

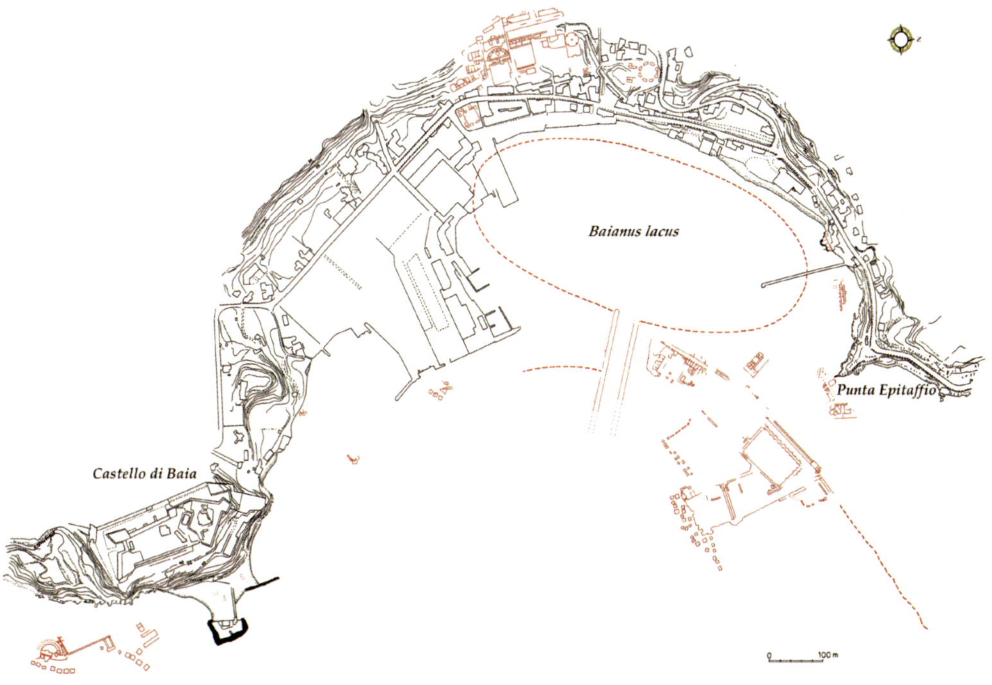

淹没的海湾和城堡的考古地图

安布拉提奥别墅，上层露台

斜的山坡，坡上长满了爱神木，站在这里可以将从尼西达岛到米塞诺角的整个波佐利湾的壮丽景色尽收眼底。另一个引人入胜的地方，是在公元前 1 世纪 90 年代由凯乌斯·瑟吉厄斯·奥拉达倡议建造的、位于附近的卢克利诺湖的牡蛎养殖场，以及他发明的新型浴室。这种浴室在地板下面设置了一个加热隔间，用于传输地下天然热量。这是别墅的主人才能享有的奢侈品。

由于这些原因，从公元前 1 世纪开始，随着别墅的大量涌现以及“别墅社会”在这一地区的盛行，罗马贵族中最重要的人物频繁出入巴亚及其沿海地带。

第一批别墅建于内战期间的巴亚，时间是公元前 75 年至公元前 31 年。在公元前 75 年，西塞罗开始执政，他见证了这片土地的沧桑；在公元前 31 年，安东尼被屋大维打败，在近一个世纪的战争之后，该地区实现了长久的和平。

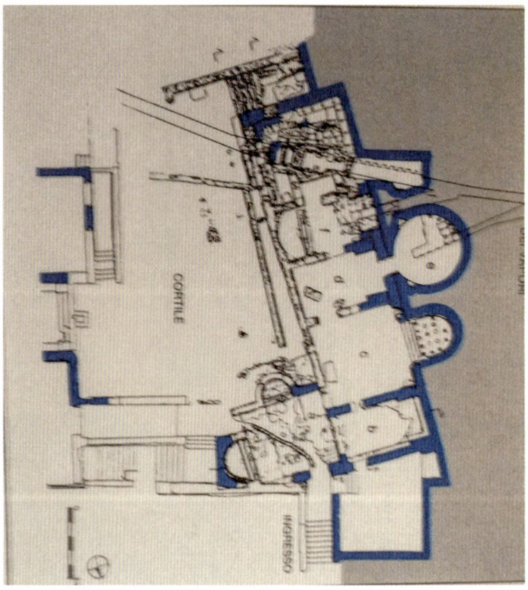

小型温泉浴场

towards the sea, offered a spectacular view of the entire Gulf of Pozzuoli from Nisida to Misenum. During the 1st century B.C., another attraction were the oyster farms in nearby Lake Lucrinus, created by Caius Sergius Orata, along with one of

原始资料记载了巴亚沿海地带别墅的十几位罗马业主的名字，其中包括将军马里奥、庞培和凯撒。他们的别墅建在高处，像是孤然耸立的堡垒，俯瞰着下方。

考古发现证实了别墅的数据资料和地形位置。这些别墅的铭文无法辨认，但根据挖掘数据和原始资料我们可以假设，塞内卡和塔西佗所引证的凯撒别墅，极有可能就是在阿拉贡城堡高地上发现的那座别墅，被纳入了名为“帕迪廖内·卡瓦列雷”的防御工事。

这些建筑物建在陡峭的海岬或山坡上，为了能够在纵向尤其是垂直方向上充分利用可用的面积，他们开发了梯形建筑结构，用来支撑上层建筑，并使用当地的火山灰砂浆（火山灰），使得墙壁的内核坚固且具有弹性。

这种建筑模式在公元前 2 世纪末至公元前 1 世纪初传播开来，最杰出的代表是安布拉提奥别墅。这个别墅大约从公元前 1 世纪中叶开始建造，有 6 个长约 100 米的露台占据了一个约 80 米高的垂直切面。也许当时这个小型温泉浴场的小桑拿区（蒸汽浴室）就属于这个别墅，这是巴亚第一个根据瑟吉厄斯·奥拉达引进的创新方法建造的、由小支柱（悬吊的）支撑、地下自然热量在地板下扩散的火坑供暖房间。

这些住宅的丰富性，仅仅通过现存的建筑来看

his inventions: a new type of bath, the balineae pensiles,which made it possible to create a chamber, heated under the floor, which allowed for the natural heat from the subsoil to be diffused. A luxury for the owners of the surrounding villa.

Because of this, starting from the 1st century B.C., Baiae and its coastline was visited by the most important exponents of the Roman aristocracy, with the onslaught of villas and the popularity of the "villa society".

The first villas were built in Baiae during the civil wars, between 75 B.C. - the year of Cicero's entry into politics (the main witness of the vicissitudes of the territory), and 31 B.C. - the year Octavian defeated Antony and the beginning of a long period of peace, after almost a century of wars.

Sources mention the names of a dozen Roman owners of villas on the coast of Baiae, including Generals Marius, Pompey, and Caesar, whose villas dominated the underlying locations, isolated like fortresses, situated in an elevated position (Seneca, ad Luc. 51,11).

Archeological evidence confirms both the numerical data and the topographical position. The epigraphy of these villas could not be identified, but it is highly possible, on the basis of excavation data and sources, that Caesar's villa cited by Seneca and by Tacitus was the one discovered on the upland of the Aragonese Castle, incorporated into the fortification called "Padiglione Cavaliere".

These buildings, which were built on steep promontories or on hilly slopes - so that they could make the most of the available surface area, both longitudinally and especially vertically - developed terraced architectures, each one supporting the one above it with the use of local pozzolan mortar (pulvis puteolanus), which made the inner core of the walls resistant and, at the same time, elastic.

的话体现得并不明显。在卡斯泰洛别墅和特里泰利山上的别墅中，人们发掘出了精致绝伦的图案装饰，就图案的精美和代表性而言，其独创性超过了维苏威别墅的当代装饰主题，充分彰显出当时社会名流的品位。

直到公元前1世纪30年代，巴亚景观还都是由几个分散的别墅和未开发的温泉组成，而在其后的几十年里，这里发生了巨大的变化，成为海岸建筑众多、人口稠密的地区。斯特拉博著名论著的第4、5节曾描述了从阿特内奥海角（坎帕内拉海岬）到米塞诺整个海湾的海岸，它就好像是一个城市，有着诸供人们居住的海滨别墅。也正是受到屋大维·奥古斯都崛起所带来的影响，他的一系列举措给人们带来了很多奢侈享受和福利：尤利乌斯港改建用

Since the beginning of the mid-1st century B.C., the most spectacular example of this architectural model - popular between the end of the 2nd and the beginning of the 1st century B.C. - was the Villa dell'Ambulatio with its six terraces, approximately 100 meters long, which occupied a vertical section measuring approximately 80 meters in height. The small sauna area (laconicum) of the "Piccole Terme" - small thermal baths, belonging to this villa, probably dates back to the same period. It was perhaps the first time that a hypocaust chamber supported by pillars (suspensurae) was used in Baiae. This was implemented for the diffusion under floors of the natural heat from the subsoil, based on an innovation introduced by Sergius Orata.

The wealth of these homes is not only evident from the surviving architecture. Excavations, for example, which involved the Villa del Castello (fig. 4), and Villa Tritoli (fig. 5), documented highly refined pictorial decorations that surpass, in their originality, the motifs and depictions of the

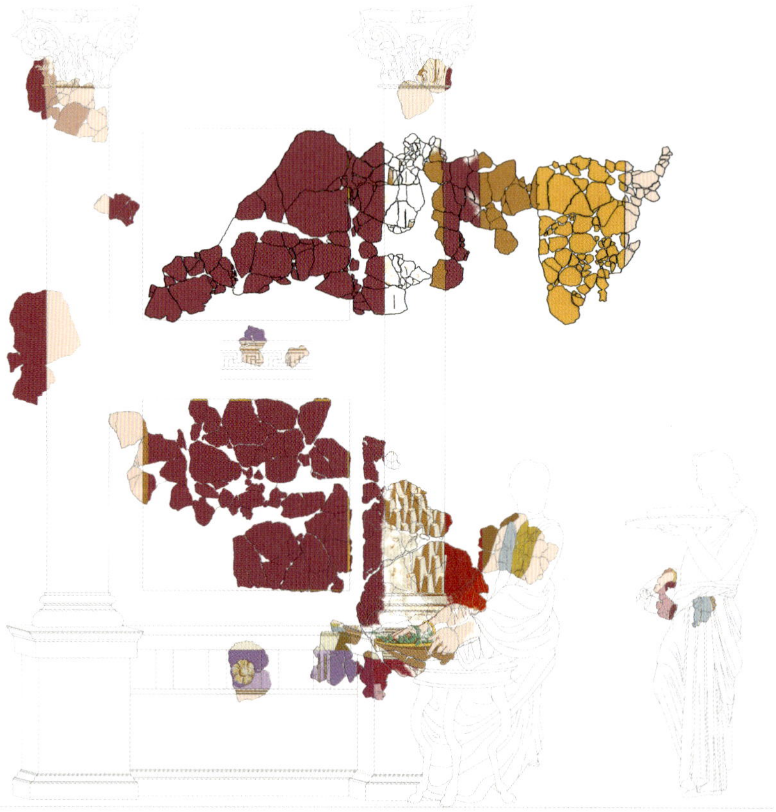

特里泰利别墅，壁画场景复原

于商业用途、军事港口转移到米塞诺，以及建造出为佛莱格瑞带来饮用水的塞利诺渡槽。所有这些措施都有利于建造新别墅、扩建现有别墅，以及建造新的温泉设施和扩建现有的小型温泉浴场。

人们相继发现了大量建造于公元前 1 世纪末和公元 2 世纪的别墅废墟，这些废墟从斯卡兰德罗内地区的卢克利诺西坡沿着海湾直到卡斯特海角，几乎没有中断。

只有一个别墅，我们或许知道它的主人，这栋别墅曾经耸立在巴亚湖东岸，现在已经被淹没。因为在那里人们发现了一个刻着“L. 皮索尼斯”名字的铅水管（铅瘘），他可能是 L. 卡尔普尔尼乌斯 · 皮索，根据有关资料，他的后人参与了反对尼禄的阴谋，这起阴谋发生在巴亚的同一栋别墅中。

还有一些房屋集中建在可以俯瞰巴亚湖海湾的山丘上，这个建筑群由被现代学者定义为“温泉浴场”的一系列房屋构成，这些房屋呈扇形分布，其中一些有着奇特的名字（安布拉提奥、莫库利奥、萨桑德拉、维纳斯和小型温泉浴场）。一些刻在 3 世纪末期玻璃瓶上的图案描绘了从海上看到的巴亚海岸“宫殿”的样子，人们认为这是一座皇宫——艾比达菲奥海岬的克劳迪乌斯的宫殿。（受到海陆升降的影响，其罗马式建筑被保存在海中，现在可以看到的是在阿拉贡城堡的雕塑，哈德良时期（公元 117 年—134 年）的浴场、维纳斯神庙及其后面的水疗区域，还有亚历山大 · 塞韦罗宫殿（公元 204 年—234 年）和狄安娜神庙及其现在已被淹没的罗马式建筑。）现今已经修复了在海中发现的数十个建筑和雕塑，其中一部分收藏在佛莱格瑞博物馆。

在巴亚帝国的前三个世纪，由于温泉的奢华和舒适，巴亚成为皇室的首选驻跸地。普林尼通过巴亚风格的语言对其进行了充分的总结，同时考古发现也反映了这种生活方式，我们可以根据宫殿中陈

contemporary decorations of the Vesuvian villas, revealing the taste of an elite society.

If until the beginning of the 1st century B.C., Baiae's landscape consisted of a few scattered villas and unexploited thermal baths, within a few decades, it changed radically and became a coastline populated with buildings. In his famous passage, V.4.5., Strabo described the coast of the entire gulf, from Capo Ateneo (Punta della Campanella) to Misenum, as one single city, so numerous were the seaside villas that populated it. The rise to power of Octavian Augustus brought luxury and well-being with his interventions: the commercial conversion of Portus Iulius, the displacement of the military port at Misenum, and the construction of the Serino aqueduct that brought potable water to all of the Phlegraean centers. All this favored the construction of new villas and the expansion of already existing ones, as well as the construction of new thermal bath complexes, such as the so-called "Tempio di Mercurio" - Temple of Mercury - and the original rooms of the so-called "Stanze di Venere" - Rooms of Venus - along with the expansion of the existing "Piccole Terme".

Between the end of the 1st century B.C. and the 2nd century A.D., the villas extended almost without interruption between the western slope of the Lucrinus, in Scalandrone, along all of the Baianus sinus, up to the promontory of the Castle.

Only in one case was it possible to attribute the name of an owner to a villa. The villa stood on the eastern shore of the Baianus lacus, which is now submerged, and the name of its owner, L. Pisonis, was found inscribed on a pipeline (fistula plumbea). He was probably L. Calpurnius Piso, whose nephew was involved in the conspiracy against Nero that, according to sources, took place in that same villa in Baiae.

The residential building development was located on the hill overlooking the inlet of the Baianus lacus, which was overly populated with the construction of a series of homes defined by modern scholars as "Terme" (Thermal Baths). This was used not only to highlight their predominant feature but, above all, to emphasize how these so-called "Sectors" were atypical and non-classifiable, with several having fancy names, such as Ambulatio, Mercurio, Sosandra, Venere, and Piccole Terme. Their interpretation, based on the term, Palatium - engraved on several late 3rd-century glass flasks depicting

列的一系列雕塑想象当时的情形。

之后，在公元 3 世纪和 4 世纪之间，海陆升降导致从波佐利到米塞诺的沿海地带的非均匀坍塌。根据最近的水下调查，我们确定与当前的海平面高度相比，罗马时代的海平面高度大约在 -4 米左右。巴亚沿海地带的建筑物逐渐废弃并被海水淹没，就像维苏威火山喷发一样，海洋封存了它们的各种装饰，正如佛莱格瑞博物馆展出的艾比达菲奥的罗马式建筑雕塑所示。

另一方面，从后古典时期的证据和皮埃特罗 · 达 · 埃波利失落的诗篇可以看出，巴亚浴场的热闹和名望并没有消失。安吉莉卡图书馆的《在波佐利湾的浴池上》（1211—1221）手抄副本中描述了浴池中每种水的优点，并用珍贵的微缩模型进行了展示。

P. 米涅洛

the coast of Baiae seen from the sea - was mainly considered a unit of imperial constructions: Claudius' palace on Punta Epitaffio with its nymphaeum - preserved below sea level, due to the phenomenon of bradyseism, with its sculptural apparatus now housed in the Aragonese Castle; the baths from Hadrian's era (117-134 A.D.) with their so-called "Tempio di Venere" - Temple of Venus, and its thermal bath area in the rear; the palace of Alexander Severus (204-234 A.D.) with the so-called "Tempio di Diana" - Temple of Diana, and its now submerged nymphaeums, from which dozens of architectural remains and sculptures recovered at sea originate, partly exhibited in the Phlegraean Museum.

During the first three centuries of the Baiae Empire, it became the favorite destination of the imperial court for its luxury and the wellness of its thermal baths, which Pliny well-summarized with the term, mos Baianus, to indicate a lifestyle that the archeological evidence - further emphasized by a series of sculptures on display - only partly demonstrates.

Then, between the 3rd and 4th centuries, bradyseism caused the non-homogeneous collapse of the coastal strip from Pozzuoli to Misenum, where recent underwater surveys made it possible to establish that the sea level in the Roman era must have been approximately -4 meters as compared to the current altitude. The buildings on the coast of Baiae were progressively abandoned and covered by the sea that, like the eruption of the Vesuvius, preserved them along with their decorative apparatus, as demonstrated by the sculptures of the Nymphaeum of Punta Epitaffio exhibited in the Phlegraean Museum.

However, the fame of and visits to the baths of Baiae did not cease, as we can see in the testimonies from the post-classical era and from the lost poem by Petrus de Ebulo, the De Balneis Puteolanis (1211-1221), copied in a manuscript of the "Biblioteca Angelica" (Angelica Library), which describes them with the virtues attributed to each type of water and illustrates them with exquisite miniatures.

P. Miniero

狄俄尼索斯与黑豹的雕像

公元 1 世纪
大理石
高 140 厘米，底座宽 60.5 厘米，底座宽 40 厘米
重 200 千克
坎皮佛莱格瑞考古公园 - 巴亚城堡中的坎皮佛莱格瑞考古博物馆，展品编号 222739

Statue of Dionysus with Panther

1st century A.D.
height 140 cm, width of plinth 60.5 cm, depth of plinth 40 cm
weight 200 kilograms
Phlegraean Fields Archeological Park - Archeological Museum of the Phlegraean Fields in the Castle of Baia Inv. 222739

狄俄尼索斯与黑豹的雕像，白色大理石（伦纳斯）制作，来自艾比达菲奥海岬（Punta Epitaffio）宫殿（东侧第一个壁龛）。这座宫殿也被称为克劳迪乌斯的罗马式建筑。狄俄尼索斯这位年轻的神有着柔和的轮廓，他的右臂依靠在一根被帷幔覆盖的柱子上，右手里有一个杯子（康塔罗斯酒杯，现已佚失），他正在从杯子里倒酒给蹲在柱子旁边的黑豹。这个组合是对罗马时代的雕塑原型的重新阐释。雕像由几个独立的部分组装而成，这种极不常见的技术是尤利乌斯 · 克劳迪乌斯王朝（公元 1 世纪）佛莱格瑞时代雕塑家常用的工艺。艾比达菲奥海岬大厅在海平面上，被认为是一个被海水三面包围的巨大水神殿。雕像被分成两组：后殿的部分与尤利西斯迷惑波吕斐摩斯的场景有关，而另一部分则代表了尤利乌斯 · 克劳迪乌斯王朝。

港口场景浮雕

公元 3 世纪后半叶
大理石
高 21 厘米，宽 31 厘米，厚 5 厘米
罗马国家博物馆 - 戴克里先浴场，展品编号 56425

Bas-Relief with Port Scene

second half of the 3rd century A.D.
height 21 cm, width 31 cm, thickness 5 cm
National Roman Museum, Baths of Diocletian Inv. 56425

浮雕描绘了一位海港的装卸工人，正从一艘小船上卸下食品货物：他肩抗一只箱子，右臂上搭着包裹箱子的布，左手紧握着一个小物件——可能是一张记有卸货劳动报酬的票券。在船头可以看到连接船坞的跳板。在奥斯蒂亚，由于港口的海床过低，大型船只无法驶入，这些特殊的小船就成了为满载货物的大船卸货必不可少的媒介，它们也被用来运送货物到城市里的仓库。此外，它们还会通过河岸上牛力的牵引，逆流经由台伯河直接驶往罗马。

UNIT III

THE DOMINION OF THE SEA

SHIPS AND SHIPBUILDING

第三单元

海上统治

船舶和船舶制造

第一部分

军舰

3A. MILITARY SHIPS

在第一次布匿战争期间（公元前 264 年—公元前 241 年），罗马为了能在大海上对抗其永恒的敌人——迦太基人而建立了海军。根据古希腊著名的历史学家波里比阿斯讲述，在此之前罗马人既没有航海的职业，也没有航海的经验。他们凭借着过人的智慧和富于冒险的精神，来到了地中海，以前所未有的超短时间建造了第一支舰队，同时仿制了迦太基人的五列桨战舰，随后在海岸线进行巡逻，这些行动有效地阻止了迦太基人越过墨西拿海峡。每艘罗马五列桨战舰都有 300 名桨手（每支桨 5 名）和 120 名士兵驾驭。其后，汉尼拔 · 罗迪奥带兵俘虏了一座巨大的帆船，那是一艘四列桨战舰（或四边桨）。他们还以此为参照范本，在公元前 242 年又建造了 200 艘战舰，并在公元前 241 年的埃加迪群岛海战中投入使用。该战役是勒班陀战役（1571 年）之前罗马所经历的最大规模的海战。得益于他们的新技术装置——乌鸦吊桥（尽管有些人对此表示怀疑），即带有挂钩的移动通道，罗马战舰可以钩住敌人的战舰并登上敌舰，让士兵像在地面一样进行战斗。

事实上，罗马在海上的军事活动可以追溯到几个世纪前——它与伊特鲁里亚海军和意大利南部的希腊城邦之间曾爆发过冲突。在布匿战争之后的几个世纪里，没有强大的对手步步紧逼，再加上罗马人对陆地的绝对统治，使其对加强舰队力量又失去了兴趣。罗马舰队一直主要由三列桨战舰组成。公元前 67 年，在庞培大帝（曾被赋予特殊权力）的命令下，一支强

The birth of one Roman military navy was particularly linked to the First Punic War (264-241 B.C.), when Rome had to face its eternal enemy, Carthage, on its own domain: the sea. The famous Greek historian, Polybius, told how the Romans - who did not have vocation for nor had experience in navigation up until then - began to venture into the Mediterranean with great resourcefulness and skill. They built their first fleet in record time, copying a Carthaginian quinquereme, which had ended up on the coast during maneuvering procedures meant to prevent them from crossing the Strait of Messina. Each Roman quinquereme had 300 rowers (five for each oar) and 120 soldiers. Subsequently, they took possession of General Hannibal Barca's large galley, the tetrere (or quadrireme), which was moved by groups of four oars each, maneuvered by a rower or by a single order of oars that were, in turn, each maneuvered by four rowers. They also used this ship as a model for constructing 200 more ships in 242 B.C. The Battle of the Aegates was won by Rome in 241 B.C. and marked the end of the largest naval war fought in the Mediterranean at least until the battle of Lepanto (1571), also thanks to the use of the corvus (although some doubts remain regarding its use). This was a mobile loading bridge equipped with a spike that the Roman ships would use to pierce and anchor the enemy ships. The soldiers would then board the ships and engage in close combat, just as they would on land.

Actually, Rome's military activities on the sea date back to previous centuries and to battles with the Etruscan navy and those with the Greek cities of southern Italy. However, the Romans became uninterested in strengthening their fleet in the centuries following the Punic wars. The urgency to battle their fearsome adversary no longer existed, so they returned to their missions on land. The fleet was mainly made up triremes, long ships with a rowing system and three levels of oars moved by single rowers. In 67 B.C., an imposing naval force under the command of Pompey the Great (to whom exceptional powers

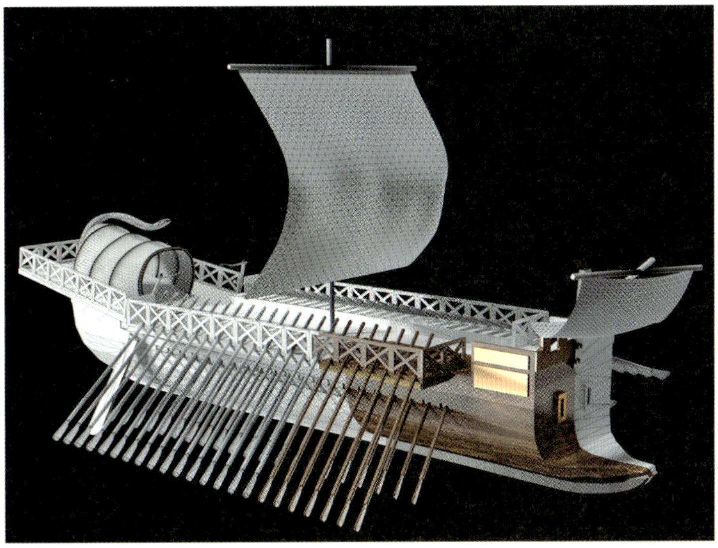

利布尼船：马泰奥·科利纳的3D重建

奇维塔韦基亚港口一艘利布尼船的部分复原重建

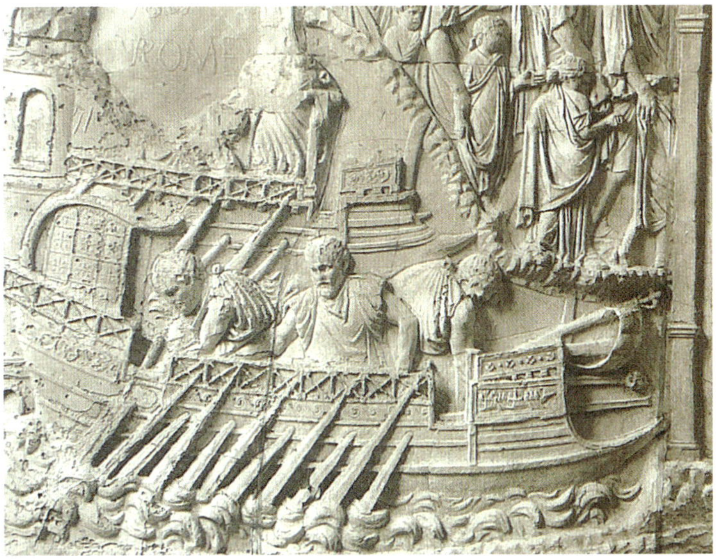

图拉真纪念碑上的第82个场景，启发了对利布尼船的复制

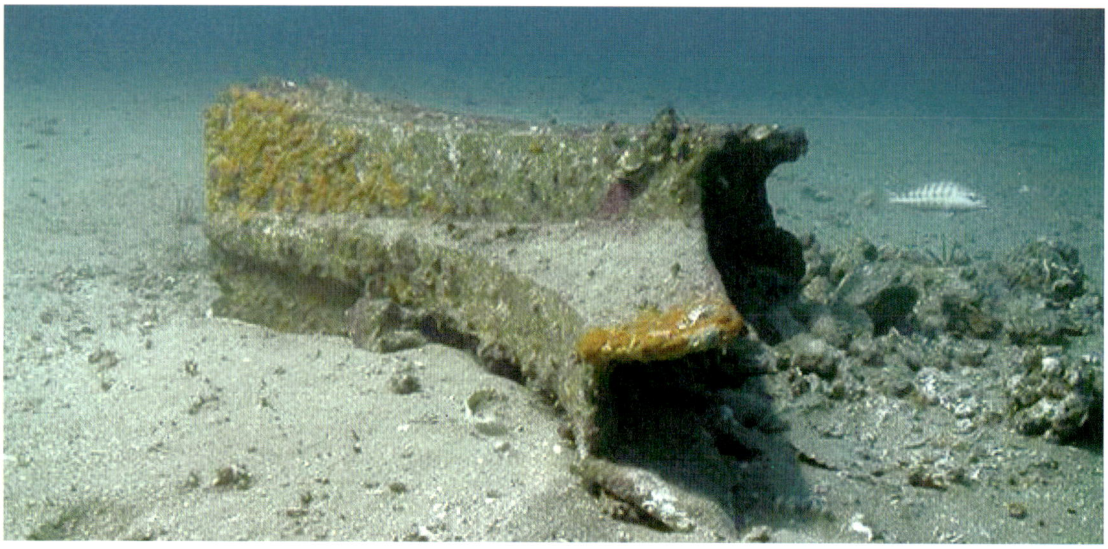

埃加迪群岛海战中战船的喙形舰首

大的海军舰队又再次以超乎寻常的速度集结起来，并成功地打击了威胁海上贸易的海盗们。

奥古斯都皇帝重组了海军，使其行动更加高效，并配备了轻型装备，使其能够适应海上治安的任务，比如从伊利里亚人手里借来行动敏捷的利布尼船，从图拉真凯旋柱浮雕上的潘诺尼亚舰队中可以看到它的身影。在公元前 1 世纪中期，双排桨样式的（每边大约 25 个）利布尼船和罗斯特拉塔船，开始取代列姆波斯船，被伊利里亚的海盗们所使用。

这种带桨的战舰，前面配有倾斜向前的弓形构造，延伸至后方为卷轴的形状，并且在甲板配备了一个厚重的青铜支撑柱，即喙形舰首，用来击毁敌人的船只。但是，支柱和龙骨是独立的，因此在撞击时，甲板可能会断裂并脱落，而船体本身不会受到损坏或卡住。目前在埃加迪群岛的水域中已经发现大约 20 个喙形舰首以及许多头盔，这是罗马在公元前 241 年赢得战争的特殊见证。事实上，战舰残骸几乎都不存在了：木质船体并不像商船那样受双层甲板的保护，也和非易腐货物（陶瓷、金属、大理石等）不同，木质船体最终都会腐朽并消失，只留下螺栓或钉子这些金属部件。

R. 奥列玛

were conferred) was again quickly and successfully formed to battle pirates who threatened maritime trade.

Emperor Augustus reorganized the navy and made it more efficient, equipping it with light ships that were suitable for policing the seas; ships such as the liburnae - agile racing ships borrowed from the Illyrians, which probably also appear in the reliefs of the Pannonian fleet on Trajan's Column - and the dikrotus. The liburna, with its double row of oars (perhaps 25 per side) and rostrum (naval ram), probably replaced the lembus, which was also used by Illyrian pirates in the middle of the 1st century B.C..

Military ships with oars had a bow that was rather bent forward, ending in a volute, onto which a powerful bronze rostrum was hooked that was used to drive into and puncture enemy ships. However, the ram and keel were independent, so that the ram could break off once it was driven into the enemy ship, without the attacking ship being damaged, or getting stuck in the other ship. About twenty rostrums were recovered in the waters of the archipelago of the Aegates, along with numerous helmets. This was an exceptional testimony of the battle won by Rome in 241 B.C.. In fact, there are few known shipwrecks of military ships: wooden hulls - unlike those of merchant ships that were protected by layers of amphorae or non-perishable cargo (ceramics, metals, marble, etc.) - deteriorated and disappeared, leaving only their metal parts, such as bolts and nails.

S. Auriemma

船型柱基座

公元 2 世纪—3 世纪
大理石
高 28 厘米，宽 57 厘米，厚 30 厘米
重 110 千克
罗马国家博物馆，展品编号 677

Column Base with Ship

2nd - 3rd century A.D.
height 28 cm, width 57 cm, thickness 30 cm
weight 110 kilograms
National Roman Museum, Baths of Diocletian Inv. 677

这艘小型船可能是一艘祭船，是水手们远征成功后专门举行庆祝活动所用，或许还具有军事性质。这艘船身处由海浪围绕的方形底座上，完全用浮雕装饰，这些浮雕位于两个水平的卧式支座：在下侧两端，分别描绘着一头朝向船头的狮子，呈攻击姿态，朝向船尾的是一条长长的螺旋状丝带。在其中心位置，一侧绘有两只海豚，鼻子朝向一个双柄大口酒坛；另一侧中心位置则绘有一个花环，常春藤的枝蔓从花环中伸展出来。而在卧式支座的上部，有一个与长矛交替出现的鹈鹕，旁边是蜿蜒的带状装饰，另一边是一系列武器，可能是表示探险队的军事用途。接下来是一个花环。此外，朝向船尾的是一排装饰有菱形的栏杆，该栏杆与卧式支座上部重叠。最后，在卧式支座上面放置的是方柱底座和柱基。

刻有海豚和铭文的石棺立面

公元 3 世纪—4 世纪
大理石
高度 28~29 厘米，整体宽度 172 厘米，厚度 2.5~3.8 厘米
重 43 ～ 45 千克
罗马国家博物馆 - 戴克里先浴场，展品编号 77305

Sarcophagus Base
3rd - 4th century A.D.
height 28-29 cm,width 172cm, thickness 2.5-3.8 cm
weight 43-45 kilograms
National Roman Museum, Baths of Diocletian Inv. 77305

这件石棺立面带有一中央桌台，桌台上面刻有铭文，两侧以极低的浮雕描绘了穿过海浪的四对海豚。平行的曲线展现了重重波浪，与海豚形成对比。海豚有凸起的鳍部和轮廓分明的眼睛。铭文设置在海军司令瓦莱里乌斯·维鲁斯（Valerius Verus）的纪念碑上，按照他的父亲瓦莱里乌斯以及他的母亲尤利亚(Iulia)的说法，他在 24 岁时亡故。他的父亲是一名因特殊任务而被召回的士兵。为死者进行“个性化签名”的是希腊海神（Thiasos），这段文字写在迪曼尼（Dei Mani）的文件表格内的上部，明确提到了对伊西斯（Iside）的崇拜——伊西斯在米塞诺舰队中两次担任了海军司令的职务。这位将领在死亡时非常年轻，功勋卓著，然而却不幸英年早逝。因此，在举行庆祝活动时，人们总是会联想到神圣的使命，而不是单纯的军事活动。

致迪曼尼·蒂亚苏斯

瓦莱里乌斯·维鲁斯，两次率领帝国的舰队驻扎在米塞诺的大将，却只活了 23 年。他的父亲瓦莱里乌斯，一名执行特别任务的士兵，和他的母亲尤利亚，为他们的儿子所立。

挂着战利品的船型瓦檐饰

公元前 1 世纪—公元 1 世纪末
陶
高 22 厘米，宽 17.2 厘米，厚 12.5 厘米
罗马国家博物馆 - 马西莫宫，展品编号 4509

Antefix
1st century B.C. - end of the 1st century A.D.
height 22 cm, width 17.2 cm, thickness 12.5 cm
National Roman Museum, Palazzo Massimo Inv. 4509

波纹状轮廓的瓦檐装饰有一个巨大的军事战利品标志。海船的船头升起，上面有一个螺旋形的牌匾和一个前台。军事战利品标志由一套盔甲、一顶头盔、一块盾牌和两把交叉的长矛组成。在其两侧，是头正朝向下方的两只飞跃的海豚。海船或海船中的一部分、海豚和各种军事战利品标志构成了奥古斯都时代各种图像的一部分。这些图像元素在公共和私人纪念物中以各种方式组合展现出来，以庆祝阿齐奥（Azio）海军战争的胜利（公元前 31 年）。在这场海军大战中，屋大维（未来的奥古斯都）最终击败了对手马克·安东尼奥，开辟了通往皇权的道路。

船上的库柏勒瓦檐饰

公元前 1 世纪—公元 1 世纪末
陶
宽 17 厘米，高 23.8 厘米，厚 9.5～11 厘米
罗马国家博物馆 - 马西莫宫，展品编号 70060

Antefix

1st century B.C. - late-1st century A.D.
width 17 cm, height 23.8 cm, thickness 9.5-11 cm
National Roman Museum, Palazzo Massimo Inv. 70060

瓦檐装饰带有海上女神西布莉（Cibele）的形象，她坐在一艘海船的船桅前、两只狮子之间的宝座上。船帆从船桅的顶部降下，铺向船头和船尾。在船体上，是方向舵和数支船桨。

西布莉的形象从一个侧面展示了在公元前 204 年罗马安纳托利亚人对神性的崇拜。这种黑色的石头就是女神的象征，它被人用海船从意大利培希努（Pessinunte）运送过来，放置在意大利帕拉蒂诺（Palatino）神庙。在那里，西布莉被罗马人敬奉为伟大的母亲。

三层桨战船浮雕石板

奥古斯都时代
白色大理石
高 84.5 厘米，宽 79 厘米，厚 8 厘米
重 190 千克
坎皮佛莱格瑞考古公园 - 巴亚城堡中的坎皮佛莱格瑞考古博物馆，展品编号 6600

Bas-Relief with Triremes

Augustan Age
height 84.5 cm, width 79 cm, thickness 8 cm
weight 190 kilograms
Phlegraean Fields Archeological Park - Archeological Museum of the Phlegraean Fields in the Castle of Baia Inv. 6600

三层桨战船浮雕石板，白色大理石材质，1761 年发掘自库迈富萨罗湖；这些石板与一个鼓形（圆桶状）的墓碑相关，让人联想起公元前 1 世纪末米塞纳特舰队的壮举。该浮雕刻画了一艘向右航行的三层桨战船，有三排桨，船首有两个浮雕图像：一个身份不明的神的形象和一个美杜莎头像，它具有消灾驱魔的作用；在船尾高甲板有军旗飘扬；除了一名舵手和一名瞭望员外，船上还可以看到七名桨手。

第二部分

商船和其他船舶

3B. MERCHANT AND OTHER SHIPS

在罗马帝国时期，商船和海军的发展达到了顶峰，船只种类繁多，从近海船（用于沿海航行和货物再分配）到大型货船（用于运输），从各种渔船到从事工程行业或特殊用途的船只，它们在绘画、马赛克画、石头和大理石纪念碑、硬币、宝石中都有丰富的图像描绘，其中最著名的当属突尼斯的阿尔西布罗斯马赛克画，画中描绘了 25 艘不同类型的船只。它们的外观和建造流派皆不相同，反映了起源的多样性，但地中海的统一和罗马长时间的和平，导致了海军技术的同质化。

商船的尺寸和吨位各不相同。它们可以具有对称的船体，但在大多数情况下是不对称的，船头具有不同的轮廓和高高的船尾。船尾很宽，为船舵留出了空间和支撑点，大多数舵的形状像铲子。船尾通常是船舱，而厨房或食品储藏室一般在船头位置，形状有凸起的（参见公元 200 年奥斯蒂亚的波尔图斯·奥古斯都的浮雕。）、直立的或凹陷的（两艘船面对面时，一艘是凸出的弓形，一艘是凹陷的弓

It was with the Roman Empire that the merchant navy reached its apogee through an extraordinary variety of ships, ranging from the cabotator (for coastal navigation and the redistribution of goods), to the large onerarias (used for transport), along with all types of fishing boats, service boats or boats for special uses, as was proven by the rich repertoire of images found on paintings, mosaics, stone and marble monuments, coins, gems, and so on, which were discovered. Among these is the famous mosaic of Altiburus in Tunisa in which 25 different ships are depicted.The variety in appearance and denomination of the ships reflects their diverse origins, but the peace and unification of Rome, and subsequent peace in the Mediterranean, led to the homogenization of naval technologies.

Merchant ships varied in size and tonnage. They either had a crescent-shaped symmetrical hull or, in most cases, an asymmetric hull, with prows in different shapes, and a high stern. The stern was wide, in order to give space to and support the rudders, which were shaped like shovels. The cabin was usually located in the stern, while the larder, or pantry, could also have been found in the bow. This was convex (see: votive bas-relief of the Portus Augusti in Ostia, 200 A.D.), or straight or concave (see: two facing ships - one with a convex bow and

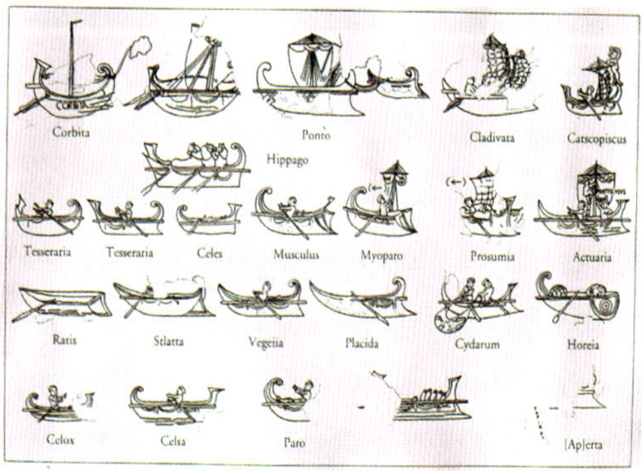

船只目录：公元3世纪末阿尔西布罗斯的突尼斯马赛克

公元200年，奥斯蒂亚的波尔图斯·奥古斯都的浅浮雕

奥斯蒂亚广场西勒克顿船的马赛克，公元2世纪晚期

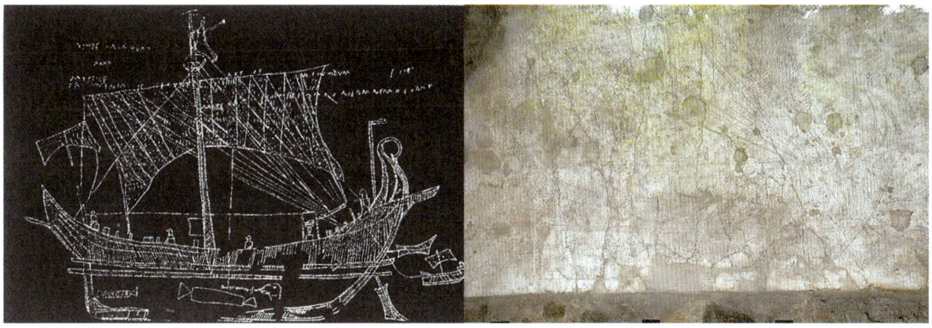

公元1世纪欧洲船只上的庞贝人涂饰

形——参见今天突尼斯萨拉克塔市奥斯蒂亚广场上的马赛克画，可追溯到公元2世纪。）

还有一种方帆，往往比较小，安置在船头，主要起到操控船舶转向的作用。帝国时代的方帆可以叠加在三角形帆上以增加其表面大小（从波尔图斯的浮雕中可见）。船尾明轮常做成天鹅脖颈的形状（参见公元1世纪欧洲船只上的庞贝人涂饰）。

特殊类型的商船，例如用于运输小麦的船只——萨摩萨塔的琉善（公元2世纪的希腊作家）所描述的爱西斯船，长55米，它可以将埃及的谷物运输到罗马城；或拉皮达里亚船，用于运输石块、石柱、大理石石棺，这类货物的最大重量可达350吨。

还有一种特殊的船只叫考迪卡里亚，它可以驶入由克劳迪乌斯皇帝和图拉真皇帝在台伯河上建造的港口。这种船可以被拖出堤坝，用于运输从大型航运单位转运到罗马河港口的货物。三艘考迪卡里亚连同其他船只（现在保存在菲乌米奇诺船舶博物馆）和克劳迪乌斯港口码头的延伸部分，在20世纪60年代被发现——当时罗马“莱昂纳多·达·芬奇”机场已经建成。

除了军舰和运输船外，当时还有许多其他类型船只。有许多渔船配备了可以沉入水中的水箱，以

the other with a concave bow - in the mosaic of the Navicularii of Syllectum [present-day village of Salakta in Tunisia] in the Piazzale delle Corporazioni in Ostia, dating back to the 2nd century A.D.) - due to the presence of a cutwater that was used as a drift.

These ships also had a square sail and often another smaller sail at the bow, which was mainly used to improve steering. During the Imperial Age, a triangular sail was often superimposed on the square sail to increase its surface (visible in the bas-relief from Portus). The sternpost often ended in a swan-neck shape with a spiral (see: Pompeian graffiti from the Europa ship, 1st century A.D.).

Special types of merchant ships, for example, were the naves frumentariae, used for transporting grain, such as the Isis described by Lucian of Samosata (Greek writer from the 2nd century A.D.) - which was 55 meters long and transported wheat to Rome from Egypt - or else the naves lapidariae, that reached 350 tons and were used to transport blocks, columns, and marble sarcophagi.

The navis caudicaria was also a particular type of ship. It was used to sail up the Tiber from the ports built by Emperors Claudius and Trajan. This ship was towed by the embankments for haulage and transported goods that were transferred from the large onerarias to the river port of Rome. Three of these ships were discovered in the 1960s, when Rome's "Leonardo da Vinci" airport was being built, along with other ships (now at the Fiumicino Ship Museum) and parts of the piers of the Port of Claudius.

描绘伊西斯吉米尼亚诺装运谷物的壁画

奥斯蒂亚广场：绘有陶罐转运场景的马赛克，公元2世纪末期

『渔夫之船』

菲乌米奇诺船博物馆藏，『菲乌米奇诺1号』木制帆船

保证鱼类存活，例如在被淹没的克劳迪乌斯港口发现的“渔夫之船”。在荷兰的古里诺河的沙床上，也发现过这种类型的船只。

在港口内还发现了用于疏浚海底的工程船。在法国马赛一个被淹没的港口也发现了两例相同的遗迹，其船体被用来容纳码头地基和支柱。

R. 奥列玛

Other vessels existed besides warships and transport ships. Many were probably fishing boats, equipped with a central tank that would be filled with water, in order to keep the fish alive. An example again derives from the buried Port of Claudius, the so-called "Barca del pescatore" (the Fisherman's Boat). Other boats of this type were found in Holland, under the silted banks of the old Rhine.

There were also service boats in the ports, used for dredging the seabed. Two examples were identified in the buried port of Marseille, in France. The hulls had been reused as caissons for the foundations of docks and piers.

R. Auriemma

第三部分
古代造船
3C. ANCIENT SHIPBUILDING

水下考古研究揭开了古代造船的原理和方法。在古地中海，最优秀的建造方法是使用承重木板即外壳来决定船体的形状，并确保其坚固性。从青铜器时代到罗马帝国时代末期的所有已知的残骸，都证实了这种技术的存在。直到古代中晚期，才逐渐出现了使用龙骨作为支撑的建造技术。

最常用的组装技术是使用榫孔和榫头拼接，木板板材切割好后并排放置（不像北欧传统工艺那样使用熟料重叠），然后通过插入孔（榫眼）中的突

Underwater archeology has investigated and revealed the principles and methods of ancient shipbuilding. In the ancient Mediterranean, the construction system par excellence was that of load-bearing planks, where the planks (shell) determined the shape of the hull and ensured its solidity, as was proven by all the shipwrecks discovered from the Bronze Age to the end of the Roman Empire. Only in late antiquity, and gradually, did the transition to the supporting frame method take place.

The mortise-and-tenon joint technique was the most commonly used construction technique for planks - with the

布林迪西的托瑞圣萨比娜号，罗马帝国晚期的船舶残骸

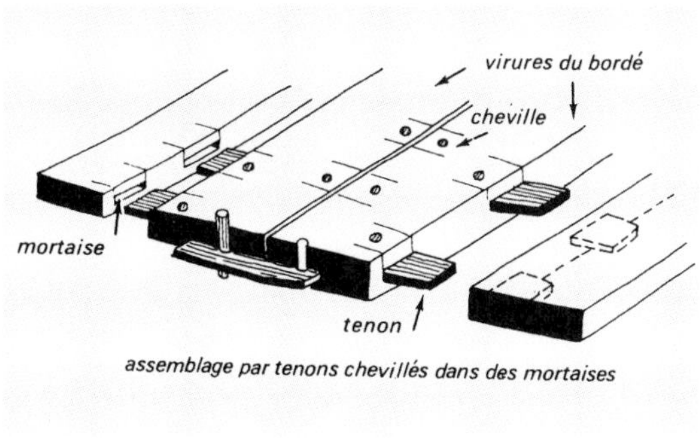

榫卯船壳板装配技术

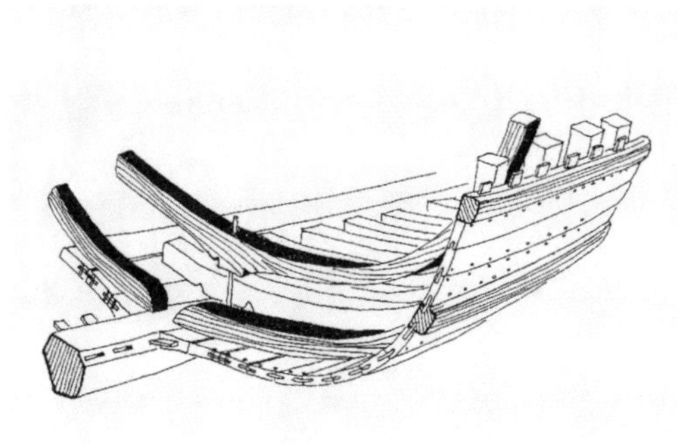

古代造船图纸

片（楔子）将木板固定在一起。在后来的沉船残骸中，楔子的数量和榫眼的深度都减少了，也不再固定在一起。

整个骨架由一个“骨干”、龙骨（包括若干个连接结实的部件）以及一系列“肋骨”组成，有序排列；那些通过龙骨轴线而没有中断的地板木材与半框架交错穿插；地板和下边沿都有延伸部分；纵向的分割以及肋骨和龙骨之间没有连接（从公元3世纪开始，才有了连接的建造方法）。这是支撑板技术的一个特征——框架只起到次要的作用。在骨架上方安装内部木板板材，通常采用典型的并排施工方法。

考古发现，仅在极少数情况下，船舶上部的痕迹能够得以保留，其基本部件是支撑船板的交叉部件（梁）的支撑物。甚至船的桅杆也很少保存下来，因为其固定在梁上，而这个梁挡住了框架结构。当时，船桅杆的底部插入一个空心腔体（即底部斜槽可以滑动的板条箱），当需要降帆时，桅杆可以朝着船尾的方向滑动放倒，这从许多描述记载中均可得知。

R. 奥列玛

cuts in the boards of the planks placed side-by-side (unlike the overlapping technique - known as clinker - used in the Nordic tradition). The planks were then held together by tabs (tenons) inserted in the holes (mortises) - formed through the thicknesses of the boards - and fixed with wooden pegs (dibbles). In shipwrecks discovered at a later date, the tabs diminished in number and depth and were no longer pegged together.

The framework included a “backbone”, the kccl - comprised of several elements that were firmly connected together - and a series of “ribs”, the frames. Those that passed through the axis of the keel without interruption (floor timbers) alternated with half frames; both had extensions. The splitting of the ribs, as well as the absence of a connection between the ribs and the keel (which began to be used in the 3rd century A.D.), is a feature of the load-bearing plank method and denotes the secondary role of the framework. The internal planking was mounted above the framework, always with the typical side-by-side construction method.

Only in a very few cases were traces of the mast and the upper parts of ships - where fundamental components, such as pillars with transversal elements (cross beams) that supported the bridge - were preserved. The masts of the ship were also rarely preserved. These were fixed to a beam, the keelson, which blocked the ribs; the foot of the mast was inserted in a cavity, the mast step, with a sliding bottom that allowed for felling the mast towards the stern when it was necessary to lower the sails, as can be seen in many images.

R. Auriemma

第四部分

卡利古拉和内米湖的船

3D. CALIGULA AND THE NEMI SHIPS

在罗马以南约 30 公里，靠近阿尔班山附近，第三罗马帝国皇帝盖乌斯·尤利乌斯·凯撒·奥古斯都·日耳曼——通常被称为卡利古拉（公元 37 年—41 年），在内米湖岸边建造了一座豪华的别墅和两艘巨大的船只（其中最大的一艘，甲板面积超过 2 000 平方米），装饰得金碧辉煌。这一惊人的壮举彰显了卡利古拉性格的本质。历史资料描述他为人古怪而奢侈，为我们展现了一个东方统治者的形象，他对奢侈和权力的追求以各种形式表现得淋漓尽致。

这两艘船作为游船，样式独特，皇帝将其打造成豪华的东方宫殿的模样，是真正漂浮在湖水中的宫殿。对于其建造形式，卡利古拉的灵感来自于杰出的先例，例如在其两个世纪之前锡拉库萨的暴君希罗二世（公元前 270 年—公元前 215 年）所建造的船。作为热爱挑战和喜欢做被认为“不可能的壮举”的人，皇帝开始建造两艘船：第一艘长 71 米，宽 20 米；第二艘长 75 米，宽 29 米，其特点是有等距离的长梁。

最近的研究表明，第一艘船是作为皇帝在湖岸上所建豪华住宅的一种附属建筑物而被建造，而第二艘船则具备仪式功能——它被认为是与伊西斯女神有关的崇拜对象的证据，这位具有埃及血统的女神与当地内米湖具有拉丁血统的女神狄安娜在神灵崇拜上被同化了。别墅—圣殿—船舶的综合体表明了皇帝对政治、宗教和建筑整体计划的精确性，船舶的装饰以及在其中发现的物品，都确切地证实了

On the shores of Lake Nemi, approximately 30 kilometers south of Rome, near the Alban Hills, the third Roman emperor, Gaius Julius Caesar Augustus Germanicus - known as Caligula, (37 - 41 A.D.) - had built a luxurious villa and two giant ships of exceptional size and decorative splendor. (The largest of the two ships exceeded 2,000 square meters).This incredible feat emphasizes Caligula's nature. Historical sources have described him as being eccentric and extravagant, providing us with an image of an oriental sovereign who loved luxury and power expressed in all its forms.

The two ships constituted a unique example of ceremonial vessels; veritable floating palaces in the waters of the lake, built by the Emperor in the image of luxurious oriental palaces. Caligula was inspired by illustrious precedents for their construction, such as the ship of the tyrant, Hiero II of Syracuse (270-215 B.C.), built about two centuries earlier. As one who loved challenges and feats deemed impossible, the Emperor started building two hulls: the first measuring 71 meters in length and 20 meters in width; the second 75 meters in length and 29 in width, characterized by the presence of long beams (which support the deck) placed at equal distances.

Recent studies have shown that the first ship was used as a sort of guesthouse for the sumptuous Imperial Palace that the sovereign owned on the shores of the lake. The second was for ceremonial functions, proven by the discovery of objects of worship linked to the goddess Isis, divinity of Egyptian origin, which was assimilated to the Roman goddess, Diana, venerated in the nearby Sanctuary of Nemi. The villa-sanctuary-ship complex responded to the Emperor's precise political, religious, and architectural program, and the decorations of the ships, as well as the objects found in them, are evident proof of this. The relationship between the ships and the cult

这一点。例如，船舶与祭祀女神狄安娜之间的联系，解释了为何动物头饰和西尔维斯特里的头饰一起保存在马西莫宫殿辉煌的栏杆支撑点上；而根据拉丁作家阿普列乌斯的记载，雕塑张开的双手手臂，与埃及伊西斯女神在游行过程中展开左手的形象似乎是相同的。

目前我们还无法探究内米湖中船舶沉没的具体原因，而这种情况其实在更早之前也曾经发生过，据推测可能的原因是在皇帝被谋杀之后，新的统治者需要“除名毁忆”，或者从集体记忆中系统地消除与被谋杀的皇帝相关的所有痕迹。然而这些神奇的记忆却深深烙印在了当地居民的心中，代代相传。当地人留传下了有关这两艘大船沉没在湖底的故事，谣言船上蕴藏着不可思议的宝藏。由于当地渔民经常能够从湖水中打捞出一些物品，因此这个传说一直流传至今。自 15 世纪以来，人们一直尝试使沉船重见天日。第一次发掘是在 1446 年，由意大利著名建筑师莱昂 · 巴蒂斯塔 · 阿尔伯蒂主持进行。而在之后的几个世纪里，为了让这些船重新浮出水面，人们进行了大量的尝试，但同时这些尝试也对船体产生了严重的影响——船只结构遭到破坏，船上的文物和木料也被洗劫一空。第一次真正意义上的保护性打捞，实施于 20 世纪末。1932 年 10 月，一家公司完成了这个时代性的壮举，他们抽空了湖水，从而使得这两艘船的残存结构露出了水面。但不幸的是，1944 年德国军队在撤军前纵火烧毁了这两艘船的大部分结构，目前这两艘船保存在内米湖畔 1940 年落成的新博物馆内。

M. 塞洛伦齐

of the goddess Diana, for example, explains the animal head decorations and the sylvan beings of the heads placed on the supports (herms) of the splendid balustrade preserved in Palazzo Massimo (Rome, Italy), while the forearms with open hands seem to recall what the Latin writer, Apuleius, referred to when writing about the image of a stretched out left hand exhibited during the solemn procession of Isis in Egypt.

The reason that led to sinking the ships in Lake Nemi is unknown. All we know is that it occurred in ancient times, perhaps after the Emperor was killed and after the damnatio memoriae that followed, that is, the systematic elimination from the collective memory of any element that could lead to his remembrance. Instead, the memory of these marvels remained well-rooted in the inhabitants of the place, who handed down stories about the existence of two large ships submerged at the bottom of the lake, rich in fabulous treasures. The legend was cyclically renewed by the objects that the fishermen recovered from the waters of the lake. Beginning in the 15th century, we know of attempts that were made to bring the ships back to light. The first, in 1446, was carried out by the famous Italian architect, Leon Battista Alberti. During the centuries that followed, numerous attempts took place to make the ships re-surface, which had dramatic consequences on the hulls, devastating the structures, and with artifacts and timber that were plundered. It was only at the end of the 20th century that the first actual project to recover these ships was implemented. The endeavor, which was colossal for that time, and which involved emptying the lake, ended in October 1932, bringing to light the surviving structures of the two ships. Unfortunately, an arson fire - probably started in 1944 by German soldiers before the troops were withdrawn - destroyed most of the two ships, which had been installed in the new museum built on the shores of Lake Nemi and inaugurated in 1940.

M. Serlorenzi

内米湖船只的青铜装饰

BRONZE DECORATIONS OF THE NEMI SHIPS

这是一件富丽堂皇的装饰品，两艘船作为炫耀性奢侈品，被视为权力的象征。

第一艘船的装饰属于动物头像组，这在古代艺术中是非常普遍的装饰图案。三只狮子和黑豹横向排列在船上，装饰了横梁的顶端，四只狼装饰了纵向梁的顶端，而圆柱形帽上的两只狮子头装饰了侧舵的长轴。所有动物的牙齿之间都有一个巨大的可移动圆环，且没有磨损痕迹，因此可以证明其不是用于系泊，而只是起到装饰作用。美杜莎的头放置在顶部，仿佛她的眼睛正在注视着一切。

在第二艘船上，四个方向舵和栏杆旁边则是用双面图形来装饰横梁。与船舶的木结构和丰富的大理石覆盖物相比，青铜装饰显得格外醒目。木制部件上或者有用热涂法（一种绘画技术，将颜料溶解在熔化的蜡中进行绘画）绘制的图案，或者覆盖着赤陶浮雕。

M. 塞洛伦齐

This is an exceptionally rich decoration that identifies in ships an example of ostentatious luxury as an expression of power.

The group of heads of animal figures - a very common decorative motif in ancient art - was part of the decoration of the prima nave, the first ship.The three lions and the panther adorned the heads of the beams arranged transversely to the ship (cross beams), the four wolves adorned the heads of the longitudinal beams, the two lion heads on the cylindrical caps crowned the long axes of the lateral rudders. All the animal heads held a solid, movable ring between their teeth. These rings showed no traces of wear and, therefore, were not used for mooring but were there only for decorative purposes. Medusa's head was placed up on top, as if put there to keep watch.

Instead, the hands that decorated the beams near the four rudders, as well as the balustrade with the double-faced heads on the supports (herms), were preserved from the seconda nave, the second ship. The bronze decorations stood out compared to the wooden structure of the ships and the rich marble coverings. The wooden parts were decorated with encaustic painting (a technique carried out using colors dissolved in melted wax) or covered with terracotta reliefs, which were also painted.

M. Serlorenzi

有手掌和前臂的船首梁头装饰

公元 37 年—41 年
铜
高 60 厘米，宽 54 厘米，厚 31 厘米
罗马国家博物馆 - 马西莫宫，展品编号 124759

Beam head with hand

37-41 A.D.
height 60 cm, width 54 cm, depth 31 cm
National Roman Museum, Palazzo Massimo Inv. 124759

这件青铜器是第二艘船船首木梁末端的装饰部件。它呈现了男性的左前臂，带有右手和前臂的对称装饰与之对应。这种装饰元素除了有艺术表现的特性，其珍贵之处还在于它的象征价值——张开的手被认为拥有消除危险的力量。此外，不排除这一主题与内米湖附近一处圣地所祭祀的狩猎女神狄安娜之间有一定联系。

狼头造型的梁头

公元 37 年—41 年
铜
高 40 厘米，宽 25 厘米，厚 50 厘米
重 40 ~ 50 千克
罗马国家博物馆 - 马西莫宫，展品编号 124755

Beam head with wolf

37-41 A.D.
height 40 cm, width 25 cm, thickness 50 cm
weight 40-50 kilograms
National Roman Museum, Palazzo Massimo Inv. 124755

这只狼头装饰在第一艘船的一根纵向木梁的末端。这种动物所展示的力量是惊人的。凶猛的眼睛、紧皱的眉毛、锋利的牙齿、脸上和下颚的毛发，都表现得栩栩如生。狼是罗马人极为喜爱的一种动物，它代表了战斗的力量和热情，是战斗民族的独特元素，也是罗马人立国之本和发展的准则。传说中，罗马城的诞生就与一只母狼的出现有关。这只母狼曾哺育过双胞胎罗穆卢斯和雷穆斯，双胞胎是在台伯河畔的帕拉廷山下被发现的。

狮头造型的梁头

公元 37 年—公元 41 年
铜
高 24.8 厘米，宽 47.5 厘米，厚 23.2 厘米
重 40 ~ 50 千克
罗马国家博物馆 - 马西莫宫，展品编号 33787

Beam head with lion

37-41 A.D.
height 24.8 cm, width 47.5 cm, thickness 23.2 cm
weight 40-50 kilograms
National Roman Museum, Palazzo Massimo Inv. 33787

狮头装饰着第一艘船的船首横梁。这只动物被压扁到几乎变形，这使得它的大嘴看起来凶猛而可怕：鬃毛乱成一团，表情紧缩，眼神凶狠，下巴咬得紧紧的。在古代，与狮子主题相关的装饰经常出现，它常与权力、王权和至高无上的价值观相联系。

第五部分

商船和船上生活

3E. MERCHANT SHIPS AND LIFE ON BOARD

在罗马帝国时期，客船——像今天的跨大西洋班轮一样，原本只是用来运送乘客的船只——并不存在。人们乘坐航行货船、繁重的船只出行，因为这些船只比军用船舶更为可靠和舒适，而且对私人旅客而言可能更方便。

商船的船员非常少，只有5～6名船员，战舰则不然。

来自沉船的材料和海军的图绘为我们展示了一幅船上的生活景象。水下考古调查的遗存可以分为两类：与船只管理和维修有关的遗存，以及与船上人员日常生活有关的遗存。

在与船舶设备有关的发现中，包含有舱载泵、与船舶操纵有关的木制部件（滑轮，用于索具的偏心轮）、锚（通常由木制轴、树桩和铅滑轮组成）和探测器（一种钟形金属物体，内部涂有油脂并系在顶部，用于探究海底的深度和性质）。沉船残骸中发现有一般的维护工具，如木槌、小型金属镐，以及一种带有树脂和沥青痕迹的容器（用于修补和填塞船体）。这些船还配备了诸如剑和匕首等武器或投掷武器（如吊索），以防在危险情况下进行防卫。

日常物品特别有趣，从中可以想象航行期间的船上生活。

与船上饮食有关的物品特别重要，这些食物以谷类和易于运输且营养丰富的干果和坚果（如核桃、枣等）为主，同时包括肉类（可能用盐腌过）和在旅行及在港口停留期间捕获到的鱼。

残存的炉子是由砖砌成的，里面尚有余烬，炉

During the Roman Empire, passenger ships - intended as ships that only transported people, like transatlantic liners today - did not exist. People traveled using cargo ships with sails, onerariae (onerarias), which were more reliable and comfortable than military ships, besides probably being more accessible to private travelers.

Merchant ships had a very small crew, 5-6 sailors, as compared to warships with oars.

The materials recuperated from shipwrecks, as well as naval iconography, give us an overall picture of life on board. The remains from underwater archeological surveys can be divided into two categories: those related to the governance and maintenance of ships and those related to the daily life of people on board.

The discoveries related to equipment on ships include bilge pumps, wooden parts used for maneuvering (pulleys, wooden blocks for rigging), anchors - usually made from wooden shafts and stumps and lead blocks - and also sounders, bell-shaped metal objects that were greased inside, tied to a line, and used to verify the depth and nature of the seabed. General maintenance tools were also found among the relics of shipwrecks. These included wooden mallets, small metal pickaxes, and containers with traces of resins and pitch, which were used to repair and caulk the hull. Weapons used as defense in the event of danger, such as swords and daggers, or launching weapons, such as slings, were also discovered.

Everyday objects are particularly interesting and help us image life on board during crossings.

Objects found that were related to the type of food eaten on board were also important. Foodstuffs included grains and fruit, which were easily transportable, and nutritious dry fruit and nuts, such as walnuts, dates, and so on. Meat was also eaten, probably salted, along with fish that was caught during the trip and when stopping at ports.

Some remains also included pieces of stoves formed by a

篦可用于烹饪，研钵用于研磨谷物，另外还有一些陶器、双耳瓶、水罐和盛液体的杯子、盛固体食物的碗和盘子等物品。在 20 世纪 60 年代菲乌米奇诺国际机场建设期间，发现了古罗马帝国皇家港口（波尔图斯港），在其中发掘出来的小型划桨渔船（“菲乌米奇诺”5 号）的残骸中，有一个带盖的碗，里面有一堆枣和坚果的残渣。在“罗恩”3 号船的残骸中——它可能是因为罗纳河的洪水而沉没的，目前保存在阿尔勒（法国，古代称为阿莱拉特）博物馆中——人们在炉边发现了船员用餐的遗迹，推断应该是急于自救或被水溺亡的人遗弃的。

在菲乌米奇诺的残骸中有一只皮革凉鞋，可能是渔民的；从大小来看，应该属于一个十几岁的男孩或女孩。

海上航行期间，在非工作时间或休息时间里，船员们一起玩游戏打发时光，有许多痕迹表明了这一点。掷骰子的游戏非常普遍，比如有的使用羊的距骨（羊蹄中的骨头）制成。用颜色对比鲜明的玻璃或骨头当棋子，将“鲁索利埃桌子”当作棋盘格——在当时可能是直接刻在船板上的。

R. 塞巴斯蒂亚尼

brick box, in which embers were placed, and a grill on which to cook, as well as mortars for grinding grains, crockery, amphorae, jugs and cups for liquids, and bowls and dishes for solid food. Among the pieces found at Fiumicino, the ancient imperial port of Rome (Portus) - in the wreck of the small fishing boat with oars (Fiumicino 5) discovered in the 1960s during the construction of the international airport - there was a bowl with a plate-lid and a mess tin with the remains of dates and nuts. In the wreck of the river barge, Rhone 3 - which probably sunk during a flood of the Rhone and is preserved in the museum of Arles (France), ancient Arelate - a hearth was found at stern with the remains of the crew's meal, abandoned in the hasty attempt to save themselves or because they faced their imminent death in the flood waters.

The remains of the wreck at Fiumicino also included a leather sandal, probably a fisherman's. From the size, it could have belonged to a teenage boy or girl.

During the crossings, those on board also rested or had time to lounge around and play games, of which there are numerous traces. Dice games were extremely common, like those using the astragals (leg bones) of sheep. With pawns made of glass or bone in contrasting colors, a kind of checkers was played on boards called "lusoria tablets", probably engraved directly on the planks of the ship.

R. Sebastiani

考迪卡里亚船模型

公元 1 世纪—公元 3 世纪船舶的复制品
木头和其他材料
长 1 米，宽 40 厘米，高 90 厘米
重 15 千克
圣塞维拉航海博物馆，展品编号 348

Model of a Navis Caudicaria

Replica of ships from the 1st - 3rd century A.D.
length 1 m, width 40 cm, height 90 cm
weight 15 kilograms
Santa Marinella Civic Museum, "Museum of the Sea and of Ancient Navigation"　Inv. 348

罗马时代的内河运输用船——考迪卡里亚船模型。考迪卡里亚船是一种特殊的大型内河驳船，用来把货物从海港运到罗马的内河港口。几个世纪以来，这种船在台伯河上日夜穿梭，从地中海各地为罗马带来了大量的物资。在古奥斯蒂亚发现的铭文中，人们经常提到船的船身是扁平的，与其他靠桨推动的船不同的是，这些船使用的是拖曳系统——也就是说它们是从岸边拖着走的。这种推进系统，一直使用到 19 世纪末。这艘船用绳索 (helciarii - tnl. hawsers) 钩住，由动物（通常是牛或水牛）或人类从河岸上拖动，逆流而上直到目的地。

2 枚铁钉

公元 1 世纪上半叶
铁
600085：高 43 厘米，四边形横截面，最长边 1.5 厘米
600086：高 30 厘米，四边形横截面，最长边 1.5 厘米
罗马考古、艺术品和景观监管局，展品编号：600085、600086

Naval Nails

first half of the 1st century A.D.
600085: height 43 cm, quadrangular sect. side max 1.5 cm
600086: height 30 cm, quadrangular sect. side max 1.5 cm
Special Superintendence of Archeology, Fine Arts, and Landscapes of Rome Inv. 600085, 600086

在古罗马河港发现的两枚造船木匠用的铁钉，经铸造和锻造而成。这些带有方形截面的大尺寸铁钉表明它们是为建造特殊的大型船只而设计。同样大小的铁钉让人想起罗马附近内米湖上的船只——卡利古拉皇帝（公元 1 世纪上半叶）建造的巨船，它们是一种“漂浮的宫殿”，皇帝将其作为仪式船使用。1944 年第二次世界大战期间，巨船的遗迹被大火烧毁。

骨质针

公元 2 世纪
骨
长 13.3 厘米，直径 0.6 厘米
重约 4.1 克
罗马考古、艺术品和景观监管局，展品编号 600049

Fibula with Needle

2nd century A.D.
length 13.3 cm,diameter 0.6 cm
approx. weight4.1 grams
Special Superintendence of Archeology, Fine Arts, and Landscapes of Rome Inv. 600049

骨质针，有一个矩形孔作为针眼，针眼上下各有一个用来系带的圆孔。此物来自罗马，2018 年在特拉斯特韦雷的莫洛西尼大道展开的发掘中被发现。

油灯

公元 1 世纪末—2 世纪中期（公元 90 年—140 年）
陶
高 4.8 厘米，长 9.2 厘米，直径 7.4 厘米
重 73.3 克
罗马考古、艺术品和景观监管局，展品编号 600060

Decorated Oil Lamp

lLate-1st.—mid-2nd century A.D. (90-140 A.D.)
height 4.8 cm, length 9.2 cm, diameter 7.4 cm
weight 73.3 grams
Special Superintendence of Archeology, Fine Arts, and Landscapes of Rome Inv. 600060

圆嘴油灯的嘴部几乎已经全部缺失了。它的身体呈圆形，圆嘴与肩部中间通过直线部分连接，带有一个垂直环状耳柄。圆盘有两个圆形凹槽与肩部分开，左边装饰着一只奔跑的羚羊形象，具有相当自然的浮雕效果。底部平坦，刻有圆环，并压印图章：C.OPPI.RES - C. Oppius Restitutus （CIL XV，6593）。油灯由米色赤陶土制成，带有红色的装饰。中轴是一层半液态的黏土，古代常用作器皿的最后一层涂料涂在容器上。油灯的生产地区是意大利中部。这件油灯于罗马特拉斯特韦雷的莫罗西尼大道的发掘中发现。特拉斯特韦是一个工匠聚集区，与这座城市的古河港相连。

小水罐

公元 1 世纪
陶
高 6.8 厘米，罐口直径 5.2 厘米
重 103.8 克
罗马考古、艺术品和景观监管局，展品编号 600050

Pot Jar

1st century A.D.
height 6.8 cm, rim diameter 5.2 cm
weight 103.8 grams
Special Superintendence of Archeology, Fine Arts, and Landscapes of Rome Inv.600050

使用赤陶在陶车上制成的未经装饰的陶罐。这些陶制器皿曾作为饮水用的杯子使用。它们的形状大小各异，有些甚至装饰得很华丽。这件陶罐非常简单，无论是在陆地还是在船上，它都是一件最常见的生活用具。这件文物于罗马特拉斯特韦雷的莫罗西尼大道开展的发掘过程中被发现。特拉斯特韦雷是一个工匠聚集区，与这座城市的古河港相连。

陶罐形建筑构件

公元 2 世纪—3 世纪
陶
高 9.8 厘米，边缘直径 4.7 厘米，罐体直径 4.9 厘米
重 89.4 克
罗马考古、艺术品和景观监管局，展品编号 600051

Architectural Element

2nd - 3rd century A.D.
height 9.8 cm, rim diameter 4.7 cm, body diameter 4.9 cm
weight 89.4 grams
Special Superintendence of Archeology, Fine Arts, and Landscapes of Rome Inv. 600051

在陶车上制造的双耳陶罐形态的建筑构件，用于拱顶的结构中。在罗马帝国时期的建筑中，类似这样的建筑元素被广泛地用于建造坚固的轻量混凝土拱顶。双耳陶罐作为一种常见的运输容器，在混凝土浇筑中得到了广泛的应用。

3 枚游戏棋子

公元 1 世纪—3 世纪
玻璃膏
天蓝色：直径 1.4 厘米，厚 0.6 厘米；
白色：直径 1.7 厘米，厚 0.7 厘米；
紫黑色：直径 1.6 厘米，厚 0.7 厘米
重 1.8 ～ 2.4 克
罗马考古、艺术品和景观监管局，展品编号 600061-62-63

Playing Pieces

1st - 3rd century A.D.
blue: diameter 1.4 cm, thickness 0.6 cm;
white: diameter 1.7 cm, thickness 0.7 cm;
purple-black: diameter 1.6 cm, thickness 0.7 cm
weight: from approx 1.8 to 2.4 grams
Special Superintendence of Archeology, Fine Arts, and Landscapes of Rome Inv. 600061, 600062, 600063

三枚分别为天蓝色、白色和紫黑色的玻璃釉棋子，采用玻璃釉颗粒熔化时的“滴釉”工艺制成。这种棋类游戏在古罗马非常流行。孩子用丢弃的坚果做棋子，而成年人则用骰子或者绵羊、山羊的腿骨。在孩子和成人中，有一种所谓的“小坑游戏”十分流行。具体的玩法无从得知，但是他们可能使用的是一种带有坑洞的棋盘，以及用玻璃膏或者其他材料制成的小球或弹珠，和“九子棋”也许有些类似。这些物品是在罗马古迹中被发掘出来的，位于特拉斯泰韦雷的莫罗西尼路，这里曾经是一个与古老河港相连的手工业区。

2 枚游戏棋子

公元 1 世纪—2 世纪
骨
展品编号 600054：直径 2.8 厘米，厚 0.8 厘米，重 5 克
展品编号 600056：直径 1.9 厘米，厚 0.3 厘米，重 1.8 克
罗马考古、艺术品和景观监管局，展品编号 600054、600056

Playing Piece

1st-2nd century A.D.
600054: diameter 2.8 cm, thickness 0.8 cm, weight 5 grams
600056: diameter 1.9 cm, thickness 0.3 cm, weight 1.8 grams
Special Superintendence of Archeology, Fine Arts, and Landscapes of Rome Inv. 600054, 600056

600054：骨质棋子采用凸圆盘形状，正面外侧装饰有同心切口，中央有钮，背面有数字。

600056：正面雕刻有同心圆装饰的凸形骨质棋子。

这两件物品来自在罗马特拉斯特韦雷的莫罗西尼大道展开的发掘过程。特拉斯特韦雷是一个工匠聚集区，与这座城市的古河港相连。

骨质棋子

公元 1 世纪—2 世纪
骨
直径 2 厘米，厚 0.2 厘米
重 1.2 克
罗马考古、艺术品和景观监管局，展品编号 600055

Playing Piece

1st - 2nd century A.D.
diameter 2 cm, thickness 0.2 cm
weight 1.2 grams
Special Superintendence of Archeology, Fine Arts, and Landscapes of Rome Inv. 600055

正面雕刻有同心圆装饰的平面骨质棋子。这件物品于对罗马特拉斯特韦雷的莫罗西尼大道展开的发掘中被发现。特拉斯特韦雷是一个工匠聚集区，与这座城市的古河港相连。

有柄的小瓷罐残片

公元 1 世纪—2 世纪
陶
高 8 厘米，宽 5.2 厘米，厚 4.5 厘米
重 57.9 克
罗马考古、艺术品和景观监管局，展品编号 600052

Small Jug

1st - 2nd century A.D.
height 8 cm, width 5.2 cm, overall thickness 4.5 cm
weight 57.9 grams
Special Superintendence of Archeology, Fine Arts, and Landscapes of Rome Inv. 600052

残缺的带柄小陶罐，装饰有葡萄枝蔓和葡萄串浮雕，浮雕使用模具工艺制成。罐身装饰最终由手工完成。该土质涂层（釉层）通过强氧化焙烧过程获得，属于“珊瑚红”类型。陶罐上有耳柄。

鱼纹油灯

公元 1 世纪初
陶
长 10.7 厘米，宽 8.5 厘米，高 3.8 厘米
罗马国家博物馆 - 马西莫宫，展品编号 189115

Oil Lamp

early-1st century A.D.
length 10.7 cm, width 8.5 cm, height 3.8 cm
National Roman Museum, Palazzo Massimo Inv. 189115

装饰着鱼类浮雕的圆盘：两只海豚、一只海狸，在灯嘴下方是一条海船，船上有两名水手，他们的头上有两个小圆盘。展开的船帆部分占据了圆盘周围的凹槽处。油灯的灯脚是环形的。三角状的灯嘴上有使用过的痕迹。

饰有骑海豚的爱神的油灯

公元 1 世纪
陶
长 11.5 厘米，宽 8.2 厘米，高 4.2 厘米
罗马国家博物馆 - 马西莫宫，展品编号 62088

Oil Lamp

1st century A.D.
length 11.5 cm, width 8.2 cm, height 4.2 cm
National Roman Museum, Palazzo Massimo Inv. 62088

带有心形嘴的油灯。灯面略微凹陷的圆盘上有三个切口连接的海洋场景：中间有一只海豚、一只螃蟹、一只龙虾，下半部分是另外一只海豚。平底部由两个切口连接而成，在平底部的中间印着“奇斯特凡”（CISTEFAN）字样。

饰有三层桨战船的油灯

公元前 1 世纪
陶
长 8.3 厘米，宽 8.5 厘米，高 4 厘米
罗马国家博物馆 - 马西莫宫，展品编号 197213

Oil Lamp

1st century B.C.
length 8.3 cm, width 8.5 cm, height 4 cm
National Roman Museum, Palazzo Massimo Inv. 197213

这件油灯有圆形的灯体，且带有两个侧面开槽的手柄。圆盘装饰有一艘三列桨座的战船，带有一个非常突出的平台和一块较低的船帆，船帆围绕着周围的凹槽。油灯底部印有难以辨认的字样。

圆形灯嘴虾纹油灯

公元 2 世纪
陶
长 10 厘米，宽 10 厘米，高 4.5 厘米
罗马国家博物馆 - 马西莫宫，展品编号 200889

Oil Lamp
2nd century A.D.
length 10 cm, width 10 cm, height 4.5 cm
National Roman Museum, Palazzo Massimo Inv. 200889

凹形的圆盘上装饰有螃蟹浮雕，蟹爪围绕着偏离中心的浇口。

饰有海豚和涡形纹饰的油灯

公元 1 世纪
陶
长 11.6 厘米，宽 6.1 厘米，高 4 厘米
罗马国家博物馆 - 马西莫宫，展品编号：190805

Oil Lamp
1st century A.D.
length 11.6 cm, width 6.1 cm, height 4 cm
National Roman Museum, Palazzo Massimo Inv. 190805

倾斜的灯肩上带有两个同心环，向下倾斜到凹陷很深的圆盘，圆盘右侧装饰有海豚图案。灯嘴为三角形，在突出的塑料蜗壳之间，有一小的通风孔。扁平的环形底部带有难以辨认的字样。

涡形纹饰油灯

公元 2 世纪
陶
长 9 厘米，宽 6 厘米，高 2.3 厘米
罗马国家博物馆 - 马西莫宫，展品编号 188948

Oil Lamp
2nd century A.D.
length 9 cm, width 6 cm, height 2.3 cm
National Roman Museum, Palazzo Massimo Inv. 188948

该油灯带有蜗壳，但没有手柄。灯肩部有两个同心圆环，用于界定两条海豚之间的凹形圆盘。凹形圆盘上装饰有海神的头像。环形脚上是平形底部。

饰有帆船的油灯

公元 2 世纪末—3 世纪初
陶
长 10.6 厘米，宽 8.2 厘米，高 2.9 厘米
罗马国家博物馆 - 马西莫宫，展品编号 10261

Oil Lamp

late-2nd - early-3rd century A.D.
length 10.6 cm, width 8.2 cm, height 2.9 cm
National Roman Museum, Palazzo Massimo Inv. 10261

油灯肩部装饰有月桂花环和同心圆环，用于界定凹形圆盘，凹形圆盘左侧有船的图案。环形灯脚，印有“奇维尔菲”（CIVLPHI）字样。

饰有渔夫的油灯

公元 1 世纪后期
陶
长 9.6 厘米
罗马国家博物馆 - 马西莫宫，展品编号 60681

Oil Lamp

second half of the 1st century A.D.
length 9.6 cm
National Roman Museum, Palazzo Massimo Inv. 60681

凹形圆盘由三个同心凹槽连接，装饰着一个钓鱼场景：一名渔夫面向左侧，戴有头饰，身着短外套，坐在岩石上，双腿交叉，拉起钓鱼线，一条鱼已经上钩。一个袋子挂在他的右臂上。油灯的平底部有一凹槽。油料进料孔呈偏心状。

UNIT IV

ALONG WATERWAYS

GOODS AND TRANSPORTATION

第四单元

浮海而行
商品与运输

贸易是一件可憎之事：它违背上帝之命，上帝有意用海水将大陆分开，却把一些不虔诚的船只引向大海……这是伟大的拉丁文诗人贺拉斯所言。然而，很显然，其他人和金口若望（生活在公元4世纪下半叶的希腊主教和神学家）有着相同的想法：上帝赐予人类海洋，使你不必在旅途中辛苦劳作。

罗马在地中海所处的位置及其霸权势力，决定了它随之而来的“消费全球化”，从某方面讲，这和当今主要商品的“非本地化”生产类似。帝国时期，罗马人可以喝到产自高卢、克里特岛和塞浦路斯的葡萄酒。此外，罗马贵族还可以买到产自坎帕尼亚或是爱琴海岛屿的名贵葡萄酒，来自希腊的蜂蜜和来自非洲、地中海东部、葡萄牙、庞贝城等各地的蜂蜜、鱼酱油和鱼酱。人们平时吃的面包是由船队从埃及和非洲进口的小麦制成。此外，大量的石油从西班牙南部的加的斯港运来，还有大批进口自安达卢西亚的铅、葡萄酒和鱼酱。

食物主要通过海运供应各地。正如戴克里先皇帝制定的价格典籍所述，由于相对成本较低，所以即使是在船只非常容易出现事故的冬季，或是不便于航行的时期（3月到11月），海运还是比陆运更受欢迎。

当时，海运是最主要的运输方式，所有种类的货物都以这种方式运输，例如食品：谷物、价廉物美的葡萄酒、橄榄油、鱼酱、鱼罐头、肉类、蜂蜜、水果、盐等；原料或半成品：毛坯玻璃、大理石、石料、金属、矿物等；建筑材料：石料、砖、火山灰（用于制作水力构造物所需水泥的火山砂）；精美的餐具；艺术作品和手工艺品，例如家具、装饰品等；由陶瓷、玻璃、青铜、琥珀、金、银、象牙、宝石、珍珠等制成的家庭和个人用品；（植物和矿物质）药品；奢侈品：熏香、药膏、香水等；可回

Trade is an abominable thing: against the decree of a wise god who wanted the lands to be separated from the waves, it leads impious ships across the seas... this is what the great Latin poet, Horace, asserted. Evidently, however, others had the same idea as John Chrysostom (Greek bishop and theologian who lived in the second half of the 4th century A.D.): God gave you the sea to sail so that you need not toil in the journey.

Following the presence and power of Rome in the Mediterranean, a sort of “globalization of consumption” occurred around this basin. During the Imperial Age, the Romans drank wines produced in Gaul, Crete, and Cyprus in large quantities. If their class was noble and elevated, they bought expensive wines from Campania or from the Aegean islands, Greek honey and Garum, and fish sauces that came from Africa, the Easter Mediterranean, far away Portugal, or Pompeii. The bread that was consumed on a daily basis was made with wheat imported from Egypt and Africa using the flotilla of large ships. Great quantities of oil sailed from southern Spain, from the port of Cadiz - where olive groves grew as far as the eye could see along the course of the Guadalquivir - as well as cargoes of lead, wine, and fish sauces from Andalusia.

The supply of food and its distribution took place mainly by sea. Usually, despite the winter periods of mare clausum, when the sea was not navigable (from March to November), and the frequent risks during navigation, transport by sea was much preferred to land because of lower costs, as we also know from Emperor Diocletian’s Edict on Maximum Prices.

Transport by sea was the preeminent means, and all types of goods traveled in this manner, such as foodstuffs: grains, inexpensive and quality wines, olive oil, sauces and fish preserves, meat, honey, fruit, salt, etc.; raw or semi-finished materials: glass, marble, stones, metals, minerals, etc.; building materials: stone, bricks, pozzolan (volcanic sand used for cement in hydraulic structures); fine tableware; works of art and artistic handicrafts, such as precious furnishings and ornaments; various objects for domestic and personal use in ceramics, glass, bronze, amber, gold, silver, ivory, precious gems, pearls; medicinal substances (vegetable and mineral); luxury goods: incense, ointments, perfumes, etc.; metals and

姆列特岛“格拉瓦特”号沉船。1989年挖掘，发现了产自第勒尼安海岸的餐具

“格拉多”号沉船中装在桶中需要回收的玻璃碎片

科马基奥市“瓦雷博迪”号沉船残骸

男性雕像“希腊王子”或“卢基乌斯·埃米利乌斯·鲍鲁斯”

收的金属、玻璃以及其他手工艺品加工材料，例如明矾、染料等；除食品外，其他易腐材料：皮革、牛皮、羊毛、丝绸等面料、木材、奴隶……

食物“成批地”进行运输，但食物的消费量会随着社会阶层的不同而有所改变，例如人口最多的古都罗马以及维苏威火山地区，坎帕尼亚范围内的繁华城镇，庞贝、赫库兰尼姆和奥普隆蒂斯古城，这些地方的分发量就会多一些。如上所述，货物从波佐利港口和奥斯蒂亚港口进口后抵达罗马或庞贝。食物免费分配给成年罗马公民，也通过水路提供给保卫帝国边境的军队。

谷物以及其他食品，在运输过程中没有被装到两耳细颈酒罐中，而是可能被直接装在袋中或直接放在货舱中。因此很多装载运输的商品至今都无从

glass to recycle; materials intended for artisanal processing, such as alum, dyes; perishable materials: besides food, also hides, leather, wool, silk and other fabrics, wood , slaves, and more...

Food was also distributed “in bulk”, and food consumption took place in different ways, depending on the social classes, both in Rome - the largest and most populated metropolis in antiquity - and also in the area of the Vesuvius, such as Pompeii, Herculaneum, and Oplontis, flourishing city centers in Campania. As mentioned, imported goods arrived to Rome or Pompeii through the ports of Pozzuoli and Ostia. Main staples were distributed for free to adult Roman citizens, and they were also supplied along the river to the troops that guarded the borders of the Empire.

Many loads of cargo left no traces: grains, for example, but also other foodstuffs were not transported using amphorae but, probably, using sacks, or even kept loose in the hold. In

奥斯蒂亚图拉真港官员浮雕，陶罐卸货场景

纳尔德奥海洋博物馆中船上货仓横截面复原

莱切省纳尔德奥的“圣卡泰里娜”号沉船残骸

考证。很多我们现在所了解的商品都是被装在粘土容器、两耳细颈酒罐中的。根据不同的地理区域和时间以及所装商品（除食品外，还有沥青、石灰、明矾、皮革加工用的液体）的不同，它们所需要的容器样式和类型也不尽相同。

一旦双耳酒罐被装满，就会用特殊的陶瓷塞和石灰或火山灰密封。为了使容器壁防水，通常会在外壁敷上一层薄薄的沥青或树脂。若容器内装的是葡萄酒和鱼酱，则内壁也会敷上一层，这不仅能防止液体被吸收，还能使葡萄酒更添风味。这些酒罐的“实用性”除了表现在装运作用上，还体现在建筑（减轻墙壁结构和屋顶结构重量）以及儿童葬礼方面。

R. 奥列玛

most cases, the goods transported were identified through the clay container used, the amphora, which was produced in different forms and types depending on the geographical area, the period, and also the content: not only foodstuffs, but also tar, lime, alum, urine for leather processing, and so on.

Once filled, the amphora was closed with special ceramic stoppers and sealed with lime or pozzolan (fig. 8). To waterproof the internal walls, the external surface was treated, while a thin layer of bitumen, tar or resin frequently covered the inner walls of amphorae used for transporting wine and fish sauce, with the dual function of preventing the absorption of the liquid and, in the case of wine, of flavoring it. Although they were “refillable”, amphorae were often reused both for new cargo loads and in construction (to lighten wall structures and roofs) and also in child burials.

R. Auriemma

罗马共和时代后期船舶残骸，“圣萨比纳塔”3号上的迦太基两耳细颈酒罐

特雷米蒂群岛的“特雷·森奇”号沉船上带软木塞的双耳细颈酒罐

第一部分

从地中海到罗马的陶罐

4A. FOODSTUFFS: AMPHORAE FROM THE MEDITERRANEAN TO ROME

在罗马时代，用于运输货物的容器包括桶、篮子、麻袋、双耳细颈瓶等，双耳细颈瓶是其中使用最广泛的，无疑也是迄今保存最完好的。

从地中海沿岸到帝国的边界，基于罗马领土扩张和由此扩大的日益复杂的市场体系，随着各省货物运抵首都与意大利半岛，同时也随着省际之间和省内区域间的交流，越来越多的双耳细颈瓶出现在人们身旁。当时，罗马市场开始逐渐涉及边境的进出口贸易，这是源于罗马军团的存在以及边境人口贸易的兴起。

随着出口量的增加，有必要将各省的农业开发与日益“标准化”的容器生产系统结合起来，以确保容器的尺寸、可容物的统一。特别是容器装载量的标准化，使商业贸易的管理与控制变得更加容易。容器的标准化也使运输船舶的装卸变得更加方便和高效。

货物是为私人贸易和国家分销而准备的，因此必须确保运输货物的质量和数量得到严格区分。这就是为什么许多双耳细颈瓶上有说明分类信息的铭文，就像我们使用的标签。特别是在货物的可追溯性必须得到保证的要求下，更是如此。

罗马人印章 / 邮戳是在加工时印在新鲜黏土上的，以便农业生产土地所有者知悉双耳细颈瓶的来源出处。双耳细颈瓶的颈部或瓶身用黑色或红色笔刷描绘的商业铭文（称为 tituli picti）提供了瓶内货物的性质、运输、货物贸易和参与人员的信息，

The different containers that were used in Roman times for transporting goods included barrels, baskets, sacks, amphorae, and so on. Amphorae were among the most widely used and, undoubtedly, those that were most preserved to date.

Their presence, from the shores of the Mediterranean to the borders of the Empire, increased over time, to the extent that Rome expanded across the territory, with a consequent expansion of a market system that became increasingly complex, based on the arrival of goods from the provinces to the capital and the Italian peninsula, but also the regional exchange between and within the provinces. Another aspect of the Roman market concerned the import and supply along borders (tn. limes - “path” in Latin - was originally a path that marked the boundary between plots of land; later, “frontier”), due to the presence of legions and of commerce with bordering populations.

With the increase in the volume of exports, it became necessary to combine the agricultural exploitation of the provincial territories with an increasingly “standardized” container production system, which would allow to ensure for size, content, and origin. In particular, the standardization of container capacities made it possible to be able to manage both commercial transactions and inspections more easily, especially within the state’s import and supply (rationings) system (“Annona”). The standardization of containers also simplified and made the cargo on transport ships more efficient.

The goods were intended for both private trade and state distributions, so it was essential to guarantee the quality and quantity of the goods that were transported in the amphorae. This is why many amphorae had inscriptions with different categories of information, somewhat like the labels we use today. This usually occurred for the state’s supply market, where the traceability of the load was indispensable.

The stamps impressed during production in clay that was still fresh, indicated information on the owners of the amphorae

以及“海关”检查和日期。

对容器的形状、黏土特征的研究，以及对装载货物和涉及货运箱生产和销售相关操作的人员的说明的调查，重现了当时的商业区域、商业开发和私人采购粮食交易的动态。

双耳细颈瓶是研究古代社会经济的基本信息档案。罗马的泰斯塔西奥山就是个典型例子。它是一座假山，位于阿文提诺山脚下的古河港口，曾经有250多年的活跃史。这座小山丘周长约1.2千米，高约30米，是由公元前1世纪至公元前3世纪期间向罗马供应食用油而使用的数以百万计的双耳细颈瓶堆积而形成的。

据估计，山上的双耳细颈瓶可装载的食用油容量，足够50万人使用250年。它们当中绝大多数（约85%）来自西班牙安达卢西亚地区（古代的贝蒂卡省）。其余则来自北非和其他地中海省份。

浸满油的双耳细颈瓶无法重复利用，因此这座山成为供国家使用的垃圾填埋场——“阿诺纳”。

而在泰斯塔西奥山上的双耳细颈瓶身所出现的“标签”、印记及标志，则使我们获知双耳细颈瓶的生产炉、所有者、油的毛重和净重，以及产品营销人员。标签还反映了罗马政府的税务检查情况，包括领事年，即罗马历中的装运日期。

对于罗马人来说，泰斯塔西奥山只是一座垃圾填埋场，而对我们来说，它是了解罗马帝国商业网络最重要的档案之一。

R. 塞巴斯蒂亚尼

production furnaces and the agricultural property. Writings (called tituli picti), painted with a brush in black or red on the neck or on the body of the amphora, provided information regarding the nature of the contents, the transport, the goods traded, the individuals involved, “customs” controls, and the date.

The study of the shapes, the characteristics of the clay, and the indications regarding the contents and those responsible for the procedures related to the production and trade of the containers, have allowed us to reconstruct the dynamics of how the territory was exploited and how the public and private trade and supply of foodstuffs was carried out.

Amphorae constituted a fundamental source of information for studying economics and societies in ancient times. An example can be found in Rome with Monte Testaccio. This is an artificial mound created over a period of 250 years, situated behind the ancient river port, the emporium, at the foot of the Aventine Hill. It has a perimeter of approximately 1.2 kilometers and is 30 meters tall, formed by the accumulation of millions of pieces of amphorae that were used to supply oil to Rome between the 1st and 3rd centuries A.D.

According to statistical calculations, the amphorae found in Monte Testaccio today could probably contain a sufficient amount of oil for the needs of 500,000 people for 250 years. There is a great majority (approx. 85%) of amphorae from the region of Andalusia in Spain (the ancient province of Betica). The rest came from North Africa and the remaining Mediterranean.

The oil amphorae would become impregnated with the contents and could not be reused, so the Monte became an organized landfill for the state’s import and supply system, the “Annona”.

The “labels” present on the amphorae found in Monte Testaccio, stamps and tituli picti, give us information on the amphora production furnaces, the owners, the tare and net content of oil, and the individuals involved in the trade of the product. The labels also indicated the Roman administrative tax inspections, including the consular year, i.e. the shipment date based on the Roman calendar.

Monte Testaccio, which was a landfill for the Romans, is instead, for us, one of the most important archives of the Roman Empire’s trade network.

R. Sebastiani

第二部分

食物：意大利葡萄酒的海上之旅

4B. FOODSTUFFS: A CARGO OF ITALIC WINE

在公元前 100 年的时候，罗马船只的货仓里装载着意大利葡萄酒。当时装葡萄酒的容器为双耳细颈瓶，呈锥形，有长长的瓶颈。公元前 2 世纪到公元前 1 世纪期间，意大利半岛伊特鲁里亚海的一侧散布着众多作坊，能够生产大量的双耳细颈瓶，用于出口优质的农产品，这种贸易在托斯卡纳、拉齐奥和坎帕尼亚地区尤为繁荣。双耳细颈瓶设计之初是为了适用于大型跨地中海贸易：尖尖的底部使双耳瓶能够嵌入覆盖在船舱底或底层双耳瓶之间的沙子或砾石上——这种设计能够合理利用船上空间，装载更多的货物（多达 5 层，11 000 件）。生产这种双耳细颈瓶所用材料的质量，以及它们的厚度，使双耳细颈瓶非常耐用。

据古书记载，这些双耳细颈酒罐里装的葡萄酒是用于交换奴隶、金属、牛、皮革的筹码；也为了交换来自坎帕尼亚的甜酒，从亚历山大港运输到西西里岛到达意大利的红珊瑚和黄金，以及香料、香草、纺织品、象牙和珍珠等物品。

意大利半岛的优质高价葡萄酒多数来自第勒尼安海区域的拉齐奥和坎帕尼亚大区，例如红葡萄酒榭库博，以及白葡萄酒色蒂诺、法拉诺、索伦托和维苏威。它们的信息会在酒罐的“标签”上体现。此外，意大利维苏威火山周围的其他地区，也是以高产和高质闻名的葡萄种植区：例如，低价性烈的葡萄酒维努库拉，以及与庞贝酒（产量大但质量较次）共同生产的西西里岛产区酒穆尔杰迪娜（也称为庞贝亚娜）。

At the turn of the year 100 B.C, Roman ships carried Italic wine in their holds. We know that the content was wine from the type of amphora used, tapered and with a long neck. These were manufactured in numerous workshops along the Tyrrhenian side of the Italian peninsula between the 1st and 2nd centuries B.C. and where used for exporting excellent-quality products produced by large agricultural companies that particularly flourished in Tuscany, Lazio, and Campania. These amphorae were made for large trans-marine trade routes: their pointed base - inserted into a layer of sand or gravel that covered the bottom of the hold of the ship, or between the amphorae of the lower layer - allowed them to be rationally stowed in merchant ships (up to 11,000 pieces in 5 layers). The quality of the material used to produce the amphorae, as well as their thickness, made them very resistant.

The wine contained in these amphorae was a bargaining chip for slaves, metal, cattle, and hides, as ancient writers recounted. In exchange for the sweet wine from Campania and red coral and gold, goods such as spices, herbs, fabrics, ivory, and pearls arrived in Italy, transiting through Alessandria to Sicily.

Excellent-quality wines, such as Cecubo - probably white - Setino, Falerno, Sorrentino, and Vesuviano came from the Tyrrhenian side of the Italian peninsula, between Lazio and Campania. These exquisite and very expensive wines were indicated on the "labels" written on the amphorae. However, in other areas around the Vesuvius, famous grape varieties were also cultivated for both their productivity, as well as their quality: the vennuncula, from which a very strong wine was obtained but that was of little value, and the murgentina - also called Pompeian - originally from Sicily, used to produce the vinum pompeianum, of which there was an abundance but that was of poor quality.

The large cargoes of wine from Tyrrhenian ports reached

『吉安斯马德拉格』号沉船残骸

『吉安斯马德拉格』号沉船残骸

从第勒尼安海港口进口的大量葡萄酒被运输到各省市，特别是地中海西部的各省市。高卢，现在的法国，是个典型的葡萄酒消费大国，葡萄酒在大型宴会仪式上不可缺少。古时众所周知的谚语“高卢人醉酒”实际上是一种社会现象，是葡萄酒进口的推动力。

这些进口品中的“最佳照片”是“吉安斯马德拉格”号沉船的货物——来自拉齐奥南部的丰迪—泰拉奇纳地区的大约 9 000 个可能盛满红酒的双耳细颈瓶。这艘船于公元前 75 年—公元前 60 年间在普罗旺斯海岸沉没。我们无比遗憾地推测，沉船上还有一群经常饮用“细颈瓶红酒”的当地精英……

R. 奥列玛

various provinces, especially in the western Mediterranean. Gaul, present-day France, was a privileged destination for wine that was ritually consumed during large banquets for thousands of people. The proverbial Gallic drunkenness - proverbial in antiquity - was actually a social institution that was the driving force of wine imports.

The best “photograph” of these imports was the cargo found in the shipwreck of the Madrague des Giens: about 9,000 amphorae of wine, probably red, from the area of Fondi-Terracina in southern Lazio. The ship had sank between 75 and 60 B.C. along the coasts of Provence, we presume with great regret for the local elite who consumed this wine in considerable quantities...

R. Auriemma

带有戳记的双耳尖底罐，德拉塞尔 6A 型

公元 1 世纪
陶
高 105 厘米，最大直径 40.7 厘米，周长 130 厘米
重约 25 千克
罗马考古、艺术品和景观监管局，展品编号 581633

Amphora
1st century A.D.
height 105 cm, max. diameter 40.7 cm, circumference 130 cm, approx.
weight 25 kilograms
Special Superintendence of Archeology, Fine Arts, and Landscapes of Rome Inv. 581633

用于运输葡萄酒的德拉塞尔 6a 型双耳陶罐。这些陶罐也被称为亚得里亚海陶罐，因为那里是生产陶罐的窑的所在地——古罗马时代的皮塞纳姆地区，位于意大利中部面向亚得里亚海的部分。双耳陶罐是当时最受欢迎和最经济的运输容器之一。这件带有戳记的双耳尖底罐是在陶车上制作的，在尚未完全干燥的陶坯上粘接了因形状而被称为“棍子”的环形耳柄（把手）。在双耳陶罐的颈上有一枚压印印章（刻在黏土上，至今仍然清晰），上面写着“P.C. T I E”。双耳陶罐发现于对泰斯塔乔地区仓库展开的发掘过程中，这些仓库毗邻古罗马河港。

双耳尖底罐，阿非利加 Ⅲ C 型

公元 4 世纪—5 世纪上半叶
陶
整体高度 97 厘米，整体直径 18 厘米
重约 10 千克
罗马考古、艺术品和景观监管局，展品编号 566828

Amphora
4th - first half of the 5th century A.D.
overall height 97 cm, general diameter 18 cm
approx.weight 10 kilograms
Special Superintendence of Archeology, Fine Arts, and Landscapes of Rome Inv. 566828

中等尺寸的圆柱形双耳陶罐。在陶车上制作，在干燥过程中粘接耳柄，分类为阿非利加 Ⅲ C 型，制造于阿非利加北部地区的泽吉塔那（Zeugitana）和比扎塞纳（Bizacena），即今天的突尼斯地区。双耳陶罐保存近乎完整，仅底部尖端部分缺失。它通常用来运输葡萄酒或鱼露（咸鱼酱），甚至还可能被用来运输橄榄油。双耳陶罐来自台伯河上的古罗马港口。

双耳尖底橄榄油罐，德拉塞尔 20 型

公元 2 世纪
陶
高 100 厘米，肩部宽 70 厘米
重约 40 千克
罗马考古、艺术品和景观监管局，展品编号 600087

Amphora
2nd century A.D.
height 100 cm, shoulder width 70 cm
approx. weight 40 kilograms
Special Superintendence of Archeology, Fine Arts, and Landscapes of Rome Inv. 600087

用于运输油的双耳陶罐，于西班牙的贝缇卡省制造（即今天的安达鲁西亚地区），分类为德拉塞尔 20 型。这件双耳陶罐保存完整，在罗马德拉伦加拉街科西尼宫花园的发掘过程中被发现。德拉塞尔 20 型双耳陶罐有一个非常容易辨认的球形结构，带有两个矮胖的圆环形手柄，适合穿过木棍或绳索以方便运输。生产于公元 1 世纪至 3 世纪之间的德拉塞尔 20 型“大肚”陶罐，在整个地中海西部和罗马帝国的西北部省份，直至比里坦尼亚都有大量发现，这证明西班牙出产的油在罗马帝国大部分地区被广泛地使用了许多个世纪。

双耳尖底罐罐盖

公元 1 世纪上半叶
陶
直径 8.5 厘米，厚 2.5 厘米
重 125.2 克
罗马考古、艺术品和景观监管局，展品编号 599843

Amphora Cap
first half of the 2nd century A.D.
diameter 8.5 cm, thickness 2.5 cm
weight 125.2 grams
Special Superintendence of Archeology, Fine Arts, and Landscapes of Rome Inv. 599843

双耳尖底罐罐盖由赤陶制成，手工成型，带有浮雕字符，出土于毗邻古罗马河港的泰斯塔乔的仓库。

油灯

公元 1 世纪末—2 世纪（公元 90 年—140 年）
陶
高 4.1 厘米，长 9.9 厘米，直径 7 厘米
重 96.2 克
罗马考古、艺术品和景观监管局，展品编号 600059

Decorated Oil Lamp

late-1st - mid-2nd century A.D. (90-140 A.D.)
height 4.1 cm, length. 9.9 cm, diameter 7 cm
weight 96.2 grams
Special Superintendence of Archeology, Fine Arts, and Landscapes of Rome Inv. 600059

带有圆形嘴的油灯，保存完整，由米黄色的陶土制成，产于意大利中部地区。它的特征是身体和嘴呈圆形，肩部中间有一个直线形附件，有两个垂直的环状耳柄。盘形部分与肩部之间有两个圆形雕刻，上面装饰着一个浮雕形象：一只兔子蹲在右侧吃着一株可能是藤蔓的植物。底部平整，并有一个雕刻的圆圈。

油灯

公元 1 世纪—2 世纪中期
陶
长 9 厘米，宽 6 厘米，高 3.5 厘米
重约 66 克
罗马考古、艺术品和景观监管局，展品编号 600073

Oil Lamp

1st - mid-2nd century A.D.
length 9 cm, width 6 cm, height 3.5 cm
approx. weight 66 grams
Special Superintendence of Archeology, Fine Arts, and Landscapes of Rome Inv. 600073

鸟头形油灯，带有横向环形耳柄。这种油灯的特点是造型和装饰非常简单，由轻质黏土制成，没有涂层或彩绘，灯体细长呈截锥形，带有铁砧形状的嘴、横向的环形耳柄（把手）和一个被称为“栅栏”的简单阴刻装饰。这种类型的油灯为家庭使用，具有标准化系列生产的特点；其特殊的灯体形状非常适合堆放包装和运输，所以它们被称为“航运”油灯。产品最早可能出现在公元 1 世纪初的罗马，生产它的作坊遍布于第勒尼安中部地区，特别是拉齐奥和坎帕尼亚，主要是为了满足当地市场的需求。这几件油灯于 2019 年在对罗马科西尼宫展开的发掘中被发现。

玻璃香膏瓶

帝国时代
玻璃
长 9 厘米，宽 2 厘米
重约 15 克
罗马考古、艺术品和景观监管局，展品编号 600076

Lacrymatory

Imperial Age
length 9 cm, width 2 cm
approx. weight 15 grams
Special Superintendence of Archeology, Fine Arts, and Landscapes of Rome Inv. 600076

罗马的吹制透明玻璃软膏罐，出土于 2018 年在特拉斯提维尔的莫洛西尼大道展开的发掘。香膏瓶为细长且薄的圆柱体，类似于现代的试管，只有一个极小的瓶颈，表现出颈部和身体之间的区别。底部突出。它类似于“管”型，但整体比这种类型的文物要薄。

玻璃细颈瓶残片

帝国时代
玻璃
长 8 厘米，底宽 4 厘米
重约 26 克
罗马考古、艺术品和景观监管局，展品编号 600077

Lacrymatory

Imperial Age
length 8 cm, width at the base 4 cm
approx. weight 26 grams
Special Superintendence of Archeology, Fine Arts, and Landscapes of Rome Inv. 600077

吹制的透明玻璃油脂瓶呈蓝色，破碎，缺少主体和底部。油脂瓶体呈圆形，底部平坦，颈部为圆柱形，较长，边缘为喇叭口形。玻璃瓶来自罗马，于 2018 年在特拉斯特韦雷的莫洛西尼大道被发掘出土。

蓝色玻璃膏制项链饰珠

帝国时代
玻璃
长 2 厘米，宽 0.5 厘米
重约 5 克
罗马考古、艺术品和景观监管局，展品编号 600078

Necklace Bead

Imperial Age
length 2 cm, width 0.5 cm
approx. weight 5 grams
Special Superintendence of Archeology, Fine Arts, and Landscapes of Rome Inv. 600078

蓝色玻璃材质的八角形项链饰珠来自罗马，于 2018 年在特拉斯特韦雷的莫洛西尼大道被发掘出土。

饰有赫拉克勒斯形象的陶瓷残片

帝国时代
陶
长 10 厘米，宽 7 厘米
重约 68 克
罗马考古、艺术品和景观监管局，展品编号 600079

Ceramic Fragment with Representation of Hercules

Imperial Age
length 10 cm, width 7 cm
approx. weight 68 grams
Special Superintendence of Archeology, Fine Arts, and Landscapes of Rome Inv. 600079

陶土碎片上刻画了赫拉克勒斯的完整形象。我们根据狮子（尼米亚狮的皮，他第一次劳动的成果）得以认出陶片上的人物是赫拉克勒斯。这件陶土碎片是在特拉斯特韦雷的莫洛西尼大道被发掘出土的。

陶土小头像

帝国时代
陶
长 6 厘米，宽 4 厘米
重约 28 克
罗马考古、艺术品和景观监管局，展品编号 600080

Clay Head

Imperial Age
length 6 cm, width 4 cm
approx. weight 28 grams
Special Superintendence of Archeology, Fine Arts, and Landscapes of Rome Inv. 600080

陶土雕像头部，颈部连接处断裂。它可能是供奉的雕像的一部分。由于遭到大面积腐蚀，雕像的脸部很难辨认。

残缺头像

帝国时代
陶
长 6 厘米，宽 4 厘米
重约 28 克
罗马考古、艺术品和景观监管局，展品编号 600081

Terracotta head

Imperial Age
length 6 cm, width 4 cm
approx. weight28 grams
Special Superintendence of Archeology, Fine Arts, and Landscapes of Rome Inv. 600081

底部断裂的没有颈部的陶土头像。头部原本可能是一件雕像的一部分。这件头像是在特拉斯特韦雷的莫洛西尼大道被发掘出土的。

面部残片

罗马帝国时代
陶
长 4.5 厘米，宽 3.5 厘米
重约 18 克
罗马考古、艺术品和景观监管局，展品编号 600082

Terracotta head

Imperial Age
length 4.5 cm, width 3.5 cm
approx. weight 18 grams
Special Superintendence of Archeology, Fine Arts, and Landscapes of Rome Inv. 600082

用浅色黏土制成的陶土面部残片，可能有装饰作用。这件残片是在特拉斯特韦雷的莫洛西尼大道被发掘出土的。

铜制钥匙

帝国时代
铜
长 5 厘米，宽 1.5 厘米
重约 6 克
罗马考古、艺术品和景观监管局，展品编号 600090

Key

Imperial Age
length 5 cm, width 1.5 cm
approx. weight 6 grams
Special Superintendence of Archeology, Fine Arts, and Landscapes of Rome Inv. 600090

小型青铜钥匙，可能用于盒子、箱子的锁或挂锁。钥匙几乎完好，但有很明显的氧化和表面腐蚀痕迹。青铜钥匙采用失蜡铸造工艺制作；有精心设计的钥匙齿，上面有很多齿状凸起。这件钥匙来自罗马，于 2018 年在特拉斯特韦雷的莫洛西尼大道发掘出土。

骨质锁具

帝国时代
骨
长 3 厘米，宽 2 厘米
重约 18 克
罗马考古、艺术品和景观监管局，展品编号 600092

Lock

Imperial Age
length 3 cm, width 2 cm
approx. weight 18 grams
Special Superintendence of Archeology, Fine Arts, and Landscapes of Rome Inv. 600092

骨质饰钮

公元 1 世纪—3 世纪
骨
A）直径 2.5 厘米，重约 4 克
B）直径 4 厘米，重约 9 克
罗马考古、艺术品和景观监管局，展品编号 600088

Studs

1st - 3rd century A.D.
A) diameter 2.5 cm, approx. weight 4 grams
B) diameter 4 cm, approx. weight 9 grams
Special Superintendence of Archeology, Fine Arts, and Landscapes of Rome Inv. 600088

两个中间有洞的骨质饰钮。一个（A）呈光滑的锥形，在穿孔的中心部分周围有圆形凹槽。另一个（B）具有略微凸起的底部，其特征是带有圆形槽，凸出较明显，仅在中心孔处变平。它们都是装饰配件。这两件文物都来自罗马，是 2018 年在特拉斯提维尔的莫罗西尼大道出土的。

3 枚骨针

帝国时代
骨
A）长 7.5 厘米，重约 3 克
B）长 9.5 厘米，重约 5 克
C）长 10.8 厘米，直径 0.4 厘米，重约 3.1 克
罗马考古、艺术品和景观监管局，展品编号 600089

Sewing needle and hair pin

Imperial Age
A) length 7.5 cm, approx. weight 3 grams
B) length 9.5 cm, approx. weight 5 grams
C) length 10.8, diameter 0.4 cm, weight 3.1 grams
Special Superintendence of Archeology, Fine Arts, and Landscapes of Rome Inv. 600089

骨质缝衣针。第一根（A）稍小，圆柱形，带有尖头，针孔略长。另一根（B）稍大，针头偏平，带有较大的矩形针孔。针的形状和大小以及针孔的大小因针的用途而有所不同。带有矩形针眼的大针更有可能用于缝纫皮革带子或粗绳子，有所不同。第三根（C）可能是一个骨制发簪，针顺着尖端逐渐变细，一端有圆形凸起。这三件文物是在特拉斯特韦雷的莫洛西尼大道被发掘出土的。

大理石研钵，残缺

公元 1 世纪 —3 世纪
大理石
长 15 厘米，宽 14 厘米
重约 0.795 克
罗马考古、艺术品和景观监管局，展品编号：600095

Mortar

1st - 3rd century A.D.
length 15 cm, width 14 cm
approx. weight 0.795 grams
Special Superintendence of Archeology, Fine Arts, and Landscapes of Rome Inv. 600095

大理石研钵的一部分。研钵呈圆形，研钵内外部表面不甚精细，带有一个四边形手柄；底部有一个圆形的凹槽。大理石研钵功能各异，不同形状和内部表面结构可表现出其用途：有些可能更适合磨碎豆科植物或调味料，尤其是那些内部表面粗糙以方便使用的；另一些则用于制作食物，甚至用于粉碎绘画颜料。

骨质茶匙

公元 1 世纪 —3 世纪
长 6.5 厘米，宽 2.6 厘米
重约 5 克
罗马考古、艺术品和景观监管局，展品编号：600084/1

Teaspoon

1st - 3rd century A.D.
length 6.5 cm, width 2.6 cm
approx. weight 5 grams
Special Superintendence of Archeology, Fine Arts, and Landscapes of Rome Inv. 600084/1

这把骨质茶匙的特征为圆形杯状部分和具有圆形截面的破损的棒状勺柄。这些物件，形状与材质（有时装饰有金圈）使它们具有广泛的用途——包括食用蛋类和贝壳类动物时，可用手柄的尖端将其取出。勺子是日常用品，在某种情况下经常与女性联系在一起。这些物品在罗马很常见，体积小、种类繁多，包括缝纫针、发簪、抹刀等。此外，它还被做成用于在蜡版上写字的工具、勺子和用于纺织的物品，例如纺锤和梭子。

骨质小勺子

公元 1 世纪—3 世纪
骨
长 5 厘米，宽 2.4 厘米
重约 4 克
罗马考古、艺术品和景观监管局，展品编号 600084/2

Teaspoon

1st -3rd century A.D.
length 5 cm, width 2.4 cm
approx. weight 4 grams
Special Superintendence of Archeology, Fine Arts, and Landscapes of Rome Inv. 600084/2

骨质茶匙，类似于前一件文物，末端缺失，带有一个完美的圆杯。

盛酒的双耳尖底陶罐

公元前 2 世纪后半叶—公元前 1 世纪前半叶
陶
高 108 ～ 127 厘米，最大直径 30 ～ 32 厘米，罐口直径 17 ～ 18 厘米
罗马国家博物馆 - 戴克里先浴场，展品编号 2002425 20B; 2002189 17C; 2002454 21B; 2002192 17C; 2002421 21B; 2002364 22A; 2002458 20B; 2002356 17B; 2002371 19B;2002436 22A; 2002353 23A; 2002367 16B

Transport Amphorae

second half of the 2nd - mid-1st century B.C.
height 108-127 cm, max. diameter 30-32 cm, rim diameter 17-18 cm
National Roman Museum, Baths of Diocletian Inv. 2002425 20B, 2002189 17C, 2002454 21B, 2002192 17C, 2002421 21B, 2002364 22A, 2002458 20B, 2002356 17B, 2002371 19B, 2002436 22A, 2002353 23A, 2002367 16B

酒罐款式为“德拉塞尔 1 型”，是公元前 2 世纪中叶至公元前 1 世纪中叶在第勒尼安海上葡萄酒运输使用范围最广的容器款式。它的名字来源于 19 世纪第一个发现这种款式并编号的德国学者海因里希 · 德拉塞尔（Heinrich Dressel）。这种罐子的特征是高口、圆柱长颈，有椭圆形的长把手，卵形渐细罐身，酒罐底部为圆柱形尖底。这种款式的罐子被用来运送产于意大利中部靠近第勒尼安海的酿酒中心所出产的葡萄酒。在地中海西部、法国、德国和不列颠等地区公元前 2 世纪中叶至公元前 1 世纪中叶之间的考古发现中，均有这种罐子的身影，见证了罗马帝国覆灭前一个世纪意大利葡萄酒的巨大产量和商业规模。

第三部分

艺术品：海底博物馆

4C - WORKS OF ART: A MUSEUM AT THE BOTTOM OF THE SEA

古代艺术品的运输和贸易也十分繁荣，这些艺术品大多是罗马帝国在战场上获得的战利品：在执政官卢西奥·穆米乌斯占领科林斯之后，大量艺术品来到罗马。人们痛骂执政官的掠夺暴行，并为陶器上那简洁刻画的神灵形象感到痛惜……罗马的裁判官皮乌斯在其门廊上使用了利西波斯所创作的亚历山大大帝的雕像作品；而弗里斯则掠夺了墨西拿的海乌斯藏品，其中包括普拉克希特列斯、米隆和波利克莱托斯的雕像作品，以及利利比乌斯的迪奥克莱斯·波皮利乌斯的雕像作品。可以说，掠夺对象从马耳他到锡拉库萨的神殿，无一幸免。这些艺术珍品激发了真正的艺术激情，并促成了第一批藏品的诞生。

这些作品最后大多被安置在公共场所，有些则被放置在胜利者特别建造的凯旋门中，以彰显他们的军事成就。其中，从希腊大神殿中盗窃来的著名希腊作品被着重展示。

大多数战利品都被运往了罗马，但殖民地也分到了一些：它们被奖赏给那些为战争胜利做出贡献的杰出公民，以装点他们的家乡。

说到这个时期繁荣的贸易，我们必须提到海洋。在海底深处就珍藏着一个美妙的“博物馆”，欢迎着那些遭遇海难的不幸船只留下的珍贵货物。

最著名的例子是里亚切的青铜器。1972 年，人们在卡拉布里亚的爱奥尼亚水域发现了两件创作于公元前 5 世纪的希腊青铜器，随之一起被发现的还有希腊的安提基希拉和突尼斯海岸的马赫迪耶的

The transport and trade of works of art also flourished in ancient times, along the wake of Roman conquests and the rich spoils that ensued. After the capture of Corinth by Consul Lucius Mummius, many works of art arrived in Rome, raising the suspicion of a scandal, and making many long for the simple images of terracotta gods... Quintus Caecilius Metellus used a statue of Alexander the Great by Lysippos in the portico he built in Rome; Verres sacked Heius' collections in Messina, including the statues of Praxiteles, Myron, and Policletus, and Diocles Popilius at Lilybaeum, without sparing the furnishings from the sanctuaries of Malta and Syracuse. These treasures unleashed a tried and true passion that led to the birth of the first art collections.

The works mostly ended up in public places. Some were also used in triumphal arches specially built by winners to enhance their military successes and exhibit the famous Greek works that were stolen, above all, from great sanctuaries in Greece.

The war spoils were mainly destined for Rome, but the colonies also received a part of them. They were distributed to citizens who became illustrious for having contributed to the victories, embellishing their hometowns.

However, what endows us with information regarding this flourishing trade is the sea, which has preserved a wonderful "museum" in its depths, welcoming the prized cargoes of the unfortunate ships that were shipwrecked.

The most famous examples are represented by the Riace Bronzes - two splendid Greek originals from the 5th century B.C. discovered in 1972 in the Ionian waters of Calabria, but also by the cargoes of Antikythera in Greece and Mahdia on the Tunisian coast, milestones in the history of research, are striking proof. An illustrious victim of ancient and modern art collecting was the "Victorious Youth", also known as the "Getty Bronze", a precious Greek original attributed to

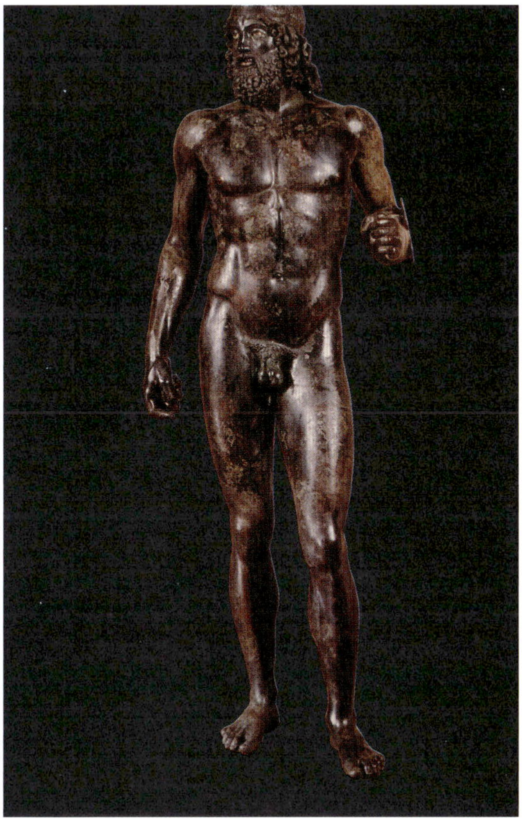

货物，这个惊人的发现成为考古史上的一座里程碑。位于法诺的竞技场收藏有大量古代和现代的杰出艺术品，其中一件珍贵的希腊作品被认为是利西波斯的手笔，它于20世纪60年代中期在马尔凯海岸地区用渔网打捞得来。神奇的是，这座雕像后来经非法手段莫名其妙地从意大利消失了，十年后才在马里布的保罗盖蒂博物馆重新出现。

最新的发现是“马扎拉·德尔瓦洛的萨提尔”，一个跳舞的裸体男性铜像。他头向后仰，秀发飘逸，有一双尖耳朵，该铜像于1998年在西西里运河一艘渔船的渔网中被发现。克罗地亚的运动员——“刮板”——1999年在克罗地亚卢西诺岛的水域浮出水面。这是一个年轻的运动员的形象，在运动后打算使用一种特殊工具清除身上的灰尘和油污。

保存至今的古老青铜雕像非常罕见，因此非常珍贵，其中许多来自海洋或河流沉船。古时候大多数雕像是用来装饰公共空间或豪宅的，后来，许多青铜雕像都被融化，以再利用这些高贵且昂贵的金属。尤其是在经济不发达的时期，很多古代艺术品因为上述原因而被摧毁，并转变为其他的物品，有时甚至是简陋的、不太值钱的物品，但是可用作生活用品。

在罗马国家博物馆里，保存着一系列在海上发现的物品。比如一匹青铜马的碎片（来自泰拉奇纳的蓬扎岛），就可能是马术团体的一部分。说到这些，其中比较有趣的是在奇维塔韦基亚发现的头像，那是一个女性的形象，被放置在船的正面，由于其特征和可识别性，成为船舶不可或缺的装饰元素。精细的工艺彰显了罗马青铜器工匠的技术能力，很多商船沿袭了这种豪华的装饰。

除了艺术品之外，还有奢侈工艺品的交易（今天我们称之为“家具配件”）：墙壁壁灯、小型雕塑、

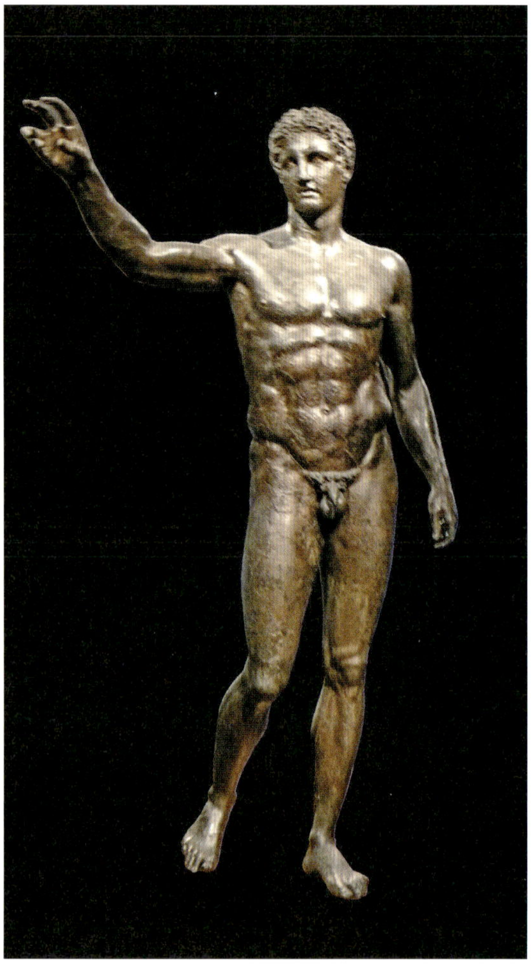

安迪基西拉岛的“青年”

Lysippos, recovered with nets in the waters of Fano on the coast of the Marche region in the mid-1960s. The statue, in fact, inexplicably and illegally disappeared from Italy to reappear ten years later in the J.P. Getty Museum in Malibu.

More recent discoveries include the “Satyr of Mazara del Vallo”, a bronze statue that depicts a dancing nude male figure, with his head thrown back, hair flowing, and pointed ears, recovered in 1998 in the nets of a fishing boat in the Strait of Sicily, and also the Croatian Apoxyomenos - the “Scraper” - the statue of a young athlete intent on removing dust, perspiration, and oil from his body using a special tool - the strigil - after exercising. The statue was discovered in 1999 in the waters of the island of Lošinj, in Croatia.

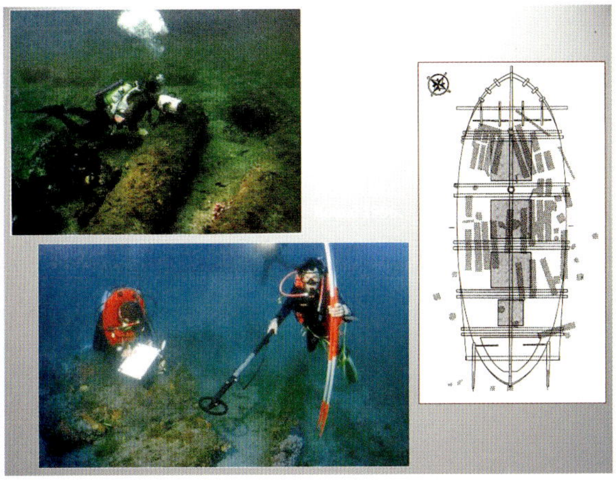

「马赫迪耶」号沉船残骸

法诺的田径运动员

The bronze statues from antiquity that have survived till now are very rare and, therefore, precious. Many derive from the sea or river wrecks, since most that reached their destinations to decorate public spaces or mansions of wealthy aristocrats in ancient times, were melted in later periods to reuse the noble and expensive metal. Ancient works were destroyed and transformed into many other objects, sometimes even humble and not very valuable but more useful for daily life, during periods of low prosperity.

A series of objects recovered at sea come from the National Roman Museum, such as the fragments of a bronze horse (from Ponza, Terracina), which was probably part of an equestrian group. To this regard, it is also interesting to mention the figurehead from Civitavecchia, in the shape of a woman. Figureheads were placed on the bows of ships as an indispensable decorative element that characterized and distinguished the ship itself. The fine workmanship of this example highlights the technical ability of Roman bronze sculptors and the decorative ostentation that was also reserved for trade vessels.

Along with works of art, trade in luxury crafts items also existed (today we would define these as "furnishings"): sconces, small sculptures, parts of furniture, vases, oil lamps, and so on. Several of the objects on display might have been furnishings used aboard ships, for example, statuettes of gods, possibly placed in a corner, dedicated to worship (sacellum

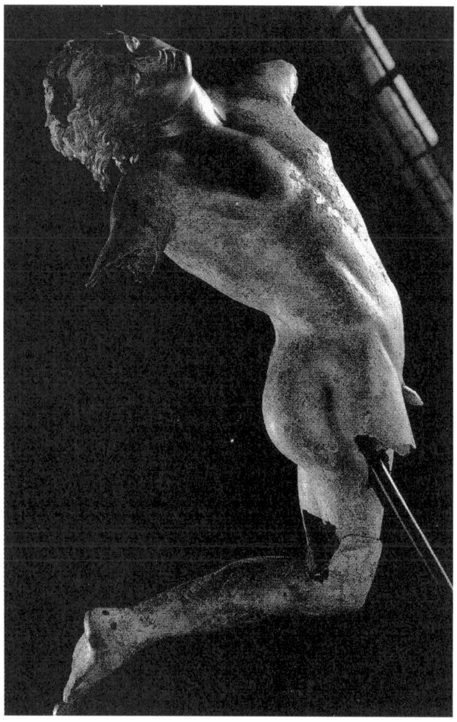

『马扎拉·德尔瓦洛的萨提尔』

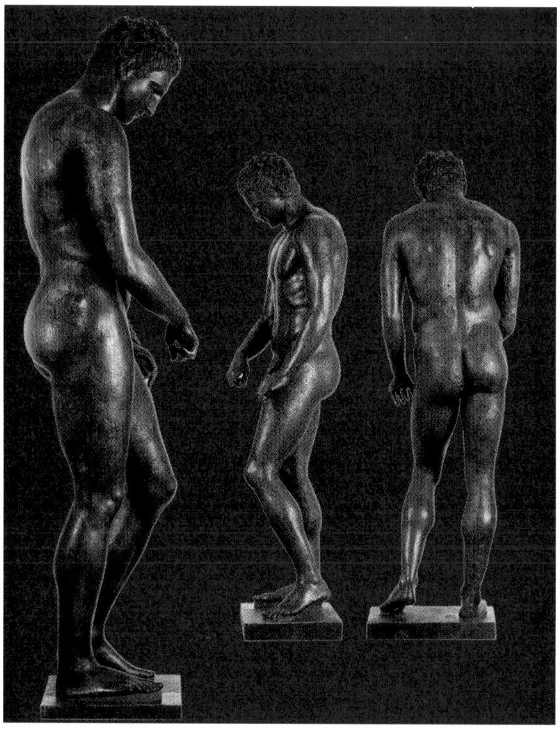

克罗地亚的田径运动员——『刮板』

家具部件、花瓶、油灯等。这次展出的一些展品可能是船上使用的家具，例如可能被放置在船角专用于祭祀的小神像。然而，它们更有可能被打算作为奢侈品出售，例如来自罗马国家博物馆的、带有站在海怪上的厄洛斯的喷泉或带有格里芬造型的桌子支架。

R．奥列玛，M．塞洛伦齐

- shrine). Most likely, however, they were luxury goods intended for sale, such as the fountain with putti (a winged infant, also known as a cherub) riding a sea monster, or the pedestal of the table (trapezophoron) with griffins from the National Roman Museum.

R. Auriemma, M. Serlorenzi

珍贵文物：塞罗内海岬铜像的 3D 还原

PRECIOUS RELICS: THE BRONZES OF PUNTA DEL SERRONE IN 3D

1992 年，在布林迪西以北的塞罗内海岬深处发现了公元前 4 世纪至公元 2 世纪时期制作的 200 块青铜像碎片，它们是神、哲学家、权力人物、古代重要家族的成员的“化身”。

这些艺术品是在帝国时代晚期“乘”船“抵达”亚得里亚海的，但由于船只遇到困难——船只沉没或是货物被抛出船外——这些作品最终沉入海底。

船只从希腊出发，在这些青铜像沉入海底、成为碎片之前，它们装饰着著名的公共或私人建筑（这从展品所呈现出的高水平可以看出来）——应该是与公元 2 世纪最富有的知识分子、诡辩家和赞助人希罗德 · 阿提库斯有关的居所。在这些雕塑中，最重要的是阿提库斯最喜欢的学生波吕丢凯斯的青铜像，它出现在这位诡辩家以众多杰作装饰的别墅里，

In 1992, just north of Brindisi, the depths of Punta del Serrone brought to light two hundred bronze fragments of statues, produced between the 4th century B.C. and the 2nd century A.D., which personified gods, philosophers, ruling figures, and members of important families.

These works of art had arrived in the Adriatic in the late Imperial Age - already reduced to pieces because they had been melted - and transported on a ship that, finding itself in difficulty, had probably thrown its cargo overboard or had been shipwrecked.

The ship originated from Greece where, before being broken into pieces, the sculptures embellished prestigious public or private buildings (as the high stylistic level of the examples indicates), associated with the figure of the richest intellectual, sophist, and patron from the 2nd century A.D., Herodes Atticus. In fact, among the sculptures, the bronze statue of central importance today is that of the sophist's favorite pupil, Polydeukes (Polydeukion) , whose image was found in the villas

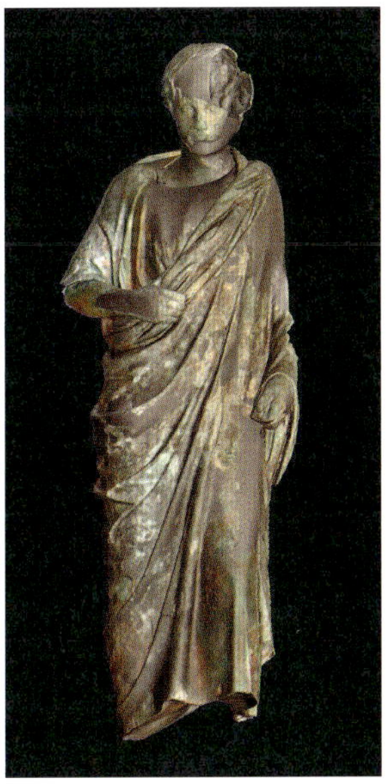
波吕丢凯斯雕塑（3D 激光扫描）

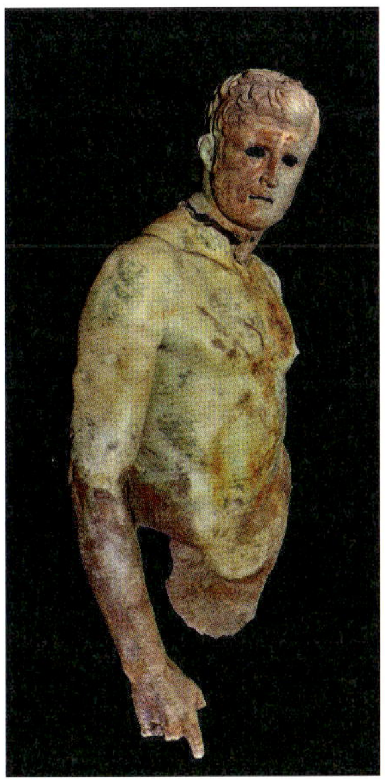
男子雕塑，也称为“希腊王子”或“卢基乌斯 · 埃米利乌斯 · 鲍鲁斯”（3D 激光扫描）

男子雕塑，也称为“希腊王子”或“卢基乌斯 · 埃米利乌斯 · 鲍鲁斯”（建模及重构复原）

也出现在古希腊城邦共同的圣地德尔斐。塞罗内海岬的铜像（也称为“布林迪西的铜像”）在希腊最初亮相时——它们很大且完好无损——一定引起了观赏者的赞叹和惊奇。

今天，为了向公众复原这些作品，“3D盒子创意试验室”与萨兰托大学SIBA合作，通过使用高分辨率激光扫描仪对碎片进行数码采集，为塞罗内海岬铜像3D建模。3D建模成功的作品中，最著名的是塞罗内海岬的铜像——“希腊王子”。这是一个真人大小的雕像，脸上的坚毅表情体现了他的活力和决心，颈部和胸部是明显的扭转姿势。他是全裸的，有着强壮的躯干、完美的背部和清晰的胸部和腹部。一件披风搭在他的下半身，遮住了他的臀部和部分腿部，但露出了部分阴毛。3D模型增强了裸露躯干外观的“活力”（人们出于库存记录目的，在他的右肩上刻有希腊字母kappa和epsilon），这个赤脚踩在帷幔上的人物形象与佛尔梅拉别墅中的赫菲斯托斯雕塑相呼应，姿势类似于“阿塔兰特赫尔墨斯”（雅典国家考古博物馆）。这两件雕塑的灵感来自于公元前4世纪的原型。

塞罗内海岬铜像可以追溯到希腊时代，当时身居要职的希腊人和罗马人摆出英雄的姿态，被描绘成充满激情的凝视形象——政治军事领域的典型代表，例如公元前168年在皮德纳打败马其顿共和国佩尔塞奥的罗马指挥官卢基乌斯·埃米利乌斯·鲍鲁斯，公元前168年在皮德纳击败马其顿的珀尔修斯的罗马指挥官。

希腊化时期出现了极富英雄主义色彩的胜利女神雕塑（或维多利亚）。从双翅羽毛的渲染暗示可以看出，女神以庄严的步态站立着，其姿态类似于“怀中抱着胜利奖杯”，这是一种希腊风格的雕像，是从帝国时代的复制品中发现的。通过3D重建，

adorned with masterpieces that Herodes Atticus owned in Greece, but it was also present in the sanctuary of Delphi. In Greece, within the context of the original exhibition, the Bronzes of Punta del Serrone (also known as the Bronzes of Brindisi) - several colossal and all still intact and impressive - must have aroused in those who observed them a strong sense of admiration and wonder.

Today, these emotions are conveyed through the three-dimensional modeling of the Bronzes of Punta del Serrone carried out, on a scientific basis, by 3D Box Creative LAB, starting from the digital acquisitions and elaborations of the fragments that Unisalento's SIBA Coordination created using a very high resolution laser scanner. In particular, using 3D modeling, a hypothetical reconstruction of the most famous among the bronzes of Punta del Serrone was created, the so-called "Hellenic prince", the life-size statue of a strong-willed individual whose energy and determination are manifested both in the resolute expression of his face and in the accentuated twist of his neck and bust. His powerful torso, with a perfectly sculpted back and well-defined chest and abdomen, was completely nude. A cape, which was lost, was draped around the lower portion, covering his hips and part of his legs, but leaving part of his pubic hair visible. The 3D model enhances the vigorous appearance of the naked torso (where the Greek letters, kappa and epsilon, were engraved on the right shoulder for inventory purposes), embodying an image of a man with bare feet planted on the ground that, in the draping, echoes Hephaestus from the Villa Formello, and resembles "Hermes from Atalante" (in the National Archeological Museum of Athens) in his pose. These two sculptures were inspired by prototypes from the 4th century B.C..

The statue of Punta del Serrone dates back to the Hellenistic age - when Greeks and Romans who held prestigious positions were represented in heroic poses and with faces that portrayed a passionate stare - depicting an exponent of the political-military sphere, most likely Lucius Aemilius Paullus Macedonicus, the Roman commander who defeated Perseus of Macedonia at Pidna in 168 B.C.

The double wings of a larger-than-life Victory (or Victoria) also date back to the Hellenistic period. As suggested by the rendering of the plumage, the goddess was represented

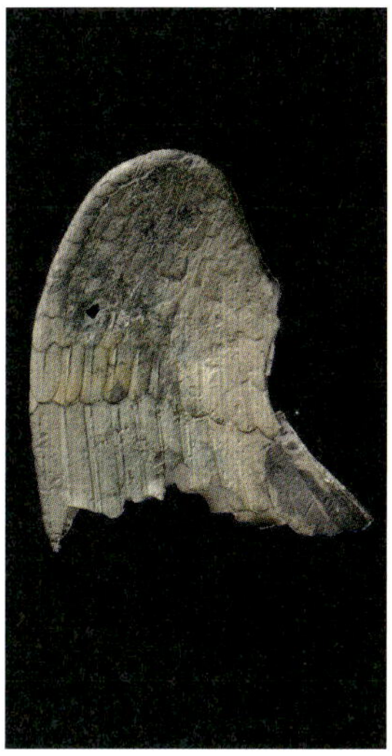

胜利女神雕塑的翅膀（3D 激光扫描）

胜利女神雕塑（建模及重构复原）

女童雕塑头部肖像及手臂部分（3D 激光扫描）

女童雕塑（建模及重构复原）

将这尊雕像“还原”为运动中的女神形象：上身裸露，下身包裹着斗篷，右臂抬起，左臂伸出，左手托着王冠。雕像头部的灵感来自“布雷西亚的胜利”，虽然布雷西亚可以追溯到早期的帝国时代（公元前 27 年—公元 2 世纪），但它与公元前 4 世纪末的原作很像。

第三个 3D 模型是一个真人大小的小女孩雕像，右臂上装饰着一只蛇形手镯，完整的头部和颈部都被保存了下来。小女孩发型独特，头发中分，发心编有一条辫子，两边分成条状，形成一个高高的发髻，别在她的后脑勺上。她是皇帝马可 · 奥勒留和女皇福斯蒂娜 · 米诺勒的女儿们收养的孩子的雕像。这些雕像用于装饰希罗德 · 阿提库斯在奥林匹亚圣所建造的纪念性喷泉。小公主的雕像通过 3D 重建得以重现在世人眼前——这是一个优雅的贵族形象，可能是希罗德 · 阿提库斯最小的女儿雅典内斯的雕像。

K. 曼尼诺

standing upright with a solemn gait, similar in attitude to the Victory with trophy, a type of Hellenistic statue that came to be known from copies created during the Imperial Age. This type of statue was copied in the 3D reconstruction of the Victory of Punta del Serrone, modeling the majestic image of the goddess in motion with the lower part of her naked body wrapped in a mantle, her right arm raised and her left arm extended, holding a crown in her hand. Instead, the head was inspired by the Winged Victory of Brescia which, although dating back to the early Imperial Age, it resembles an original from the end of the 4th century B.C..

The third 3D model is a life-size statue of a little girl of which the right arm, adorned with a snake bracelet, and full-head portrait with neck, were also preserved. The peculiar hairstyle of the little girl - hair gathered in the middle in a braid and divided on the sides into flat bands, forming a high bun pinned to the back of her head - was adopted by the daughters of Emperor Marcus Aurelius and Empress Faustina Minor in the statues that adorned the monumental fountain built by Herodes Atticus in the Sanctuary of Olympia. The statues of the two young princesses were, therefore, used as a model to reconstruct the image of the girl from Punta del Serrone; a delicate aristocrat in which perhaps Athenais, the youngest daughter of Herodes Atticus, can be recognized.

K. Mannino

格里芬造型的桌子支架

公元 1 世纪
铜
高 62.5 厘米，厚 13 厘米
重 5 千克
罗马国家博物馆 - 马西莫宫，展品编号 126105

Griffin-Shaped Support

1st century A.D.
height 62.5 cm, depth 13 cm
weight 5 kilograms
National Roman Museum, Palazzo Massimo Inv. 126105

这种台面支架可能支撑的是圆形或方形的小尺寸桌子，它在拉齐奥海岸前的海床中被发现。桌子支架是一个功能性的部件，有一只巨大的爪子作为装饰，上面是格里芬的头。格里芬是一种巨大的动物，长有公羊的角和一对翅膀，以植物为食。在希腊神话中，格里芬是一种奇妙的动物，栖息于偏远地区，具有极具个性的弯曲的嘴（希腊语中的术语 GRYPÒS 恰恰是“弯嘴”的意思）。

贝尔维德尔的阿波罗雕像左手模具残件

帝国时代
石膏
高 17 厘米，宽 13.5 厘米
重约 1 千克
坎皮佛莱格瑞考古公园 - 巴亚城堡中的坎皮佛莱格瑞考古博物馆，展品编号 174521

Fragment of a Mold

Roman Age
height 17 cm, width 13.5 cm
approx.weight 1 kilograms
Phlegraean Fields Archeological Park - Archeological Museum of the Phlegraean Fields in the Castle of Baia Inv. 174521

巴亚的索珊德拉浴场观景楼的阿波罗雕像的左手模具残件。石膏模具直接使用希腊青铜器原件制作，罗马雕刻家制作大理石复制品时使用这一方法，有时他们会修改模具原件，适应客户不断变化的需求。因此，它是众多不知所踪的希腊青铜雕像的直接“记录”；最重要的是，它是证明希腊雕塑如何成为罗马雕塑和现代雕塑起源的明确证据。1954 年偶然发现的约 430 块巴亚残片，在 30 多年的时间里被弃置一旁，无人研究，他们是唯一流传下来的古代石膏模具。

马匹部分残件

公元 1 世纪
出土于蓬扎，特拉西那
铜
高 138 厘米，长 145 厘米，宽 63 厘米
罗马国家博物馆 - 戴克里先浴场，展品编号 124547

Bronze Horse

1st century A.D.
height 138 cm, length 145 cm, width 63 cm
National Roman Museum, Baths of Diocletian Inv. 124547

两块碎片来自一尊用失蜡法浇铸而成的铜制雕塑，展现了一匹马的后身，包括右腿到膝盖部位。马尾（只保留下了一半）的动态、右腿的肌肉张力以及骑士衣服裙摆位置非常靠近马背，这些特征表明，这匹马原本可能是腾跃的姿态。这尊雕塑又或许是一组受希腊艺术家利西波斯启发而造的雕塑群中的一部分。利西波斯曾创造出一组雕塑群来纪念亚历山大大帝在格拉尼库斯（Granico）河与波斯人的战役（公元前 334 年）中战死的伙伴，之后，这组雕塑群被亚历山大大帝放在迪翁（Dion）的神庙中，献给宙斯。根据古文献记载，这组雕塑群在公元前 146 年被罗马指挥官昆图斯 · 凯西里乌斯 · 梅特卢斯（Quinto Cecilio Metello）运往罗马。

女性半身像船头饰

公元 1 世纪—2 世纪
出土于奇维塔韦基亚
铜
高 18 厘米，宽 31 厘米，深 23 厘米
罗马国家博物馆 - 马西莫宫，展品编号 74014

Figurehead

1st - 2nd century A.D.
height 18 cm, width 31 cm, depth 23 cm
National Roman Museum, Palazzo Massimo Inv. 74014

“船头饰”是指船头尖部的装饰雕塑。将这个梯形盒子插到船头上，用五枚钉子固定。这五枚钉子穿过长边对齐的孔，女性上半身便覆盖了最尖端的部分。

自古以来人类就使用船头饰，这不仅满足了装饰的需要，而且人们认为雕饰可以对船起到保护作用。船可通过其船头雕饰进行识别，并且以其船头饰进行命名。

最具代表性的船头饰都是来自神话和宗教，但也有些取自动物和历史。船舶因其船头雕饰而显示出个性，船员因其船头饰而自豪，他们认为这些船头饰可以对付来自海洋的各种潜在敌对性和破坏性危险。这些船头饰可以乘风破浪，并能够指出最安全的路线。

第四部分

往昔之景：钱币及纪念章上的船舶及港口

4D. IMAGES OF MEMORIES: SHIPS AND PORTS ON COINS AND MEDALS

第一节　硬币和奖章上的船舶和港口

4D.1. SHIPS AND PORTS ON COINS AND MEDALS

“硬币有三个要素：金属、图案和重量。缺少其中任何一项特性，都不能将该对象视为货币。”

圣依西多禄是一位生活在公元 6 世纪到 7 世纪之间的博学多才的教会学者，他在著作《词源》的第十六章中对“硬币”一词做了定义（圣依西多禄，《词源》，第十六章，18，12）。《词源》是一本百科全书式的著作，致力于记录所有已知词汇的起源和演变，其中词汇按照类别分类。

货币本质上是一种支付媒介，这一普遍而自发的观点往往导致人们优先考虑其经济因素，而不会对其中出现的图像和文字给予重视。但是，当一定重量的金属被定义为货币时，必须由国家或担保它的政府给予印记。这种印记转化为一种图像，以某种表现形式或简单的刻印体现，以此传递着精确的信息：硬币这种小金属物体，其本质和形式能够广泛地渗透到每一寸领土和每一个社会阶层，可以超越所有界限，并成为一种特殊的交流方式和快速传播的工具。换句话说，支付者通过货币对接收者发送信息。为了让每个人都清楚地知道信息内容，有必要使用人人都能理解的语言。而通过货币图像的暗示，使它们通过充满信息的视觉语言与观察者交流并在观察者的记忆中扎根，证明了这是一种有效的交流方式，是一种绝妙的过程和思想语言。罗马

“Three elements are sought for in coins: metal, design, and weight. If any of these is missing, the object cannot be considered a coin”. This is what Isidore of Seville, an erudite Doctor of the Church who lived at the turn of the 6th and 7th centuries, wrote about the term “coin” in the sixteenth chapter of his Etymologiae (Isid., Orig. , XVI, 18, 12), an encyclopedic work dedicated to the origin and evolution of all known words, sorted and divided into categories. The common and spontaneous consideration that coins are essentially a means of payment often reductively induces us to consider economic aspects as being preponderant and a priority, and we do not give the right importance to the images and words that appear on them. But, to be defined as currency, a piece of metal of a given weight must receive a stamp from the State or from the authority that guarantees for it. This stamp translates into an image, expressed in a representation or simply an inscription that, in turn, transmits a precise message. And, so, the coin - a small metallic object that, by its very nature and form, is capable of extensively penetrating into every land and social stratum, exceeding all boundaries - also becomes an exceptional means of communication and a rapid vehicle of dissemination. There is, therefore, a sender that exists who sends information through coins and a recipient who receives it. Yet, in order for the message to be clear to everyone, a language must be used that everyone can understand. And the power exercised by the suggestion of images on coins, their ability to communicate with the viewer through a visual language full of messages, and to take root in the memory of the observer, proves to be an effective means of communication. A coveted manifesto of programs and ideas. The strong communicative power of coins was

人很快就明白了货币所具备的强大交流作用，他们把它作为政治、意识形态和社会宣传的手段，向人们传递货币在提高个人地位、纪念公共建筑、庆祝军事征服、重现社会价值等方面发挥的作用。

货币是艺术的表达，而艺术是沟通的载体。货币是一种微型艺术，其想要传达的信息依赖于雕刻师的专业技能和创造力。圆形小硬币正面和反面呈现的图案，通常伴有便于理解的铭文。它们可以是神灵、拟人物、肖像、纪念碑、建筑群、物体、工具、符号或平民生活、政治和宗教活动的场景，每一个都具有象征意义，并与其所在时代的历史、意识形态和宗教环境密切相关。因为货币永远不会成为过时的信息，货币的表征意义必须始终与产生它们的历史时刻以及为某一特定问题而采用它们的人物有密切联系。因此，与同一历史时期或神话故事相关的表征意义可具有不同的含义，这与孕育它们的时代是直接相关的。

货币通过使用国家的背书使其购买力合法化，成为一种有效的交流工具，是一个民族历史与文化的非凡见证。这些金属硬币被锁在商人的马鞍包里，或塞进船只的钱柜里，沿着尘土飞扬的商队路线或古老的地中海路线航行，穿越边境，流通到发行地之外，它们的历史和发行它们的国家一样长久。

奖章，难免因其外在形式和代表的意义而被拿来与货币类比，但又与货币有着很大的不同。因为奖章纯粹的艺术价值使其不受任何世俗或繁琐要求的限制，那些不受国家权威约束的个人和显赫的庆祝者赋予其广泛的代表意义，用来纪念永恒记忆中的人物、事件或行为，巧妙地塑造和诠释了不同雕刻者的个人品位和艺术能力，但也不可避免地受到当时历史现实和风格趋势的影响。

本次展览中展示了地中海航行及很多相关方面的内容，包括商业、军事、民俗、神话等，并且专门展出了部分硬币和奖章，它们在整个展览行程中如钻石般珍贵。由于拥有藏品的重要性和一致

immediately clear to the Romans, who used them as a means of political, ideological, and social propaganda to which they entrusted messages of personal exaltation, commemoration of public buildings, celebration of military conquests, and the re-enactment of social benevolence.

Coins are an expression of art and art is communication. The art on coins is miniature art, which entrusts the message that it wants to convey to the expertise and creativity of engravers. The choice of the images that appear on the two sides of a small round coin, the back and front, often accompanied by an inscription that facilitates its understanding, is never accidental: be they gods, personifications, portraits, monuments, architectural complexes, objects, instruments, symbols or scenes of civilian, political, and religious life, each is nevertheless full of emblematic meanings, closely connected to the historical, ideological, and religious circumstances of the era that generated them because the message that is conveyed by coins is isolated from the time that created it, and the images on coins must always be read and interpreted in close relationship to the historical moment that produced them and the figures who adopted them for a given issue. So much so that images related to the same historical or mythological episode can takc on different meanings, directly related to the era that conceived them.

Validated by the seal of the State that guarantees their purchasing power, coins become an effective vehicle of communication, an extraordinary document of the history and culture of a people. Tucked away in a merchant's saddlebag or crammed into the coffers of ships, metal coins traveled dusty caravan roads or sailed along the ancient routes of the Mediterranean, circulating and crossing the boundaries of the land that generated them and often surviving the same State that created them.

Even medals - which are instinctively assimilated to coins due to their form and narrative composition, but are very much different than the latter because of their purely artistic value, free from commercial or ponderal requirements, and also due to their private and eminently celebratory character, which is free from constraints with the State authority - entrust to the wide range of their images the commemoration of figures, episodes or deeds of everlasting memory, cleverly shaped and variously interpreted by the personal taste and artistic ability of the engraver, but inevitably influenced by the historical reality and stylistic tendencies of the moment.

性，罗马国家博物馆是该领域在罗马国内和国际上最重要和最负盛名的机构之一，其奖牌藏品非常丰富。随着时间的推移，罗马奖牌藏品库里堆满了硬币、奖章、重硬币、镶嵌物、硬币类物品和宝石、金器以及珍贵的家具。如今，古代、中世纪和现代的藏品已经超过五十万件。这些非凡的财富描述了一个关于海洋的故事。几个世纪以来，这片海洋一直是许多文明的摇篮，是展示交通、交流、冲突、人类和货物旅途的舞台。记忆的图像镌刻在圆形的小金属品中，文明和时代的珍贵见证和记忆交替追逐着这单一的旅程：海洋。在奇维塔韦基亚（展品编号 19.M329-1.1、展品编号 18098），安齐奥和泰拉奇纳港口（展品编号 18695），克劳迪乌斯和图拉真（展品编号 91923、展品编号 92328）所在的古罗马帝国时代和教皇时代的古老建筑和船舶交相呼应，它们才是海洋真正的主角，是权力和财富的象征，唤起了关于战争（展品编号 63354、展品编号 18077、展品编号 85511、展品编号 19.M329-1.8）与和平的回忆（展品编号 85576、展品编号 19.M329-1.11、展品编号 92493、展品编号 19.M329-1.10）。而古老的神话故事，作为幻想的产物——没有历史根据但通常是以历史为基础——在讲述故事中发挥着重要作用。故事的主要讲述者就藏在海洋里：善变的海神尼普顿（展品编号 92552），以裸体形象示人，手持独一无二的三叉戟作为权杖；以及他迷人的新娘、海洋女神安菲特里忒（展品编号 83673）；还有结合了人类和鱼类双重特点的特里同，虽然其拥有迷人的身姿，却是居住在深渊中的怪物（展品编号 85644、展品编号 85234），以可怕的外表恐吓人类（展品编号 83671）——这是水手和船员们在充满危险和神秘的宽广海洋中漂泊冒险所经历的恐惧与焦虑的象征。

G. 安杰利 · 布法利尼

The exhibition, dedicated to navigation in the Mediterranean and to its many commercial, military, "civilian", and mythological aspects, includes a section dedicated to a selection of coins and medals - like a precious diamond set in its itinerary - deriving from the very rich collections of the Medagliere of the National Roman Museum, among the most important and prestigious in the sector, nationally and internationally, due to the importance and consistency of the collections it preserves. Coins, medals, coin weights, tesserae, mintage items, gems, goldsmith objects, and precious furnishings have filled the vaults of the coffers of the Medagliere in Rome over time. Today, its collections amount to over half a million pieces from Antiquity, the Middle Ages, and the Modern Age. This extraordinary wealth was tapped into, in order to help tell the story of a sea that has been the cradle of civilizations. The undisputed stage of traffic, exchanges, conflicts, and expeditions of peoples and goods. Images of memories impressed in those small, round pieces of metal. Precious testimonies of civilizations that alternate with past and present times following a single theme: the sea. During the time of the Papacy, the new structures of the ports of Civitavecchia (Inv. 19.M329-1.1, 8098), Anzio, and Terracina (Inv. 18695), as well as ships - the true protagonists of the sea, symbols of power and wealth, able to evoke tales of war (Inv. 63354,18077,85511,19.M329-1.8) and scenarios of peace (Inv. 85576,19.M329-1.11,92493,19.M329-1.10) - echoed the ancient Ports of Claudius and Trajan depicted on Roman coins (figs. 8,9). Even mythology, in its accepted meaning in fabulous narrations - product of an imagination without a historical foundation, but which often feeds on history - plays an important role in recounting a story that has the sea as its main protagonist: the imposing figure of Neptune (Inv.92552) - the mercurial god of the sea, represented in his vigorous nudity with a trident as a scepter, along with his charming bride, Amphitrite (Inv.83673), from whose union Triton, half man and half fish, was born - evokes fantastic figures and also monstrous beings who inhabited the abysses (Inv.85644,85234) and terrorized man with their horrible appearance (Inv.83671); symbols of the fears and anxieties that have accompanied navigators and sailors in their adventures across the immense expanse of the sea, full of danger and mystery.

G. Angeli Bufalini

第二节 从罗马帝国到罗马教皇国的港口

4D.2. PORTS: FROM IMPERIAL ROME TO THE ROME OF THE PAPACY

港口管理着密集的商业交通网络，每天将货物和人员运送到罗马各地，这是体现古人专业技术的一个例子，罗马硬币传承了这一历史记忆。这枚尼禄大帝（公元54年—68年）时期的硬币（展品编号91923），是为了纪念奥斯蒂亚（罗马）宏伟的港口建设而发行，该港口从前任君主克劳迪乌斯（公元41年—54年）在位时就开始建设。硬币再现了停有船只的两个码头，上部为阶梯式结构，可能是位于港口入口处一座小岛上的灯塔，被海神尼普顿的雕像所覆盖。尽管为了建造港口人们付出了许多努力，但由于台伯河的泥沙堆积问题，盆地淤塞时有发生，因此需要经常进行疏浚作业。为了解决这些问题，图拉真（公元98年—117年）在克劳迪乌斯时期之后又建造了一个新的港口设施，并通过一条航运运河连接（见第二单元）。图拉真货币的背面有特殊的六角形植物，人们还可以看到许多与港口活动相关的建筑物，如在硬币右侧可见两层建筑物中有可识别的仓库（展品编号92328，见第二单元—第一部分—第一节）。随着西罗马帝国在公元476年的垮台，港口逐渐遭到废弃：缺少维护，盆地被沙子所覆盖，建筑物破败，港口设施无法继续使用。几个世纪之后，教皇统治下的罗马继承了罗马帝国的港口，以恢复罗马帝国繁荣昌盛的海上贸易网络。自16世纪开始，教皇启动了重要的修复和改造工程，当时的硬币和奖章记载了这段历史。奇维塔韦基亚（古罗马时称为森图姆塞利）的情况就是这样，从教皇尤利乌斯二世（1503年—1513年）委托建造的雄伟堡垒开

The dense network of commercial traffic that transported goods and people to Rome on a daily basis was managed by the ports. An example of the technical expertise of the ancient population, which was handed down in memory through Roman coins. This is the case of a sestertius of Emperor Nero (54-68 A.D.) (Inv. 91923), which commemorates the construction of the grandiose port of Ostia (Rome), begun by his predecessor Claudius (41-54 A.D.), of which the coin reproduces the two piers occupied by several boats and a structure with steps in the upper portion, probably the lighthouse that was located on a small island at the entrance of the port, unusually topped by a statue of Neptune, god of the sea. Despite the efforts made to construct this port, the problem of the basin silting up soon occurred, caused by the deposits of debris transported by the Tiber river. This led to the need for frequent dredging procedures. To overcome these drawbacks, Trajan (98-117 A.D.) built a new port facility behind the one commissioned by Claudius, connected to it by a navigable canal (see Chap. 2). The peculiar hexagonal plant is found on the reverse side of a sestertius of Trajan, where one can also see the numerous buildings that were functional to port activities, such as the horrea (warehouses), which seem to be the two-story structures visible on the right of the coin (Inv. 92328; see: Chap. 2a.1).With the fall of the Western Roman Empire in 476 A.D., the ports were subjected to progressive abandonment. Without maintenance, the basins became covered with sand and the buildings deteriorated, often making the port facilities unusable. Centuries later, the Rome of the Papacy inherited the ports of Imperial Rome to restore part of that dense network of maritime trade that had contributed to the greatness and prosperity of the Roman Empire. Starting in the 16th century, the Pontiffs began important restorations and renovations, of which coins and medals preserve the memory. This was the case of Civitavecchia, the ancient Roman Centumcellae that, starting from the imposing fortress commissioned by Pope Julius II (1503-1513) (Inv. 19.M329-

始（展品编号 19.M329-1.1、展品编号 18098），它的港口和防御结构不断扩大，以致成为抵御土耳其入侵的安全堡垒，并成为罗马进口和供应的主要来源。改造工作还涉及罗马的河流结构：教皇克莱门特十一世（公元 1700 年—1721 年）对里佩塔港口进行了改造，并在 1703 年用罗马斗兽场中的石灰石建造了一座宏伟的码头。遗憾的是，码头在同年爆发的地震中损坏了。教皇格里高利十六世（公元 1831 年—1846 年）则使拖吊服务现代化，用更高效的蒸汽船取代水牛的拖曳系统（展品编号 18695），服务对象为驶向里帕格兰德港口的大型船只。但是，统治阶级对奇维塔韦基亚港表现出浓厚兴趣，意味着罗马教皇对其他港口建设的冷落。这就是安齐奥（罗马）当时的情况。直到 17 世纪末，在教皇英诺森十二世（公元 1691 年—1700 年）的命令下，港口才得以重建。为了实现这一目标，部分古罗马建筑重新投入使用。同样地，教皇庇护六世（公元 1775 年—1799 年）将泰拉奇纳港搬迁到被古罗马港口建筑物包围的地区，而教皇格里高利十六世则重建了码头和防御工事（展品编号 18715），并开始开凿运河，使船舶靠岸更加方便和安全。18 世纪，安科纳港逐步复兴。经历一段时间的荒废后，由于教皇克莱门特十二世（公元 1730 年—1740 年）对商业特许权的授予做出了让步，港口商业交通恢复繁荣状态，同时加强了港口的建设，以满足新的需求。还建造了一个新的建筑物（拉扎雷托），用于货物存储和人员居住（展品编号 18505）。

S. 博卡迪

1.1, 8098), was affected by progressive expansions of the port and defensive structures, so much so as to become a safe bastion against Turkish incursions and the main source of import and supply for Rome. Renovation work also involved river structures in Rome: Pope Clement XI (1700-1721) had the port of Ripetta restructured, building a monumental quay in 1703, thanks to the use of travertine taken from the Colosseum, which had been damaged by the earthquake that occurred in the same year. Instead, Pope Gregory XVI (1831-1846) modernized the towing system for the large ships that came from the sea to the port of Ripa Grande, replacing the towing system - that used buffalos - with more efficient steamboats (Inv. 18695). However, the ruling class's prevailing interest in the port of Civitavecchia meant that the other port facilities pertaining to the Rome of the Papacy were the object of general disinterest. This was the case with Anzio (Rome). Its ports, for which parts of the ancient Roman structures were reused, were reconstructed only at the end of the 17th century, at the behest of Pope Innocent XII (1691-1700). Similarly, Pope Pius VI (1775-1799) intervened in the port of Terracina, relocated in the area occupied by the ancient Roman port structure, while Pope Gregory XVI (1831-1846) (Inv. 18715) restructured the dock, the fortifications, and provided in reclaiming the canal, in order to facilitate and make the landing place for ships safer. The 18th century also marked the recovery of the port of Ancona. After a period of strong decline, thanks to the concession of the commercial franchise granted by Pope Clement XII (1730-1740), thriving trade traffic resumed in the port, while building interventions strengthened the port facilities to meet new demands. A new Lazaret, a quarantine station for goods and people (Inv. 18505), was also built.

S. Boccardi

尼禄时期的塞斯太尔斯（公元 54 年—68 年）

带有克劳迪乌斯港口图案的古罗马货币
约公元 64 年
铜
直径 33.04 毫米
重 29.34 克
罗马国家博物馆，古钱收藏，展品编号 91923

Sestertius of Nero (54-68 A.D.) - Roman Coin with the Port of Claudius

approx. 64 A.D.
diameter 33.04 mm
weight 29.34 grams
National Roman Museum, Medagliere - Numanistic Collection Inv. 91923

这款塞斯太尔斯（Sesterzio）硬币是为了纪念奥斯蒂亚市新罗马港的落成典礼而发行的。这个港口是为这座城市提供物资的基础设施，也是克劳迪乌斯皇帝（公元 41 年—54 年）的希望之所在。但是，港口修建工程却是由他的继任者尼禄皇帝（公元 54 年—68 年）完成的。从图案描绘的港口结构中，我们可以看到，硬币从上方再现了一个图景：两只桥墩，有一些船只在航行，上部有一阶梯式的结构，可能是位于小岛上的灯塔，灯塔出现在港口的入口处，不同寻常地“顶”着海神尼普顿的雕像。这样处理是一种技术上的权宜之计，如此可以在狭小的空间内插入更多的建筑元素。躺着支撑着舵的人物形象，还有一只海豚，可以从不同角度解读为台伯河或港口的象征。

图拉真时期塞斯太尔斯（公元 98 年—117 年）

带有图拉真港口图案的古罗马货币
约公元 112 年—114 年夏天
铜
直径 34.61 毫米
重 27.32 克
罗马国家博物馆，古钱收藏，展品编号 92328

Sestertius of Trajan (98-117 A.D.) - Roman Coin with the Port of Trajan

ca. 112 - summer 114 A.D.
diameter 34.61 mm
weight 27.32 grams
National Roman Museum, Medagliere - Numanistic Collection Inv. 92328

在图拉真大帝统治的年代，公元 110 年—112 年间一个新的港池拔地而起。这个港池在硬币的图案上位于克劳迪乌斯皇帝（公元 41 年—54 年）“肩膀”的后面，连接了一条可通航的运河。一方面，新的港池加强了对向罗马运送货物的船只的管理；另一方面，又为城市提供了一个港湾。它很少暴露于恶劣天气中，并且几乎不会被沙土淤塞，避免了昂贵的维护成本。在图拉真港口，这枚硬币再现了特有的六角形设施，它的每个侧面约为 36 米长，围绕着约 32 公顷面积的土地。硬币上有许多与港口活动相关的建筑物，例如硬币背面右侧的仓库，可以看出它有两层结构。

教皇尤利乌斯二世时期纪念币（公元 1503 年—1513 年）

带有奇维塔韦基亚港口图案的教皇古币
重新评估为约 19 世纪
铜
直径 41.00 毫米
重 48.48 克
罗马国家博物馆，古钱收藏，展品编号 18098

Medal of Julius II (1503-1513) - Papal Medal with the Port of Civitavecchia

Possible 19th-century recoin
diameter 41.00 mm
weight 48.48 grams
National Roman Museum, Medagliere - Numanistic Collection Inv. 18098

这款硬币旨在纪念教皇尤利乌斯二世（公元 1503 年—1513 年）建设奇维塔韦基亚港口的功绩。最初，罗马中心被人们称为森图姆塞利（Centumcellae），几个世纪以来，历代教皇兢兢业业，前赴后继，将此地变成了教皇国海军的中枢。教皇尤利乌斯二世负责在海岸上建造用于保护港口的新堡垒工程。该工程于 1508 年年底开始启动，1522 年完工。建筑采用四边形设计，内部有庭院，四角处有四座威武的塔楼，庄严肃穆，主体工程是一座八角塔，每侧长 12 米。

教皇乌尔巴诺八世时期纪念币（公元 1623 年—1644 年）

带有奇维塔韦基亚港口图案的教皇古币
重新评估为约 19 世纪
铜
直径 40.50 毫米
重 32.45 克
罗马国家博物馆，古钱收藏，展品编号 18262

Medal of Urban VIII (1623-1644) - Papal Medal with the Port of Civitavecchia

Possible 19th-century recoin
diameter 40.50 mm
weight 32.45 grams
National Roman Museum, Medagliere - Numanistic Collection Inv. 18262

奇维塔韦基亚港是教皇国防御土耳其人入侵的堡垒。在 16 和 17 世纪期间，奇维塔韦基亚港历经了无数次的重建。这枚硬币背面的图案再现了由教皇乌尔巴诺八世（Urbano VIII）（公元 1623 年—1644 年）主导的工程：港口码头的各种设施得到了加强，还配备了防止非法登陆的锁链，修复了教皇保罗五世（Paolo V）时期（公元 1605 年—1621 年）建造的灯塔，并新建了第二座灯塔。此外，为了容纳更大吨位的船舶，乌尔巴诺八世增加了港池的海床深度，同时将防波堤扩建到海中，这样可以保证系泊船舶的安全。

教皇亚历山大七世时期纪念币（公元 1655 年—1667 年）

带有奇维塔韦基亚港口图案的教皇古币
重新评估为约 19 世纪
铜
直径 41.50 毫米
重 29.27 克
罗马国家博物馆，古钱收藏，展品编号 18335

Medal of Alexander VII (1655-1667) - Papal Medal with the Port of Civitavecchia

Possible 19th-century recoin
diameter 41.50 mm
weight 29.27 grams
National Roman Museum, Medagliere - Numanistic Collection Inv. 18335

教皇亚历山大七世主持建造了奇维塔韦基亚港口的兵工厂，用于建造新的舰船。这项工程具体由吉安·洛伦佐·贝尼尼（Gian Lorenzo Bernini）负责施工。工程包括三个建筑物，呈扇形分布，共有六个建筑工地，每个建筑工地都可以容纳一艘两桅帆桨战船。在硬币的背面可以看到新的设施，位于教皇乌尔巴诺八世的防御性堡垒城墙和教皇尤利乌斯二世的堡垒之间。从其中一个新的设施上，我们可以看到右边的城墙。该兵工厂在第二次世界大战期间毁于对奇维塔韦基亚港口的轰炸。

教皇克莱门特十世时期的皮阿斯特（公元 1670 年—1676 年）

带有奇维塔韦基亚港口图案的教皇古币
1672 年
银
直径 43.68 毫米
重 31.94 克
罗马国家博物馆，古钱收藏，展品编号 19.M329-1.1

Piaster of Clement X (1670-1676), Papal Coin with the Port of Civitavecchia

1672
diameter 43.68 mm
weight 31.94 grams
National Roman Museum, Medagliere - Numanistic Collection Inv. 19.M329-1.1

克莱门特十世也为奇维塔韦基亚港口做出了重要贡献：他强化了港口的防御设施，确保了商业的繁荣，保证商人可以自由进入港池，并且免征关税。因为这一系列措施，商人获得了经济财富，刺激了商业交通的发展。在这枚硬币的背面，突出显示了各种经常往来港口的船只以及明确的宣传信息：“这样您就可以获得更多的财富。”

教皇克莱门特十三世（公元 1758 年—1769 年）时期的皮阿斯特

带有奇维塔韦基亚港口图案的教皇古币
重新评估为约 19 世纪
铜
直径 34.50 毫米
重 19.33 克
罗马国家博物馆，古钱收藏，展品编号 18553

Medal of Clement XIII (1758-1769) - Papal Medal with the Port of Civitavecchia

Possible 19th-century recoin
diameter 34.50 mm
weight 19.33 grams
National Roman Museum, Medagliere - Numanistic Collection Inv. 18553

克莱门特十三世进一步加强了奇维塔韦基亚港口的设施。具体来讲，这位教皇增加了与卸货有关的设施，以解决长期以来各商家业主一直抱怨卸货设施不足的缺陷。他还新建了仓库，满足了更大的物流量需求。在硬币的另一面显示了新的码头，称为“财源滚滚”，一些港口运营商正在从三艘锚定在码头上的船上卸货。在背景中可以看到港口城市利沃诺（Livorno），克莱门特十三世专门在教皇乌尔巴诺八世主导建造的城墙上增加了新的入口。

教皇克莱门特十三世时期的皮阿斯特

罗马教皇对奇维塔韦基亚港口进行宗教访问图案的教皇古币
重新评估为约 19 世纪
铜
直径 36.00 毫米
重 21.12 克
罗马国家博物馆，古钱收藏，展品编号 18554

Medal of Clement XIII (1758-1769), Papal Medal for the Pope's Visit to the Port of Civitavecchia

Possible 19th-century recoin
diameter 36.00 mm
weight 21.12 grams
National Roman Museum, Medagliere - Numanistic Collection Inv. 18554

克莱门特十三世对奇维塔韦基亚城及其港口的关注在 1762 年时达到高潮——这一年，教皇访问了这座城市。为了纪念这一事件，这枚硬币的背面展示了克莱门特十三世在随从簇拥下祝福一艘帆船的情景。这艘大船名叫圣卡洛（San Carlo），是港口造船厂建造的前两艘大型船只之一，与大船圣克莱门特（San Clemente）一起加入教皇船队——这样教皇国就能够节省购买国外生产的船只的费用。除了其他方面的细节，这枚硬币的图案还强调了船尾悬挂的旗帜，硬币雕刻师在方寸之间展示了大量的细节。

教皇克莱门特十一世时期半皮阿斯特（公元 1700 年—1721 年）

带有瑞佩塔（罗马）港口图案的教皇古币
1706 年
银
直径 39.53 毫米
重 15.91 克
罗马国家博物馆，古钱收藏，展品编号 19.M329-1.2

Half Piaster of Clement XI (1700-1721) - Papal Coin with the Port of Ripetta (Rome)

1706
diameter 39.53 mm
weight 15.91 grams
National Roman Museum, Medagliere - Numanistic Collection Inv. 19.M329-1.2

在克莱门特十一世（Clemente XI）时期，罗马配备了一个城市河港，自中世纪以来第一次拓宽了现有河流，并且更新了相关设施，这样一来为城市运送食物的船只可以更加方便地停泊。在教皇倡导下，台伯河上修建了瑞佩塔（前期的名称为“小瑞帕”，Ripa Piccola）港口，也被称为克莱门蒂诺（Clementino）港。这个建于 1703 年的港口位于罗马市中心，使用了斗兽场的石灰材料。同年，因为地震遭受了破坏。硬币的反面图案是港口的大码头，连接到了两个巨大的侧阶梯和一个带有喷泉的大露台。硬币的下半部分描绘有两个躺着的人物，象征着台伯河和阿涅内河。19 世纪后期，随着台伯河河岸的重建，该港口消失。

教皇格里高利十六世时期纪念币（公元 1831 年—1846 年）

带有罗帕格兰德（罗马）港口图案的教皇古币
1842 年
铜
直径 57.00 毫米
重 80.46 克
罗马国家博物馆，古钱收藏，展品编号 18695

Medal of Gregory XVI (1831-1846) - Papal Medal with the Port of Ripa Grande (Rome)

1842
diameter 57.00 mm
weight 80.46 grams
National Roman Museum, Medagliere - Numismatic Collection Inv. 18695

在瑞佩塔（Ripetta）港的旁边，有另一个叫罗帕格兰德（Ripa Grande）的河港，它是从大海到达罗马的大型船只的停泊地，这些大型船只被多头水牛拖曳进入台伯河。为了使与港口相关的活动现代化，人们设计了一种新的汽船以提供牵引服务，这种牵引服务在教皇格里高利十六世时期繁盛起来。这枚硬币记载了这一现代化的过程：画面中可见一艘汽船，随后是一些帆船，抵达了罗帕格兰德的河港。这枚硬币的背景中显示了圣米迦勒使徒医院，这是 19 世纪台伯河河岸重建工程之后唯一可见的建筑物；就像瑞佩塔（Ripetta）港口一样，教皇罗马港的痕迹也被抹去了。

教皇英诺森十二世时期的皮阿斯特(公元 1691 年—1700 年)

带有安齐奥港口图案的教皇古币
1699 年
银
直径 44.96 毫米
重 32.02 克
罗马国家博物馆，古钱收藏，展品编号 19.M329-1.3

Piaster of Innocent XII (1691-1700) - Papal Coin with the Port of Anzio

1699
diameter 44.96 mm
weight 32.02 grams
National Roman Museum, Medagliere - Numismatic Collection Inv. 19.M329-1.3

古代的安提乌姆城离罗马不远，在这里诞生了皇帝卡利古拉和尼禄。尼禄为实现克劳迪乌斯的愿望建造了安齐奥港。随着西罗马帝国（公元 476 年）的垮台，港口被废弃了。在 17 世纪末，教皇英诺森十二世（公元 1691 年—1700 年）开始重建安齐奥港口。该港口工程在这枚硬币的背面图案中得到体现。港口的建设从 1697 年直至 1702 年。在图案中，第一个项目涉及恢复古老的尼禄港，而一个更受欢迎的新码头连接罗马城的左边，它的港池更宽阔。但这种方案没有解决英诺森十二世港口严重的垃圾填埋问题，直到今天仍然需要持续地进行维护。

教皇格里高利十六世时期纪念币（公元 1831 年—1846 年）

带有特拉西那港口图案的教皇古币
1843 年
铜
直径 43.50 毫米
重 33.37 克
罗马国家博物馆，古钱收藏，展品编号 18715

Medal of Gregory XVI (1831-1846) - Papal Medal with the Port of Terracina

1843
diameter 43.50 mm
weight 33.37 grams
National Roman Museum, Medagliere - Numismatic Collection Inv. 18715

特拉西那（Terracina）是一个位于罗马以南约 100 公里的小镇，和奇维塔韦基亚市和安齐奥市一样，它也有一个罗马港口。在西罗马帝国灭亡后，这个港口被逐渐废弃了，仅在 18 世纪进行过重建工作。受教皇庇护四世（公元 1775 年—1799 年）的委托，施工方治理了周边的沼泽地，并重新确立了城市港口的功能。特拉西那港所在地原址为古罗马港口，今天我们仍然可以看到图拉真时代的北部码头。这枚硬币描绘了特拉西那港运河的景观，回顾了自 1839 年以来所进行的现代化工作，具体涉及码头、港口的防御工事和运河修复——对众多的商船而言，这样一来停泊更容易更安全。

教皇克莱门特十二世时期纪念币（公元 1730 年—1740 年）

带有安科纳港口图案的教皇古币
重新评估为约 19 世纪
铜
直径 32.50 毫米
重 14.37 克
罗马国家博物馆，古钱收藏，展品编号 18505

Medal of Clement XII (1730-1740) - Papal Medal with the Port of Ancona

Possible 19th-century recoin
diameter 32.50 mm
weight 14.37 grams
National Roman Museum, Medagliere - Numismatic Collection Inv. 18505

教皇在奇维塔韦基亚港的扩建和防御工程上花费了大量的精力，这意味着此阶段教皇国的其他港口基本处于弃置状态。17 世纪，安科纳港口达到了鼎盛阶段，之后开始走下坡路。当时的商业交通急剧下降，港池亦有被沙土掩盖的风险，航行变得日益困难。然而，18 世纪这种趋势出现逆转。随着克莱门特十二世政策的实施，港口再次得到了蓬勃的发展，商业特许权的施行也保证了贸易的迅速恢复。关于这项政策，我们可以从硬币另一面的描绘中得到一些启示，而港口的视图也突出显示了为增强港口结构而进行的建筑工程：码头延伸，为其内部的船只提供了更好的保护；除此之外，灯塔也得到了加固。

教皇克莱门特十二世时期纪念币（公元 1730 年—1740 年）

带有安科纳拉扎雷托城市和港口图案的教皇古币
重新评估为约 19 世纪
铜
直径 72.00 毫米
重 154.51 克
罗马国家博物馆，古钱收藏，展品编号 18507

Medal of Clement XII (1730-1740) - Papal Medal with the Port and Lazaret of Ancona

Possible 19th-century recoin
diameter 72.00 mm
weight 154.51 grams
National Roman Museum, Medagliere - Numismatic Collection Inv. 18507

新拉扎雷托（Lazzaretto）城市港口的建造始于 1733 年，在克莱门特十二世的主持下于 1738 年年底结束。这枚硬币显示了该工程的五角形平面结构图，这座建筑用于保护货物和人，并进行“检验检疫”工作。建筑物两侧开放的大型拱廊，保证了新鲜空气的对流。由于与港口关系密切，这一工程结构承担了重要的军事功能：在拿破仑时期，这个堡垒对击破法国军队的包围起到了决定性作用。第一次世界大战期间和第二次世界大战期间，该港口均被征用，当时原有的建筑部分受到了损坏。

第三节　从罗马共和国到海上共和国的船舶

4D.3. SHIPS FROM THE REPUBLIC OF ROME TO THE MARITIME REPUBLICS

作为地中海的真正主角，船舶将食物、货物和人从罗马帝国的一个地区运送到另一个地区，同时也扮演着征服或捍卫边界的强大工具的角色；硬币上描绘的船只突出了商业、“民用”和军事方面的不同功能（见第三单元）。

需要特别强调的是关乎重要军事成就的舰船图像，例如古罗马铸造的第一批青铜硬币中的舰船图像（展品编号 63354），其中，船头很可能暗示着古罗马迦太基舰队的伟大胜利。公元前 260 年，第一次布匿战争期间，罗马人在米拉佐大胜。马克·安东尼这枚硬币上描绘的军舰（展品编号 85511）展示了他与未来的奥古斯都皇帝屋大维间即将发生的冲突，后来安东尼在公元前 31 年被击败。几个世纪之后，硬币和奖章上再次出现同样令人回味的图像，船舶作为防御或者征服领土的基础，仍被认为是庆祝胜利的标志。教皇加里斯都三世奖章的背面（公元 1455 年—1458 年）（展品编号 18077）则是回顾了教皇以极大的努力准备面对土耳其的海军远征威胁，而庇护五世（公元 1566 年—1572 年）的硬币则描绘了庆祝 1571 年基督教舰队在勒班陀对抗奥斯曼帝国取得胜利的场景。除了对“战争时期”船舶的描绘，货币形象也承载着记录与和平时刻相关的事件的重担：哈德良皇帝（公元 117 年—138 年）当时的情况就是这样，他在硬币上篆刻了无数次旅行的记忆，切实反映了帝国各省终于得到了和平状态（展品编号 92493）的现实。这些“真实”事件经常伴随着意识形态价值的主题，例如波斯图末硬币（公元 260 年—269 年）上所描绘的船舶，

Ships, the true protagonists of the Mediterranean, transported food, goods, and people from one region to the other of the Roman Empire, also playing the role of a powerful instrument for the conquest or defense of borders. The images of ships on coins and medals highlight the various commercial, “civilian”, and military functions assigned to them (see Chap. 3).

Particular emphasis was given to the images of ships that alluded to important military successes, such as the one that appears on one of the first Roman cast bronze coins issued (Inv.63354), where the ship’s bow likely represents the victory, recounted by the Romans, over the Carthaginian fleet in Milazzo in 260 B.C. during the first Punic war. The military ship depicted on the coins of Marc Antony (Inv.85511) introduces the imminent clash with Octavian, the future Emperor Augustus, then defeated by him in 31 B.C.. Even after centuries, the same evocative intentions reappeared unchanged on coins and medals where ships, which were fundamental for the defense or the conquest of the territories, continued to be celebrated. Therefore, the back of the medal of Pope Callistus III (1455-1458) (Inv.18077) recalls the naval expedition prepared with great effort by the Pope, in order to face the Turkish threat, while Pius V (1566-1572) celebrated the victory by the Christian fleet against that of the Ottoman Empire at Lepanto in 1571. Alongside these images of ships in “times of war”, the images on coins also evoke events linked to moments of peace, such as in the case of Emperor Hadrian (117-138 A.D.). His numerous journeys through the provinces of the Empire, finally pacified, were remembered on coins (Inv.92493). These “real” events were joined by themes of ideological value, such as the depiction of a ship on a coin of the Emperor Posthumus (260-269 A.D.), which alludes to the transport of joy, happiness, and prosperity as products of his good governance. It is quite clear that ports and ships were important means for economic well-being and a symbol of power. Topics dear to both Rome and the subsequent maritime

其暗示了充满快乐、幸福和繁荣的运输，这是其良好治理的产物。很明显，港口和船舶是追求经济福祉的重要手段和权力的象征——罗马和随后的海上大国，如威尼斯，都非常看重这两者，它们在海上建立了自己的声望。从 1726 年莫塞尼戈时的阿尔维斯三世公爵统治时期的威尼斯货币上（展品编号 19.M329-1.8），可以看出当时其下定决心打击在地中海海域肆虐的土耳其海盗或利用武装储备保护商船的信息，而货币传播了这些信息。威尼斯作为一座海滨城市，采用直接与海洋有关的徽记：威尼斯共和国的象征是布基特罗，它作为最有代表性的船，曾载着国王和王后进行国事访问、庆祝“海上婚姻”——一个象征着威尼斯海上统治的仪式。莫塞尼戈时的阿尔维斯三世公爵在一枚硬币上描绘了布基特罗，其于 1727 年建成，并使用了丰富的装饰，包括帷幔、灰泥和镀金雕刻（展品编号 19.M329-1.10）。1797 年，拿破仑 · 波拿巴占领了威尼斯共和国，这艘宏伟的船也被法国军队烧毁了。

正如威尼斯一样，利沃诺的繁荣也集中在港口。其重要性体现在意大利进出口贸易货物的数量和质量中：从大米、果酱、凤尾鱼、鱼子酱、鲑鱼、橄榄油、葡萄酒、葡萄等食品，到乳香、药品、大麻、丝绸、地毯、亚麻籽、白银、黄金和钻石等货物，利沃诺每天都有船只来来去去，在海上航行驶向目的地，这些可从柯西莫三世 · 德 · 梅第奇（公元 1670 年—1723 年）所铸造硬币上的船舶图像中得到证实（展品编号 19.M329-1.5）。

S. 博卡迪

powers that, like Venice, founded their prestige on the sea. The message of the determination to oppose the Turkish piracy that infested the waters of the Mediterranean, or of the use of armed guards to defend the merchant ships, is diffused by the images of the coins produced by the Venetian Republic, as it appears on an osella of the Doge Alvise III Mocenigo in 1726 (Inv. 19.M329-1.8).The identification of Venice as a maritime city also translated into the use of emblems directly referable to the sea: the symbol of the Venetian Republic was the Bucentaur, a representative ship used to transport sovereigns and queens on state visits, or to celebrate the “Marriage of the Sea”, a ceremony that symbolized the maritime dominion of Venice. The Bucentaur depicted on a coin of the Doge Alvise III Mocenigo was inaugurated in 1727 and was endowed with rich decorations that included draperies, stucco, and gilded carvings (Inv. 19.M329-1.10). This magnificent ship was set on fire in 1797 by the French troops of Napoleon Bonaparte, conqueror of the Venetian Republic.

Like Venice, Livorno’s prosperity was also centered around its port. Its importance was also demonstrated in the quantity and quality of the goods that arrived to be traded in Italy or from Italy: from foodstuffs such as rice, jams, anchovies, caviar, salmon, oil, wine, grapes to merchandise such as frankincense, myrrh, hemp, silk, carpets, linseed, silvers, gold, and diamonds. Livorno was a coming and going of ships that each day sailed the sea to reach its docks, as proven by the iconography of a ship on a coin of Cosimo III de’ Medici (1670-1723) (Inv. 19.M329-1.5).

S. Boccardi

阿司

带有船艏图案的古罗马货币
公元前 225 年—公元前 217 年
铜
直径 67.31 毫米
重 294.50 克
罗马国家博物馆，古钱收藏，展品编号 63354

Aes Grave - Roman Coin with Bow of a Ship
225-217 B.C.
diameter 67.31 mm
weight 294.50 grams
National Roman Museum, Medagliere - Numismatic Collection Inv. 63354

在硬币上出现的众多船舶图案中，与海军战争胜利有关的纹样特别引人注意。这里描述的硬币就是属于这种情况。阿司是罗马早期发行的一种青铜货币，这款硬币的图案中首次出现了海船弓形的船首，可能反映了公元前 260 年罗马人在米拉佐的第一次战争——这场海战中罗马人战胜了迦太基人。

卢塔蒂奥 · 塞科时期的第纳尔

带有海船图案的古罗马货币
公元前 109 年，或公元前 108 年
银
直径 19.79 毫米
重 3.90 克
罗马国家博物馆，古钱收藏，展品编号 84250

Denarius of Q. Lutatius Catalus - Roman Coin with Ship
109 B.C.or 108 B.C,
diameter 19.79 mm
weight 3.90 grams
National Roman Museum, Medagliere - Numismatic Collection Inv. 84250

这枚硬币背面的图案反映了罗马人第一次反对迦太基人的战争，罗马战舰的标志物是橡树的树冠，这是公民和国家得到拯救的象征。发行这枚硬币是为了纪念公元前 241 年发生在意大利西西里岛西部埃加迪岛的迦太基舰队和罗马舰队之间的决战，罗马舰队由大约 200 艘船组成，由加尤斯 · 卢塔齐奥 · 卡图洛（Gaio Lutazio Catulo）大将指挥，其名字的缩写出现在了海船的船首之上。

庞培时期的第纳尔

带有海船图案的古罗马货币
公元前 49 年
银
直径 19.02 毫米
重 3.74 克
罗马国家博物馆，古钱收藏，展品编号 85208

Denarius of Gnaeis Pompeius Magnus (Pompey the Great) and Calpurnius Piso - Roman Coin with Ship

49 B.C.
diameter 19.02 mm
weight 3.74 grams
National Roman Museum, Medagliere - Numismatic Collection Inv. 85208

这枚硬币是由庞培（Pompeo Magno）发行的。庞培是一位伟大的罗马领导人，因其多次战胜罗马的敌人而闻名。这艘船的船首象征了打败海盗的战争，这些海盗来自意大利西西里岛的东部地区，数十年间，一直掠夺商船，威胁港口城市。一场于公元前 67 年结束的战争进一步推动了罗马在东方的扩张。海神尼普顿作为“代表”出现在硬币正面，进一步强调了庞培的海上霸权。

纳希迪乌斯时期第纳尔

带有海船图案的古罗马货币
公元前 44 年—公元前 43 年
银
直径 21.18 毫米
重 3.35 克
罗马国家博物馆，古钱收藏，展品编号 85526

Denarius of Q. Nasidius - Roman Coin with Ship

44-43 B.C.
diameter 21.18 mm
weight 3.35 grams
National Roman Museum, Medagliere - Numismatic Collection Inv. 85526

硬币的反面是一艘罗马军舰，地方行政官员的说明告诉我们，这枚硬币的发行者是纳西迪乌斯（Q. Nasidius）。他是继领导人庞培的儿子塞斯托 · 庞培（Sesto Pompeo）之后的罗马舰队指挥官，负责意大利南部岛屿的军事行动。几年前（公元前 48 年），在与尤利乌斯 · 凯撒（Giulio Cesare）的战争中阵亡的塞斯托 · 庞培的肖像被描绘在了硬币的正面，另外还有三叉戟和海豚，他们归属于海神尼普顿。这种表现方式将庞培同化为了神，他的儿子塞斯托 · 庞培因此拥有了神圣的血统。

马克 · 安东尼时期第纳尔

带有三只船橹图案的古罗马货币
公元前 32 年—公元前 31 年
银
直径 18.86 毫米
重 3.66 克
罗马国家博物馆，古钱收藏，展品编号 85511

Denarius of Mark Antony - Roman Coin with Trireme Ship
32-31 B.C.
diameter 18.86 mm
weight 3.66 grams
National Roman Museum, Medagliere - Numismatic Collection Inv. 85511

这枚硬币描绘了一艘罗马战舰——马克 · 安东尼(Marco Antonio)与克利奥帕特拉(Cleopatra)一起组建舰队，为后来与奥古斯都皇帝屋大维进行战斗而做准备工作。这枚硬币代表了一系列“军团”问题的一部分——也就是说，代表了马克 · 安东尼指挥的 23 个军团的军饷。硬币的正面分别提到了这 23 个军团。在这枚硬币中，第二十军团被“铭记”了下来。

教宗加里斯都三世时期纪念币（公元 1455 年—1458 年）

为对抗土耳其人的战争而发行的教皇古币
重新评估为约 19 世纪
铜
直径 41.00 毫米
重 37.51 克
罗马国家博物馆，古钱收藏，展品编号 18077

Medal of Callixtus III (1455-1458) - Papal Medal for the War Against the Turks
Possible 19th-century recoin
diameter 41.00 mm
weight 37.51 grams
National Roman Museum, Medagliere - Numismatic Collection Inv. 18077

在西罗马帝国灭亡（公元 476 年）近一千年之后，硬币上的这艘船仍然在为防御敌人或征服战争服务，它在遥远的领土斗争中发挥了重要作用。因此，教皇加里斯都三世（Callisto III，公元 1455 年—1458 年）硬币的反面记录了教皇针对土耳其人而做出的海军远征。他们做了大量的准备工作：组成教皇舰队离开罗马，25 艘船集结开往地中海东部，他们在那里取得了好几次胜利，打垮了土耳其的舰队。

教宗庇护五世时期的纪念币（公元 1566 年—1572 年）

带有海军战争图案的教皇古币
重新评估为约 19 世纪
铜
直径 42.50 毫米
重 35.27 克
罗马国家博物馆，古钱收藏，展品编号 18160

Medal of Pius V (1566-1572) - Papal Medal with Naval Battle

Possible 19th-century recoin
diameter 42.50 mm
weight 35.27 grams
National Roman Museum, Medagliere - Numismatic Collection Inv. 18160

这枚硬币纪念了 1571 年基督徒舰队在勒班陀（Lepanto）对抗奥斯曼（Ottomano）帝国的胜利。基督徒舰队由大约 8 万人和 200 艘海船组成，他们受罗马教会指挥。除了教皇国的部队之外，还包括由威尼斯和热那亚共和国、萨沃伊和乌尔比诺公国、那不勒斯和西西里王国以及托斯卡纳大公国组成的联盟军队。

哈德良时期的塞斯太尔斯（公元 117 年—138 年）

带有海船图案的古罗马货币
公元 132 年—134 年
铜
直径 32.87 毫米
重 25.92 克
罗马国家博物馆，古钱收藏，展品编号 92493

Sestertius From the Reign of Hadrian (117-138 A.D.) - Roman Coin with Ship

132-134 A.D.
diameter 32.87 mm
weight 25.92 grams
National Roman Museum, Medagliere - Numismatic Collection Inv. 92493

硬币上对船只的描绘，不仅涉及战争事件，还记录了海上旅行的情况。这就是哈德良时期（Adriano）硬币的情况。硬币的反面描绘了一艘海船，记录了皇帝在帝国各和平省份巡视的事情。虽然哈德良的统治实际上受到了犹太人（公元 132 年—135 年）起义的困扰，但硬币的铭文强调了皇帝在旅行目的地获得的快乐。

卡拉卡拉时期的第纳尔（公元 198 年—217 年）

带有海船图案的古罗马货币
公元 201 年—206 年
银
直径 18.67 毫米
重 2.86 克
罗马国家博物馆，古钱收藏，展品编号 89903

Denarius From the Reign of Caracalla (198-217 A.D.) - Roman Coin with Ship

201-206 A.D.
diameter 18.67 mm
weight 2.86 grams
National Roman Museum, Medagliere - Numismatic Collection Inv. 89903

这枚硬币描述了与“罗马皇帝之旅”相关的另外一个主题。在硬币反面的图案中，游船旁边的铭文宣布皇帝卡拉卡拉（Caracalla）和塞蒂米奥·塞韦罗（Settimio Severo）抵达了帝国的某个地方。

塞蒂米奥·塞韦罗时期的第纳尔（公元 193 年—211 年）

带有海船图案的古罗马货币
公元 202 年—210 年
银
直径 19.81 毫米
重 2.83 克
罗马国家博物馆，古钱收藏，展品编号 89738

Denarius From the Reign of Septimius Severus (193-211 A.D.) - Roman Coin with Ship

202-210 A.D.
diameter 19.81 mm
weight 2.83 grams
National Roman Museum, Medagliere - Numismatic Collection Inv. 89738

这枚硬币的发行是为了纪念塞蒂米奥·塞韦罗统治十周年。硬币背面图案的内容可能是指公元 202 年为了庆祝这个纪念日而举行的比赛，人们在罗马的马西莫（Massimo）竞技场内设置了一艘能容纳约 400 只动物的海船。在庆祝活动期间，打开海船，狮子、黑豹、野牛和鸵鸟等异国动物蜂拥而出。硬币背面的铭文传播了塞蒂米奥·塞韦罗政府所保证的“幸福时代”以及和平年代的信息。

波斯图莫时期的双塞斯太尔斯（公元 260 年—269 年）

带有海船图案的古罗马货币
大约公元 260 年—269 年
铜
直径 32.29 毫米
重 20.73 克
罗马国家博物馆，古钱收藏，展品编号 93959

Double Sestertius From the Reign of Postumus (260-269 A.D.) - Roman Coin with Ship

ca. 260-269 A.D.
diameter 32.29 mm
weight 20.73 grams
National Roman Museum, Medagliere - Numismatic Collection Inv. 93959

这枚硬币记载了与罗马皇帝的旅行和访问相关的事件，通过货币的形象，传播了事件所伴随的纯粹的意识形态主题。在这枚硬币中，船舶的形象代表了皇帝波斯图莫（Postumo，公元 260 年—269 年）的惠民政策为罗马带来的幸福、快乐和繁荣。在独立于罗马之外的高卢（Gallie）地区，在罗马帝国的危机时刻，皇帝波斯图莫亲自平息了叛乱，取得了胜利，带来了幸福，并由此被北方各省的军队拥戴为皇帝。

科西莫三世·德·美第奇时期的泰勒（公元 1670 年—1723 年）

带有利沃诺港口图案的托斯卡纳大公国货币
1692 年
银
直径 43.42 毫米
重 27.07 克
罗马国家博物馆，古钱收藏，展品编号 19.M329-1.4

Thaler From the Reign of Cosimo III de' Medici (1670-1723) - Coin of the Grand Duchy of Tuscany with the Port of Livorno

1692
diameter 43.42 mm
weight 27.07 grams
National Roman Museum, Medagliere - Numismatic Collection Inv. 19.M329-1.4

这枚硬币再现了当年利沃诺港的景象。利沃诺是托斯卡纳大公国的一座港口城市，在 17 世纪，这座港口城市成了商人们的目的地，丝绸从这里进口，佛罗伦萨的面料等意大利生产的珍贵商品从这里运出。硬币背面的图案再现了这一港口的繁华。17 世纪上半叶，费迪南德二世大公对此进行了加固工程，包括建造一个新的码头和挖掘海床，这样一来，大型船舶就可以更为方便地停泊。随着 1676 年自由港的建立，这座港口城市取得了显著的发展，政府通过了一项经济措施，减轻商人的税收负担，极大地促进了当地经济。

科西莫三世·德·美第奇时期的泰勒（公元1670年—1723年）

带有帆船图案的托斯卡纳大公国货币
1683年
银
直径38.66毫米
重13.11克
罗马国家博物馆，古钱收藏，展品编号19.M329-1.5

Half Thaler From the Reign of Cosimo III de' Medici (1670-1723) - Coin of the Grand Duchy of Tuscany with Sailing Ship

1683
diameter 38.66 mm
weight 13.11 grams
National Roman Museum, Medagliere - Numismatic Collection Inv. 19.M329-1.5

利沃诺港举足轻重的地位体现在这里所集结的大量优质的、销往意大利和海外地区的货物。每天来来往往的船只，从利沃诺港靠岸又奔赴下一站，装载着从食品到用品等各种各样的商品，例如大米、果酱、凤尾鱼、鱼子酱、鲑鱼、油、葡萄酒、葡萄、熏香、药品、大麻、丝绸、地毯、亚麻籽、金银钻石。这也是为什么硬币背面会有帆船图案的原因。

共和国执政官马克·安东尼奥·朱斯提尼亚尼时期的威尼斯银币（公元1684年—1688年）

带有威尼斯海湾图案的威尼斯共和国货币
1684年
银
直径36.97毫米
重9.69克
罗马国家博物馆，古钱收藏，展品编号19.M329-1.6

Osella of the Doge of Venice, Marcantonio Giustinian (1684-1688) - Coin from the Republic of Venice with View of the Venetian Port Basin

1684
diameter 36.97 mm
weight 9.69 grams
National Roman Museum, Medagliere - Numismatic Collection Inv. 19.M329-1.6

威尼斯共和国的财富和军事力量主要来自港口和舰队。在硬币背面的图案中，这座城市和海域相结合，重现了城市中从码头可以望到圣马可广场以及停泊船只的场景。硬币上刻有圣马可和圣特奥多罗广场的圆柱、钟楼、执政官所在的威尼斯公爵宫以及圣马可大教堂。

共和国执政官卢多维克·马宁时期的威尼斯银币（公元 1789 年—1797 年）

带有帆船战争图案的威尼斯共和国货币
1790 年
银
直径 31.78 毫米
重 9.82 克
罗马国家博物馆，古钱收藏，展品编号 19.M329-1.7

Osella of Doge Ludovico Manin (1789-1797) - Coin from the Republic of Venice with Battle Scene Between Two Sailing Ships

1790
diameter 31.78 mm
weight 9.82 grams
National Roman Museum, Medagliere - Numismatic Collection Inv. 19.M329-1.7

18 世纪，土耳其海盗在地中海海域横行肆虐，严重威胁到威尼斯共和国的繁荣发展。因此，威尼斯共和国海军的一项重要任务就是打击海盗。硬币描绘了一艘威尼斯共和国船只与一艘悬挂着土耳其国旗的船战斗的场景，这也影射出好战的威尼斯人希望控制该海域的决心。

共和国执政官阿尔维斯三世·莫塞尼戈时期的威尼斯银币（公元 1722 年—1732 年）

带有大帆船战舰和商船图案的威尼斯共和国货币
1726 年
银
直径 37.39 毫米
重 9.72 克
罗马国家博物馆，古钱收藏，展品编号 19.M329-1.8

Osella of Doge Alvise III Mocenigo (1722-1732) - Coin from the Republic of Venice with a War Galleon and Merchant Ships

1726
diameter 37.39 mm
weight 9.72 grams
National Roman Museum, Medagliere - Numismatic Collection Inv. 19.M329-1.8

硬币背面描绘的是威尼斯战舰和几艘商船的图案，背景清晰可见。这一图案暗示了威尼斯共和国用战舰护送商船使其免受土耳其海盗掠夺的决心。

共和国执政官保罗·莱尼尔时期的威尼斯银币（公元 1779 年—1789 年）

带有威尼斯军械库战舰图案的威尼斯共和国货币
1785 年
银
直径 32.12 毫米
重 9.66 克
罗马国家博物馆，古钱收藏，展品编号 19.M329-1.9

Osella of Doge Paolo Renier (1779-1789) - Coin from the Republic of Venice with Ship, in the Venetian Arsenal

1785
diameter 32.12 mm
weight 9.66 grams
National Roman Museum, Medagliere - Numismatic Collection Inv. 19.M329-1.9

贸易给威尼斯共和国带来的利益和财富，使市政当局对船队和港口设施尤为关注。硬币背面描绘了一艘战舰穿过威尼斯军械库的场景。图案暗指保罗·莱尼尔（Paolo Renier）执政官在 1782 年访问威尼斯军械库，并就发现的一些违规问题给出解决方案的事件。

共和国执政官阿尔维斯三世·莫塞尼戈时期的威尼斯银币（公元 1722 年—1732 年）

带有大型画舫图案的威尼斯共和国货币
1727 年
银
直径 37.61 毫米
重 9.75 克
罗马国家博物馆，古钱收藏，展品编号 19.M329-1.10

Osella of Doge Alvise III Mocenigo (1722-1732) - Coin from the Republic of Venice with a Bucentaur Ship

1727
diameter 37.61 mm
weight 9.75 grams
National Roman Museum, Medagliere - Numismatic Collection Inv. 19.M329-1.10

威尼斯共和国欢庆盛宴的标志是海上画舫。作为代表性船只，国王和皇后每逢国事访问或庆祝由执政官主持的“海上婚姻”时，都会搭乘画舫。这种婚姻仪式由现任执政官主持，是威尼斯统治海域的一种象征。硬币呈现的画舫造于 1727 年，拥有富丽堂皇的配饰，包括帷幔、粉饰和镀金雕刻。这美轮美奂地象征着威尼斯共和国权势的船只，于 1797 年被威尼斯共和国的侵略者——拿破仑·波拿巴所领导的法国军队烧毁。

第四节 海洋的神话和寓言

4D.4. MYTHS AND ALLEGORIES OF THE SEA

海神尼普顿能够释放风暴，也能使泉水涌起，其力量甚至可以延伸到河流和湖泊中。尼普顿一般被描绘成手持三叉戟（捕鱼工具）的形象，挥舞它，海岸的岩石都会颤抖。因此，哈德良皇帝（公元 117 年—138 年）用它在铜币上代表了自己——手里拿着船尾上部的装饰品（展品编号 92552）。其他时候，尼普顿常被描绘为乘着海马（类似于海马的神话生物）拉的战车的形象。尼普顿旁边经常搭配有安菲特里忒的形象（展品编号 83673），这个女孩从神灵身边逃走并前往海洋深处，被海豚发现并带到尼普顿身边，与尼普顿结婚。在对海洋世界或多或少怀有仁慈之心的神灵旁边，也存在着一些可怕的生物，他们居住在海洋和沿海地区，威胁着毫无戒心的不幸旅行者的生命。其中包括塞壬（展品编号 85644）——一半是女人、一半是鸟或鱼的生物。根据神话所述，塞壬居住在意大利南部海岸的一座岛屿上，她们用美妙的歌声吸引从附近经过的水手。然而，塞壬带给水手们的只有悲惨的命运：当他们驶近岛屿时，船会在礁石间搁浅，塞壬乘机吞噬不幸的人。美杜莎，三个蛇发女妖之一，海神的女儿，水手们特别害怕她。神话传说中，她们是拥有着漂亮头发的女孩，这引起了女神密涅瓦的嫉妒，于是女神将她们的头发变成了蛇。美杜莎的这一形象出现在硬币上（展品编号 83671），人们被她的目光吓坏了；女神密涅瓦将美杜莎的头砍下，放置在她的盾牌或盔甲的中心，用来防御和攻击敌人——美杜莎死后力量仍然存在。在所有的海洋生物中，最为恐怖的当属“斯库拉”（展品编号 85234）——一个生活在意大利墨西拿

Neptune was the god of the sea, capable of unleashing storms, but also making springs flow, with a power that probably extended to running waters and lakes. Neptune was generally depicted with a trident (a three-pronged spear) that, if brandished, was able to make the rocks of the coasts tremble. This is how Emperor Hadrian (117-138 A.D.) was represented on a sestertius, holding an aplustre, a decoration that adorned the upper part of the stern of ships (Inv.92552); other times he was also often depicted on a chariot drawn by hippocampi, mythological creatures similar to seahorses. Neptune was often accompanied by the Nereid, Amphitrite (Inv.83673). After having escaped the god's first approaches by hiding in the depths of the ocean, Amphitrite was found by dolphins and brought back to Neptune, who then took her in marriage. Along with the more or less benevolent gods of the marine world, frightening creatures that threatened the lives of unsuspecting and unlucky travelers dwelled in the seas and on the coastal areas. Among these were the Sirens (Inv.85644): creatures that were half-woman and half-bird or fish who, according to mythology, inhabited an island on the coast of southern Italy and who, with their persuasive song, attracted sailors navigating nearby. However, a sad fate was reserved for these sailors. As they approached the island, the ships would run aground between the rocks, where the sirens would then devour the unfortunate men. Medusa, one of the three Gorgons - the daughters of sea gods - was also particularly feared by sailors. The myth depicts her as a woman with hair so beautiful that it aroused the envy of the goddess Minerva, who then turned Medusa's hair into snakes. Her countenance, portrayed in images on coins (Inv.83671), was feared by the men who she would then petrify with her stare. A power that persisted even after Medusa's death. Her severed head was placed by the goddess Minerva on her own shield, or in the center of her armor, to be used as a defensive or offensive weapon against enemies. But among all the sea creatures, Scylla (Inv.85234) - a monster that inhabited the Italian coasts of the Strait of Messina - was the one that incited

海峡的怪物，上半身是女人，下半身是凶猛的狗。神话故事传说，斯库拉本来是一个漂亮女孩，她的美丽吸引了尼普顿的注意，海神之妻安菲特里忒因为嫉妒抓住机会将她变成了怪物；而神话的另一个版本是尼普顿本人将斯库拉变成了一个怪物，以此作为拒绝他追求的惩罚。

古代海洋的极限，标记在西边的赫拉克勒斯之柱上（展品编号 228271）。赫拉克勒斯则是与之名字相关的半神半人，神柱以他的功绩之名建立，一个放置在欧洲的直布罗陀海峡，另一个矗立在非洲休达，以此标记海的边界，并通过上面的铭文告诫人们：“不可再进一步。”除了神话故事之外，大海还通过动人的图像来唤起人们对历史事实和事件的回忆，这些图像每次都有不同的风格，在之后的岁月里被重新诠释，作为对古老而伟大的遗产的见证，而图像也通过货币这一特殊的媒介广泛传播。一个例子是在屋大维的硬币上描绘的胜利女神站在船头上的形象。屋大维是未来的奥古斯都皇帝，图像描绘的是他在公元前 31 年打败马克·安东尼和克利奥帕特拉所取得的胜利（展品编号 85576）。同样的图像主题也出现在韦斯巴芗君主（公元 69 年—79 年）的硬币上，他是新王朝的缔造者，希望能够彰显其作为奥古斯都政权继承人的身份。与展现奥古斯都荣光的想法一样，东哥特国王狄奥多里克（公元 534 年—536 年）的硬币上也使用了类似的图案。一千多年后，以意大利国王维托里奥·埃马努埃莱三世（公元 1900 年—1946 年）为代表的对经典造币风格的追捧，意味着同样的古代主题在现代造币中获得了重新诠释。硬币上，站在船首的人物形象衣襟随风飘扬，巧妙地展示了意大利的艺术之美（展品编号 19.M329-1.11）。

S. 博卡迪

the most fear (Inv.18077). With a woman's upper body and a lower body from which protruded the heads of fierce dogs, according to mythology, Scylla was originally a girl whose beauty attracted Neptune's attentions. In a fit of jealously, Amphitrite, Neptune's bride, turned her into a monster. According to another version of the myth, it was Neptune himself who transformed Scylla into a monster as punishment for refusing his attentions.

The boundaries of the sea of the ancients was marked to the west by the Pillars of Hercules (Inv.228271). Related to the demigod from which they received their name, according to the myth, they had been erected by Hercules following one of his amazing labours: one pillar was placed on the European coast, in Gibraltar, and the other on the African coast, in Ceuta, to mark the navigable boundary of the sea, as reiterated by the inscription above it, ne plus ultra, literally, "no more beyond". In addition to mythological tales, the sea could evoke historical facts and events through the use of eloquent images. With a style that differed each time, they were later reinterpreted as a reminder of an ancient and grandiose legacy, widely spread by currency, an exceptional tool of communication. An example of this is the figure of the Victory on a ship's bow depicted on a coin of Octavian (Inv.85576), the future Emperor Augustus, which recalls his great naval victory in 31 B.C. against Mark Antony and Cleopatra. The same iconography is repeated on a coin of the Emperor Vespasian (69-79 A.D.), progenitor of a new dynasty, who wanted to demonstrate his succession to Augustus' politics. The coin of the Ostrogoth king, Theodatus (534-536 A.D.), alluded to the same idea of continuity with the glorious Rome of Augustus, although the iconography regarding the Victory did not actually reflect the events of war that marked his brief reign. More than a thousand years later, the revival of the classical taste that characterized the coinage of the Italian king, Vittorio Emanuele III (1900-1946), meant that the same ancient schemes of the Victory were used and reinterpreted in modern coinage, as was represented in the skillful engraving of Italy on the bow of a ship with its soft robes moving in the wind (Inv. 19.M329-1.11).

S. Boccardi

哈德良时期的塞斯太尔斯（公元 117 年—138 年）

带有海神图案的古罗马货币
公元 125 年—128 年
铜
直径 33.18 毫米
重 27.92 克
罗马国家博物馆，古钱收藏，展品编号 92552

Sestertius From the Reign of Hadrian (117-138 A.D.) - Roman Coin with Neptune

125-128 A.D.
diameter 33.18 mm
weight 27.92 grams
National Roman Museum, Medagliere - Numismatic Collection Inv. 92552

水手们启程前会向众神祈祷，祈祷的对象中就有海王星，即海神。海神能激起暴雨海啸，使泉水涌出，他的力量甚至能控制流水湖泊。海神尼普顿的形象通常被描绘成持有一把三叉戟（叉鱼工具）的样子，若他挥舞叉戟，海岸礁石也要为之晃动。哈德良时期的这枚小银币，背面图案就描绘了这位海神的形象：手持三叉戟站在船头，船尾配有各种装饰。

克雷普雷斯五世 · 马尔库斯 · 菲卢斯 · 鲁库斯时期的第纳尔

带有海神尼普顿和海马战车图案的古罗马货币
公元前 72 年
银
直径 18.54 毫米
重 4.02 克
罗马国家博物馆，古钱收藏，展品编号 83675

Denarius Serratus of Q. Crepereius Rocus - Roman Coin with Neptune on Chariot with Hippocampi

72 B.C.
diameter 18.54 mm
weight 4.02 grams
National Roman Museum, Medagliere - Numismatic Collection Inv. 83675

如果说三叉戟和简朴是海神的标志，那么海马就是伴随他四处旅行的神话生物。这些海马类似于马，牵引着海神尼普顿的战车前进，在这枚由执政官发行的古罗马银币背面图案的底部，还刻有执政官的名字：克雷普雷斯五世 · 马尔库斯 · 菲卢斯 · 鲁库斯（Q.Creperei M.f Rocus）。

克雷普雷斯五世 · 马尔库斯 · 菲卢斯 · 鲁库斯时期的第纳尔

带有安菲特里忒图案的古罗马货币
公元前 72 年
银
直径 19.39 毫米
重 3.99 克
罗马国家博物馆，古钱收藏，展品编号 83673

Denarius Serratus of Q. Crepereius Rocus - Roman Coin with Amphitrite

72 B.C.
diame 造词 ter 19.39 mm
weight 3.99 grams
National Roman Museum, Medagliere - Numismatic Collection Inv. 83673

银币正面图案描绘的是内雷奥之女同时也是海神尼普顿的妻子——安菲特里忒。相传这位羞怯的少女为了逃避尼普顿热烈的追求，逃到了大海深处的赫拉克勒斯之柱，后来海神在一只海豚的帮助下找到了安菲特里忒并迎娶了她。

科奥迪乌斯洛夫斯 IIIVIR 时期的第纳尔

带有骑在海豚上的丘比特图案的古罗马货币
公元前 46 年
银
直径 18.86 毫米
重 3.67 克
罗马国家博物馆，古钱收藏，展品编号 83582

Denarius of Mn. Cordius Rufus IIIVIR - Roman Coin with Cupid on Dolphin

46 B.C.
diameter 18.86 mm
weight 3.67 grams
National Roman Museum, Medagliere - Numismatic Collection Inv. 83582

硬币正面描绘了爱与美的女神维纳斯，背面是她的儿子丘比特骑着海豚的画面。与大海有关的很多古老传说都讲到了女神诞生的过程：其中一个传说讲到，古老的神乌拉诺斯的性器官被割断，落入海中便成了女神；还有故事说到，维纳斯是由安菲特里忒的父亲内雷奥抚养长大的。银币背面刻画了年轻的丘比特与海豚玩耍的场景，也暗指女神与大海有千丝万缕的联系。

奥古斯都时期的第纳尔（公元前 27 年—14 年）

带有塞壬图案的古罗马货币
约公元前 19 年
银
直径 19.19 毫米
重 3.82 克
罗马国家博物馆，古钱收藏，展品编号 85644

Denarius From the Reign of Augustus (27 B.C. - 14 A.D.) - Roman Coin with Siren

ca. 19 B.C.
diameter 19.19 mm
weight 3.82 grams
National Roman Museum, Medagliere - Numismatic Collection Inv. 85644

除了仁厚善良的海神，还有一些可怕的生物栖息在海洋和沿海地区，攻击毫无戒心的不幸旅者。奥古斯都时期（公元前 27 年—公元 14 年）铸造的一种钱币的背面，便描绘了一种这样凶残的生物：身体一半是女人、一半是鸟类的塞壬。相传，塞壬生活在意大利南部海岸的一座小岛上，她们用动人的歌声引诱附近的航海者。当他们靠近这座岛屿时，便只剩悲惨的命运在等待他们了——船只在礁石间搁浅后，塞壬便现身将他们吞食。

库索蒂及萨布拉时期的第纳尔

带有美杜莎头像图案的古罗马货币
公元前 74 年
银
直径 19.88 毫米
重 4.07 克
罗马国家博物馆，古钱收藏，展品编号 83671

Denarius of Lucius Cossutius Sabula - Roman Coin with Medusa's Head

74 B.C.
diameter 19.88 mm
weight 4.07 grams
National Roman Museum, Medagliere - Numismatic Collection Inv. 83671

这枚古罗马货币正面刻画的图案，是海妖刻托的三个女儿之一，生活在海中的可怕神灵美杜莎。相传少女美杜莎拥有一头美丽的秀发，这引起了密涅瓦嫉妒，将她的头发变成了蛇发。她有着令人惧怕的巨大的獠牙和翅膀。人们的眼睛只要触及她的目光便会被石化。只有海神尼普顿敢与她亲近，并与她生下帕伽索斯，即银币背面刻画的生有双翼的神马。美杜莎的头颅被割下后仍然具有用眼睛石化他物的能力，雅典娜将其放置在自己的盾牌或盔甲中心，用来作战。

塞斯托 · 庞培时期的第纳尔

带有斯库拉图案的古罗马货币
公元前 42 年—公元前 40 年
银
直径 18.40 毫米
重 3.88 克
罗马国家博物馆，古钱收藏，展品编号 85234

Denarius of Sextus Pompey - Roman Coin with Scylla

42-40 B.C.
diameter 18.40 mm
weight 3.88 grams
National Roman Museum, Medagliere - Numismatic Collection Inv. 85234

传说，古代地中海海域，意大利墨西拿海峡海岸生活着一种特别恐怖的海怪——上半身像女人，下半身是猛犬爪牙的斯库拉。相传，斯库拉原本是一名美丽的少女，但由于海神尼普顿倾慕她，激起了海神新娘安菲特里忒的怒火，便将斯库拉变成海怪。另有神话传言，斯库拉是因为拒绝了海神的追求而被海神变为怪物的。银币上描绘斯库拉挥舞船舵的破坏性行为，暗指在公元前 36 年，塞斯托 · 庞培（奥古斯都未来的皇帝）对抗屋大维战舰获得胜利。正是凭借这一胜利，他获得了对西西里岛、撒丁岛和科西嘉的统治权。

查理五世时期的四分之一第纳尔（公元 1519 年—1556 年）

带有赫拉克勒斯之柱图案的米兰大公国货币
1551 年
银
直径 27.70 毫米
重 9.11 克
罗马国家博物馆，古钱收藏，展品编号 228271

Scudo From the Reign of Charles V (1519-1556) - Coin From the Duchy of Milan with the Pillars of Hercules

1551
diameter 27.70 mm
weight 9.11 grams
National Roman Museum, Medagliere - Numismatic Collection Inv. 228271

除了神灵和海洋生物，神话传说还塑造了许多现实具体的概念。赫拉克勒斯之柱的图案便是这样一个例子。神话相传，赫拉克勒斯是半人半神的英雄，他的一个功绩便是将大陆撕裂，分为了欧洲海岸直布罗陀和非洲海岸休达。由此，古代的航海边界开始形成，而并非（“不再”）是连接在一起的大陆了。神圣罗马帝国皇帝查理五世（公元 1519 年—1556 年）时期的硬币背面便描绘并讲述了这一概念：赫拉克勒斯之柱原意为连接两岸的海峡，后被转译为“更加”，也是“更进一步”之意，用来描述勇敢的君王领导政府征服欧洲大陆。后来，1492 年克里斯托弗 · 哥伦布发现了美洲大陆，查理五世由此获得了古代界定的大陆之外的财产。

奥古斯都时期的第纳尔

带有胜利图案的古罗马货币
约公元前 29 年—公元前 27 年
银
直径 20.18 毫米
重 3.69 克
罗马国家博物馆，古钱收藏，展品编号 85576

Denarius from the Reign of Octavian - Roman Coin with Victory on the Bow of a Ship

ca. 29-27 B.C.
diameter 20.18 mm
weight 3.69 grams
National Roman Museum, Medagliere - Numismatic Collection Inv. 85576

货币除了其本身的用途之外，也有庆祝建筑建成或通过图像宣扬神话、讲述历史事件的作用。奥古斯都皇帝屋大维时期的这枚银币，正面描绘了屋大维于公元前 31 年在阿齐奥（Azio）带领船队对抗马克·安东尼和克利奥帕特拉并取得胜利的事件。他击败了最后的对手，制订政治计划，成为罗马帝国第一位元首。

韦斯巴芗时期的阿司（公元 69 年—79 年）

带有胜利图案的古罗马货币
公元 71 年
铜
直径 26.71 毫米
重 10.97 克
罗马国家博物馆，古钱收藏，展品编号 94264

As From the Reign of Vespasian (69-70 A.D.) - Roman Coin with Victory on the Bow of a Ship

71 A.D.
diameter 26.71 mm
weight 10.97 grams
National Roman Museum, Medagliere - Numismatic Collection Inv. 94264

皇帝韦斯巴芗（Vespasiano）在其统治时期发行的货币上使用了代表胜利的象征图案——皇冠和棕榈树枝，它沿袭了罗马帝国开辟者屋大维时期货币所代表的含义，以此昭示自己为帝国继承人。

狄奥多里克时期的弗里斯（公元 534 年—536 年）

带有胜利图案的东哥特王国货币
约公元 534—535 年
铜
直径 26.93 毫米
重 10.63 克
罗马国家博物馆，古钱收藏，展品编号 103631

40 Nummi Coin (Follis) from the Reign of Theodahad (534-536 A.D.) - Coin from the Kingdom of the Ostrogoths
ca. 534-535 A.D.
diameter 26.93 mm
weight 10.63 grams
National Roman Museum, Medagliere - Numismatic Collection Inv. 103631

西罗马帝国灭亡后，公元 493 年，由赋予了罗马帝国新生命的君王狄奥多里克（公元 493—526 年）领导的哥特族日耳曼人占领了意大利半岛。狄奥多里克继承了罗马帝国奥古斯都的理念，他发行的硬币同样描绘了代表胜利的图案：皇冠和棕榈树枝。然而这一胜利的象征并不代表这一国家也会常胜——东罗马帝国查士丁尼军队的持续扩张（守住罗马后，向西攻占领土），迅速终结了狄奥多里克的统治。

维托里奥 · 埃马努埃莱三世时期的 5 分里拉（公元 1900—1946 年）

带有意大利拟人化图案的意大利王国货币
1908 年
黄铜
直径 25.07 毫米
重 4.91 克
罗马国家博物馆，古钱收藏，展品编号 19.M329-1.11

5 Cents From the Reign of Victor Emmanuel III (1900-1946) - Coin From the Kingdom of Italy with Italy Represented on the Bow of a Ship
1908
diameter 25.07 mm
weight 4.91 grams
National Roman Museum, Medagliere - Numismatic Collection Inv. 19.M329-1.11

意大利国王萨沃依家族的维托里奥 · 埃马努埃莱三世（公元 1900 年—1946 年）所铸造货币的特点是古典风格的复兴。作为一名狂热的意大利硬币鉴赏家和收藏家，他采用古老的风格来铸造新王国的货币，意大利女子坐在船头优雅的造型以及长袍随风飘扬的画面，唤起了他的灵感。

维托里奥 · 埃马努埃莱三世时期的 10 里拉（公元 1900 年—1946 年）

带有意大利拟人化图案的意大利王国货币
1936 年
银
直径 27.02 毫米
重 10.01 克
罗马国家博物馆，古钱收藏，展品编号 19.M329-1.12

10 lira Coin From the Reign of Victor Emmanuel III (1900-1946) - Coin From the Kingdom of Italy with Italy Represented on the Bow of a Ship

1936
diameter 27.02 mm
weight 10.01 grams
National Roman Museum, Medagliere - Numismatic Collection Inv. 19.M329-1.12

20 世纪 30 年代的意大利正处于殖民扩张时期。1936 年，维托里奥 · 埃马努埃莱加冕为埃塞俄比亚皇帝，这枚银币的背面描绘了埃马努埃莱统治整个国家的事件，阐释了古老船头胜利的图案意象（nn.158-160）。根据当时人们的品位，意大利被拟人化描绘为短发气势雄伟、凶猛的形象；胜利的翅膀，暗喻海战胜利以及法西斯胜利，也是第二次世界大战的象征。

UNIT V

NAVIGIA FUNDO EMERGUNT

STORY OF THE FINDINGS

第五单元

海底沉船
光芒重现

躺在海底的船比在海面航行的船还多。

——P. 马特维耶维奇

There are more ships lying at the bottom of the sea than there are above it.

(P. Matvejević)

海底沉船：光芒重现。

在《历史》的第四卷中，著名的拉丁文作家盖乌斯·萨卢斯提乌斯·克里斯普斯讲述了船只（或其残骸）被西西里岛的卡里迪漩涡吞噬后，在水下被拖曳60英里，从海底重新出水的故事。然后人们意识到海底有更多的古老船只（P. 马特维耶维奇）：地中海是“液态水泥”，也是沿岸生活的人们的通衢。几千年来，其海底深处一直悄悄地保存着人类交通、货物、知识、技术、语言和宗教不断变迁的痕迹，而船只装载的正是这些由人类的聪明才智创造的迷人而复杂的作品。

然而直到最近，这种意识才转变成一种研究，其目的是了解和重建航线和商业线路、沿海景观及明晰其演变和交流的方式，并最终形成这段历史密集的故事情节：海洋，“在陆地之间”。

水下考古的历史与皮埃兹·卢兹的史诗级壮举（法国称其为水面潜水者）以及潜水史密不可分。采集海绵的渔民从18世纪开始使用潜水服。他们冒着生命危险，完成了很多征服海洋深处的英勇壮举。而在爱琴海畔采集海绵的渔民则充分利用了潜水服，他们已经能够深入到自由潜水的最深处。他们中的一些人在20世纪初期找到了令人难以置信的艺术品，这些艺术品都是在希腊的安提凯希拉岛和突尼斯海岸的马赫迪耶岛附近随船沉没的。水下考古史的另一个里程碑是内米湖沉船发现，它标志着人们对古代舰船建造的认识有了一个巨大飞跃。

Navigia Fundo Emergunt: Bring Back to Light.

In book IV of *the Historiae*, the famous Latin author, Gaius Sallustius Crispus, tells of ships (or their relics) re-emerging from the bottom of the sea after being swallowed by the Charybdis vortex, in the Strait of Sicily, and dragged for sixty miles by underwater currents. The awareness that there are more ships lying at the bottom of the sea than there are above it (P. Matvejević) is ancient. The Mediterranean was “liquid concrete” and a bridge for the people who lived and still live along its banks. For millennia, its depths have jealously preserved the traces of the incessant movements and passages of men, goods, knowledge, techniques, languages, and religions aboard those fascinating and complex works of human ingenuity that are ships.

Only in recent times, however, has this awareness turned into research oriented towards the knowledge and reconstruction of routes and commercial circuits, of coastal landscapes and their evolution, and of contacts and exchanges, which have formed the story line that is full of the history of this sea “between the lands”.

The history of underwater archeology is inextricably linked to the epic feats of pieds lourds - as surface-supplied divers were called in France - and of diving. The protagonist of the heroic feats aimed at conquering the depths of the sea were sponge fishermen who, from the end of the 1700s, began using diving suits, risking fatal accidents. Significant use of these were made by the fishermen in the Aegean sea, who already reached very great depths with free-diving. It was precisely several of these fishermen who - during the early years of the last century - discovered and recovered the incredible cargoes of works of art shipwrecked near the island of Antikythera, in Greece, and on Mahdia on the Tunisian coast. Another milestone in the history of underwater discoveries was the

1932 年，经过了之前几个世纪的徒劳和冒险尝试，最终卡利古拉皇帝的这两艘豪华舰船在内米湖干涸后得以重见光明（见第三单元第四部分）。

1943 年，法国海军军官雅克 - 伊夫 · 库斯托和工程师爱米尔 · 加尼安研制出了足以改变潜水活动进程的伟大发明：现代化的可调节式空气呼吸器）。此后，越来越多的潜水员开始通过这种新型设备进行水下潜水活动。然而在最初，因为这种呼吸器的使用，水下遗产遭到了严重破坏：自水下空气呼吸器面世以来，在 1946 年之后的十年间，仍旧有许多沉船，尤其是法国和利古里亚沿海地区的沉船，遭到部分或全部破坏。尽管如此，这对水下考古学来说仍然是一个重大的进步 。这种呼吸器首次应用于马赫迪耶的考古公司。1948 年，在库斯托和泰莱兹的指挥下，法国海军的水下研究组（水下搜寻部队，GERS）进行了首次应用尝试。

而那段时期恰逢意大利水下考古探索的高峰时

colossal undertaking of the Nemi ships, which marked a great leap forward in the knowledge of ancient naval architecture. In 1932, after centuries of useless and adventurous attempts, the luxurious ships of the Emperor Caligula, which had sunk to the bottom of Lake Nemi, were brought to light after the lake was drained (see par. 3d, 3d.1).

In 1943, French naval officer Jacques-Yves Cousteau and Engineer Emile Gagnan developed the invention that would modify the course of underwater activities: the self-contained underwater breathing apparatus, our modern-day scuba gear. With this new device, diving then became easier and more accessible to an ever increasing number of divers. Initially, this caused serious damage to underwater archeological heritage. In the decade following 1946, the first year during which the underwater breathing apparatus was put on the market, many wrecks, especially along the coasts of France and the region of Liguria in Italy, were partially or totally destroyed. But, in spite of everything, it was a momentous advancement for underwater archeology, which immediately and progressively developed. The self-contained breathing apparatus was used for the first time during an archeological venture in Mahdia, during the expedition of the Groupe d'Etudes et de Recherches

内米湖：露出水面的一号船（1983 年，乌切利）

雅克 - 伊夫 · 库斯托和 A.R.A（1990 年，贝洛莫）

密斯脱拉，第一款水下空气呼吸器（1990 年，贝洛莫）

期。1950 年，“意大利水下考古学之父”阿尔本加·尼诺·兰博利亚发现了迄今最大的货船：该船长约 40 米，宽 10～12 米，至少有 5 层空间，船上装载了超过 11 000 只双耳细颈瓶，其中只有一小部分被发现并回收。在这艘船上还发现了黑釉陶瓷，它们堆放在双耳细颈瓶之间的空隙里。在船里发现了 6 个头盔，说明船上的水手们还可以装备并使用武器。几年之后，兰博利亚建立了阿尔本加沉船考古研究中心，该中心现在仍然在运营。二十年来，该中心在意大利各地进行考古研究和挖掘活动，例如巴亚海床的绘制等项目（见第二单元第二部分第二节）。

水下考古学家按照陆地挖掘的标准进行的第一次挖掘活动，是在土耳其南部的彻利多尼亚开展的，当时的挖掘对象是一艘青铜时代的沉船，这艘沉船在公元前 1200 年左右被损毁，当时船上载有铜锭、锡锭和金属废料。那时人们回收金属废料用来重新生产青铜。早在 1960 年，美国水下考古记者彼得·斯洛克莫顿和宾夕法尼亚大学考古学家乔治·巴斯就曾经指挥发掘过该项目。这是历史上考古学家们第一次穿着潜水服、戴着氧气瓶在水下进行科学研究！

Sous-marines (GERS) of the French Navy, directed by Cousteau and Taillez in 1948.

That period coincided with the great season of underwater archeology in Italy. In 1950, in Albenga, Nino Lamboglia - the “father” of Italian underwater archeology - began the excavation of the largest cargo ship that was found to date: about 40 meters long and 10-12 meters wide, with a load of over 11,000 amphorae in at least five layers, of which only a small part was recovered. The ship also carried black-glazed pottery, stacked in the spaces between the amphorae. Armor or weapons were available on the ship for sailors, like the 6 helmets that were discovered. A few years later, Lamboglia also founded the Experimental Center of Underwater Archeology in Albenga, which still exists and that, for twenty years, performed research and excavation activities throughout Italy, for example, by mapping the sea beds of Baia (see 2b.2).

However, the first excavation conducted by underwater archeologists using the scientific criteria of land excavations was that of the wreck of Cape Gelidonya, in southern Turkey: a ship from the Bronze Age, shipwrecked around 1200 B.C., which carried copper, tin, and metal scraps destined to be recycled and to produce new bronze. The expedition was directed by the American underwater archeology journalist, Peter Throckmorton, and by the archeologist, George Bass, of the University of Pennsylvania in 1960. For the first time, an archeologist wore a wetsuit and tanks to conduct underwater scientific research!

阿尔本加沉船残骸

卡波凯利多尼亚沉船残骸的考古过程

从此之后，地中海与其他地区海底考古的报告、发现、研究和修复工作一直不断地进行着。但不幸的是，与此同时，由于缺乏分享、管理和积极的保护政策，许多历史遗产被遗弃或遭到了掠夺和破坏。2001 年 11 月 2 日，联合国教科文组织代表国际社会针对这种倒退的行为制定了国际公约。该公约的主要目的是通过国家措施和国际合作，确保和加强对水下文化遗产的保护。对遗产的就地保护被视为最优先的解决办法，并最终否定了过去非常普遍的观点，即保护水下文化遗产的唯一方法是将它们从所在的水下环境中移走。

如今的新技术开辟了另一个领域，一个对人类来说似乎无法逾越的领域：深海。新技术创造了良好的条件，给人们带来出乎意料的惊喜。人可以乘坐小型潜艇探测深海沉积物，或者用机器代替人。这些机器可以记录数据并进行恢复工作。但只有人，可以写出迷人动听的海上航行的故事……

R. 奥列玛

Since then, sightings, findings, research, and recoveries have continued at a relentless pace in the Mediterranean and elsewhere. Unfortunately, at the same time, the lack of a sharing, management, and active protection policy has condemned an enormous part of the underwater heritage to abandonment, looting, and destruction. The UNESCO Convention of November 2nd, 2001 was the response of the international community to this degradation. Its main purpose, in fact, is to ensure and consolidate the protection of underwater cultural heritage through the adoption of national measures and international cooperation. The conservation in situ of the findings must be considered a priority, finally rejecting the previously very popular opinion that the only way to protect submerged cultural assets was to remove them from the underwater environment where they were found.

Today, new technologies have opened up another frontier that seemed insurmountable to man: the deep sea, which holds exceptional surprises in an excellent state of preservation. Man reaches its depths inside small submarines or is replaced by machines, which document and recover in his place. But it is always man who writes the fascinating stories of travels by sea...

R. Auriemma

文托泰内沉船的海中残骸：陶罐的照片

文托泰内沉船的海中残骸：声呐影像

结语
EPILOGUE

合上历史，转身当下。

海洋是各国经贸文化交流的天然纽带之一。从古至今，海上丝绸之路作为文明接触的现场，留下了大量文化交往和融合的历史印记。

2013 年，习近平总书记提出“依海富国、以海强国、人海和谐、合作共赢”的发展道路，主张通过和平、发展、合作、共赢的方式实现目标。海洋强国建设离不开海洋文化建设，海洋文化是海洋资源的重要组成部分，确立海洋文化自信是海洋文化建设的前提，是实现海洋文化创新的基础。

如今，古老的海上丝绸之路萌发出前所未有的生机与活力。“21 世纪海上丝绸之路”已在南中国海上重新起航，书写新的辉煌。

Close the long scroll of history, turn to the present.

The ocean is one of the natural bonds of economic trade and cultural communication between countries. From ancient times to the present, the Maritime Silk Road, as a site of civilization encounter, has left a great number of historical imprints of cultural exchanges and integration.

In 2013, Secretary-General Xi Jinping proposed a way of development that “enriches and prospers the country by relying on the ocean, sustains harmony between human and ocean, and creates win-win results by cooperative effort”, advocating achieving the goal through peace, development, cooperation and win-win approach. The building of a maritime power is inseparable from the construction of maritime culture, which is an important part of maritime resources. Establishing maritime cultural self-confidence is the premise of maritime cultural construction and the basis for realizing maritime cultural innovation.

Today, the ancient Maritime Silk Road unleashed unprecedented vitality and dynamism. The “21st Century Maritime Silk Road” makes sail again on the South China Sea, writing a new glory.

附录

APPENDIX

插图目录
ILLUSTRATED CATALOGUE

第四单元　浮海而行：商品与运输

图 1 - 姆列特岛格拉瓦特号沉船：1989 年挖掘，产自第勒尼安海岸的餐具（照片来自克罗地亚保护研究所 - M.Orli）。

图 2 - 布林迪西省立考古博物馆 - 男性雕像“希腊王子”或“卢基乌斯 · 埃米利乌斯 · 鲍鲁斯”。（博达德勒塞罗内铜像，2010 年；G. 罗杰洛数字处理 - 数字成像实验室 - 萨兰托大学）。

图 3 - “格拉多”号沉船：装在桶中需要回收的玻璃碎片（2018 年奥列玛）。

图 4 - 科马基奥市瓦雷博迪：正在挖掘沉船残骸的场景（照片来自艾米利亚罗马涅大区保罗博物馆）。

图 5 - 罗马，托洛尼亚系列：奥斯蒂亚图拉真港官员浮雕，陶罐卸货场景（帕米等人，1997 年）。

图 6 - a - 莱切省纳尔德奥的“圣卡泰里娜”号沉船残骸；b. 纳尔德奥海洋博物馆中船上货仓横截面复原。

图 7 - 罗马共和时代后期残骸 圣萨比纳塔 3（Torre S. Sabin）：复原的迦太基双耳细颈酒罐。（照片来自萨兰托大学文化遗产部）。

图 8 - 特雷米蒂群岛：“特雷 · 森奇”号沉船：带软木塞的双耳细颈酒罐（照片来自阿跨立思）。

第二部分　食物：意大利葡萄酒的海上之旅

图 1-2 - “马德拉格 · 德吉斯”号沉船残骸（1978 年，Madrague des Giens）。

第三部分　艺术品：海底博物馆

图 1 - 雷焦卡拉布里亚，国家考古博物馆：里亚切的青铜器。

图 2 - 雅典，国家建筑博物馆：安迪基西拉岛的“青年”。

图 3 - “马赫迪耶”号沉船残骸。

图 4 - 马里布，保罗盖蒂博物馆，法诺的田径运动员。

图 5 - “马扎拉 · 德尔瓦洛的萨提尔”。

图 6 - 洛希尼岛，雕塑博物馆 - 克罗地亚的田径运动员 - “刮板”。

珍贵文物：塞罗内海岬铜像的 3D 还原

图 1 - 布林迪西，弗朗西斯科里贝索省级考古博物馆：波吕丢凯斯雕塑。3D 激光扫描（A. 班迪拉制作，萨兰托大学高校数字图书馆）

图 2 - 布林迪西，弗朗西斯科里贝索省级考古博物馆：男子雕塑，也称为“希腊王子”或“卢基乌斯 • 埃米利乌斯 • 鲍鲁斯”。3D 激光扫描（A. 班迪拉制作，萨兰托大学高校数字图书馆）

图 3 - 布林迪西，弗朗西斯科里贝索省级考古博物馆：男子雕塑，也称为“希腊王子”或“卢基乌斯 • 埃米利乌斯 • 鲍鲁斯”。建模及重构复原（M. 托列罗制作，3D 盒子创意实验室）

图 4 - 布林迪西，弗朗西斯科里贝索省级考古博物馆：胜利女神雕塑的翅膀。3D 激光扫描（A. 班迪拉制作，萨兰托大学高校数字图书馆）

图 5 - 布林迪西，弗朗西斯科里贝索省级考古博物馆：胜利女神雕塑。建模及重构复原（M. 托列罗制作，3D 盒子创意实验室）

图 6 - 布林迪西，弗朗西斯科里贝索省级考古博物馆：女童雕塑头部肖像及手臂部分。3D 激光扫描（A. 班迪拉制作，萨兰托大学高校数字图书馆）

图 7 - 布林迪西，弗朗西斯科里贝索省级考古博物馆：女童雕塑。建模及重构复原（M. 托列罗制作，3D 盒子创意实验室）

第四部分 往昔之景：钱币及纪念章上的船舶及港口

图 1 - 教宗克莱门特十世（1670 年—1676 年）硬币，带有奇维塔韦基亚港口（罗马）的图案。
图 2 - 教宗格里高利十六世（1831 年—1846 年）纪念章，带有特拉西那港口的图案。
图 3 - 罗马共和时代（公元前 225 年—公元前 217 年）的阿斯硬币，带有船头的图案。
图 4 - 教宗卡利斯图斯三世（1455 年—1458 年）纪念章，为纪念对抗土耳其的海军远征（约 19 世纪复刻）。
图 5 - 罗马共和时代（公元前 74 年）卢修斯 · 科苏修斯 · 萨布拉的第纳尔硬币，带有美杜莎的图案。
图 6 - 罗马共和时代（约公元前 29 年—公元前 27 年）的屋大维硬币，带有船头上有翅膀的胜利女神的图案。
图 7 - 意大利王国萨伏依王朝的维托里奥 · 埃马努埃莱三世（1900 年 -1946 年）5 分硬币，带有船头上的意大利标志。
图 8 - 尼禄大帝（公元 54 年—68 年）古罗马小银币，带有奥斯蒂亚的克劳迪乌斯港口（罗马）的图案。
图 9 - 图拉真皇帝（公元 98 年—117 年）古罗马小银币，带有奥斯蒂亚的图拉真港口（罗马）的图案。
图 10 - 教宗尤利乌斯二世（1503 年—1513 年）纪念章，带有奇维塔韦基亚堡垒（罗马）的图案（19 世纪复刻）。
图 11 - 教宗格里高利十六世（1831 年—1846 年）纪念章，带有里帕大码头（罗马）的图案。
图 12 - 教宗克莱门特十二世（1730 年—1740 年）纪念章，带有安科纳传染病医院的图案（18 世纪复刻）。
图 13 - 罗马帝国时代的马克 · 安东尼（公元前 32 年—公元前 31 年）硬币，带有船的图案。
图 14 - 哈德良皇帝（公元 117 年—138 年）古罗马小银币，带有船的图案。
图 15 - 莫塞尼戈时的阿尔维斯三世（1722 年—1732 年）威尼斯银币，带有战船和商船的图案。
图 16 - 莫塞尼戈时的阿尔维斯三世（1722 年—1732 年）威尼斯银币，带有古代威尼斯执政官乘坐的大型画舫的图案。
图 17 - 科西莫三世 · 德 · 美第奇（1670 年—1723 年）银币，带有船的图案。
图 18 - 哈德良皇帝（公元 117 年—138 年）古罗马小银币，带有海神的图案。
图 19 - 罗马共和时代，Q. 克莱佩里·洛库斯（公元前 72 年）硬币，带有美杜莎的图案。
图 20 - 奥古斯都大帝（公元前 27 年—公元 14 年）硬币，带有塞壬的图案。
图 21 - 罗马共和时代的塞斯托 · 庞培（公元前 42 年—公元前 40 年）硬币，带有绵枣花的图案。
图 22 - 查理五世（1519 年—1556 年）25 分银币，带有赫拉克勒斯之柱的图案。

第五单元 海底沉船：光芒重现

图 1 - 内米湖：露出水面的一号船（1983 年，乌切利）。
图 2 - 雅克 - 伊夫 · 库斯托和 A.R.A（1990 年，贝洛莫）。
图 3 - 密斯脱拉，第一款水下空气呼吸器（1990 年，贝洛莫）。
图 4 - 阿尔本加沉船残骸。
图 5 - 卡波凯利多尼亚沉船残骸。
图 6a-b - 文托泰内沉船的海中残骸：a. 陶罐的照片；b. 声呐影像。

UNIT II WHERE LAND AND SEA ROUTES MEET: PORTS OF ROMAN ITALY

2a. The Ports of Rome - From the Sea to the City, Sailing up the Tiber

2a.2 . The Pietra Papa River Dock .

Fig.1 - Reconstruction of Pietra Papa (Simone Boni).

Fig.2 - Photo.

Fig.3 - Plan of the Pietra Papa excavations.

Fig.4 - Detailed plan of Rooms D-E and 3D reconstruction.

Fig.5 - MNR - Pietra Papa - The mosaic in Room D.

Fig.6 - Photos of the excavations, the moorings.

Fig.7 - 3D Reconstruction of Room D.

Fig.8 - Plan of hypogeum structures.

Fig.9 - MNR - Pietra Papa - Mosaic threshold.

Fig.10 - MNR - Pietra Papa - Details of ships.

Fig.11 - MNR - Pietra Papa - Details of fish.

UNIT III THE DOMINION OF THE SEA: SHIPS AND SHIPBUILDING

3a. Military Ships

Fig.1a - Liburna: 3D reconstruction by Matteo Collina.

DA CONTROLLARE LICENZE https://www.google.com/search?q=liburna&source=lnms&tbm=isch&sa=X&ved=0ahUKEwjR6eyb-aHhAhUFsaQKHd2OBkwQ_AUIDigB&biw=1138&bih=516#imgrc=ZQ1TemHjxSSTsM

Fig. 1b - 3D reconstruction of a part of a Liburna in the Port of Civitavecchia.

Fig. 2 - Scene LXXXII of the Trajan Column that inspired the reproduction of the Liburna.

Fig. 3 - Naval rams of ships from the battle of the Aegates (Maritime Superintendancy, Sicily).

3b. Merchant and Other Ships

Fig. 1 - Catalog of ships: Tunisian mosaic from Althiburos, late 3rd century A.D. (Bardo Museum, Tunis). ACQUISTARE RIPRODUZIONE NEL SITO https://www.alamy.es/bateaux-mosaico-althiburos-1930-image184455197.html

Fig. 2 - Votive bas-relief of Portus Augusti in Ostia, 200 A.D.

Fig. 3 - Mosaic of the navicularii of Syllectum, Piazzale delle Corporazioni in Ostia, end of the 2nd century A.D.

Fig. 4 - Pompeian graffiti of the ship Europe, 1st century A.D.

Fig. 5 - Rome, Vatican Museums. Fresco depicting Isis Giminiana's ship, with a scene of grain being loaded onto a navis caudicaria, from the Ostiense necropolis along the Via Laurentina (from: Pomey et al. 1997).

Fig. 6 - Ostia, Piazzale delle Corporazioni. Mosaic with scene of transfer of amphorae onto a navis caudicaria, 2nd century A.D.

Fig. 7 - Museo delle navi di Fiumicino (Fiumicino Ship Museum): Fumicino 1, navis caudicaria. https//www.ostiaantica.beniculturali.ititaree-archeologica-e-monumentaliporti-imperiali-di-claudio-and-traianomuseo-of-ships-of-fiumicino

Fig. 8 - Museo delle navi di Fiumicino (Fiumicino Ship Museum): fishing boat.

3c. Ancient Shipbuilding

Fig. 1 - Late-Imperial shipwreck of Torre S. Sabina, Brindisi (ph. University of Salento).
Fig. 2 - Mortise and tenon plank assembly technique.
Fig. 3 - Ancient shipbuilding plan.

UNIT IV ALONG WATERWAY: GOODS AND TRANSPORTATION

Fig. 1- Shipwreck of Glavat, Mlijet: cargo of flatware of Tyrrhenian production from the 1989 excavation project (ph. Croatian Conservation Institute - M. Orlić).
Fig. 2 - Brindisi, Museo Archeologico ProvincialE (Provincial Archeological Museum): male statue, "Hellenic Prince" or "Lucius Aemilius Paullus Macedonicus" (from the Bronzes of Punta del Serrone , 2010; digital elaboration by G. Ruggiero - Digital Imaging Laboratory - University of Salento).
Fig. 3 - Shipwreck of Grado: fragments of glass to be recycled, contained in barrel (from Auriemma 2018).
Fig. 4 - Valleponti, Comacchio: Shipwreck being excavated (ph. Polo Museale Emilia Romagna - Emilia Romagna Museum Center).
Fig. 5 - Rome, Torlonia collection: Relief of the Tabularii of the port of Traiano in Ostia with unloading of amphorae scene (from: Pomey et al. 1997).
Fig. 6 - a) Shipwreck of S. Caterina di Nardò, Lecce: Photo-mosaic of the cargo of amphorae; b) reconstruction of a cross section of the hold in the Museo del Mare (Museum of the sea) of Nardò.
Fig. 7 - Late-Republican shipwreck, Torre S. Sabina 3: Recovery of a Punic amphora from the cargo (ph. Department of Cultural Heritage - University of Salento).
Fig. 8 - Tremiti Islands: Shipwreck of the "Tre Senghe": Wine amphora with cork from cargo (ph. Aquarius).

4b. Foodstuffs: A Cargo of Italic Wine

Figs. 1-2 - Shipwreck of the Madrague des Giens (from: Madrague de Giens 1978).

4c. Works of Art: A Museum at the Bottom of the Sea

Fig. 1 - Reggio Calabria, National Archeological Museum: the Riace Bronzes.
Fig. 2 - Athens, National Archeological Museum: Antikythera Ephebe.
Fig. 3 - Shipwreck of Mahdia.
Fig. 4 - Malibu, P. Getty Museum: the "Victorious Youth" from Fano.
Fig. 5 - Statue of the "Satyr of Mazara del Vallo".
Fig. 6 - Losinj, Museum of the Apoxyomenos. Croatian athlete - the "Scraper".

4c.1. Precious Relics: the Bronzes of Punta del Serrone in 3D

Fig. 1: "F. Ribezzo" Provincial Archeological Museum, Brindisi. Statue of Polydeukion (3D laser scanning; created by: A. Bandiera, Coordinated by: Siba - Unisalento).
Fig. 2 : "F. Ribezzo" Provincial Archeological Museum, Brindisi. Male statue, "Hellenic Prince" or "Lucius Aemilius Paullus Macedonicus". (3D laser scanning; created by: A. Bandiera, Coordinated by: Siba - Unisalento).
Figs. 3 : "F. Ribezzo" Provincial Archeological Museum, Brindisi. Male statue, "Hellenic Prince" or "Lucius Aemilius Paullus Macedonicus". (modeling and hypothetical reconstruction; created by: M. Toriello, Coordinated by: 3D Box Creative Lab).

Fig. 4: "F. Ribezzo" Provincial Archeological Museum, Brindisi. Wing from Victory (or Victoria) statue. (3D laser scanning; created by: A. Bandiera, Coordinated by: Siba - Unisalento).

Fig. 5: "F. Ribezzo" Provincial Archeological Museum, Brindisi. Statue of Victory (or Victoria). (modeling and hypothetical reconstruction; created by: M. Toriello, Coordinated by: 3D Box Creative Lab).

Figs. 6: "F. Ribrezzo" Provincial Archeological Museum, Brindisi. Portrait and arm of little girl statue. (3D laser scanning; created by: A. Bandiera, Coordinated by: Siba - Unisalento).

Figs. 7: "F. Ribrezzo" Provincial Archeological Museum, Brindisi. Portrait and arm of little girl statue. (modeling and hypothetical reconstruction; created by: M. Toriello, Coordinated by: 3D Box Creative Lab).

4d. Images of Memories: Ships and Ports on Coins and Medals

Fig. 1 - Plate of Pope Clement X (1670-1676) with the port of Civitavecchia (Rome).

Fig. 2 - Medal of Pope Gregory XVI (1831-1846) with the port of Terracina.

Fig. 3 - Anonymous axe from the Roman Republican Age (225-217 B.C.) with ship's bow.

Fig. 4 - Medal of Pope Callistus III (1455-1458) for the naval expedition against the Turks (19th-century recoining ?).

Fig. 5 - Denarius of Lucius Cossutius Sabula from the Roman Republican Age (74 B.C.) with Medusa.

Fig. 6 - Denarius of Octavian from the Roman Republican Age (ca. 29-27 B.C.) with winged Victory on a ship's bow.

Fig. 7 - Republic of Italy. 5 cents of Vittorio Emanuele III of Savoy (1900-1946) with the representation of Italy on the bow of the ship.

Fig. 8 - Sestertius of Nero (54-68 A.D.) with the port of Claudius in Ostia (Rome).

Fig. 9 - Sestertius of Trajan (98-117 A.D.) with the port of Trajan in Ostia (Rome).

Fig. 10 - Medal of Pope Julius II (1503-1513) with the fortress of Civitavecchia (Rome) (19th-century recoining ?).

Fig. 11 - Medal of Pope Gregory XVI (1831-1846) with the port of Ripa Grande (Rome).

Fig. 12 - Medal of Pope Clement XII (1730-1740) with the Lazaret of Ancona (19th-century recoining ?).

Fig. 13 - Denarius of Marc Antony from the Roman Imperial Age (32-31 B.C.) with a ship.

Fig. 14 - Sestertius of Hadrian (117-138 A.D.) with a ship.

Fig. 15 - Osella of the Doge Alvise III Mocenigo (1722-1732) with a war vessel and merchant vessels.

Fig 16 - Osella of the Doge Alvise III Mocenigo (1722-1732) with a Bucentaur.

Fig. 17 - Half a thaler of the Grand Duke Cosimo III de' Medici (1670-1723) with a ship.

Fig. 18 - Sestertius of Emperor Hadrian (117-138 A.D.) with Neptune.

Fig. 19 - Denarius of Q. Crepereius Rocus from the Roman Republican Age (72 B.C.) with Amphitrite.

Fig. 20 - Denarius of Emperor Augustus (27 B.C. - 14 A.D.) with a siren.

Fig. 21 - Denarius of Sextus Pompeius from the Roman Republican Age (42-40 B.C.) with Scylla.

Fig. 22 - Quarter of a scudo of Charles V (1519-1556) with the Pillars of Hercules.

UNIT V NAVIGIA FUNDO EMERGUNT: STORY OF THE FINDINGS

Fig. 1 - Lake Nemi: The first ship to emerge (from: Ucelli 1983).

Fig. 2 - J.J. Cousteau with the A.R.A. (from: Bellomo, Vitale 1990).

Fig. 3 - The Mistral, the first air-powered self-contained underwater breathing apparatus (from Bellomo, Vitale 1990).

Fig. 4 - Shipwreck of Albenga.

Fig. 5 - Shipwreck of Capo Chelidonia.

Fig. 6a-b - Shipwreck of Ventotene in deep waters: a) photo of cargo of amphorae; b) sonar image.

参考资料
BIBLIOGRAPHY

第二单元 海陆交汇：意大利古罗马海港

第一部分 从海洋到城市，追溯台伯河

第一节 克劳迪乌斯和图拉真的港口

S. 凯伊等，2005 年。《港口：罗马帝国港口的考古调查》，英国罗马学派考古专著 15，伦敦。

S. 凯伊、L. 帕洛利等人（编辑）。《港口和其海岸：最近的考古学研究。》，2011 年，英国罗马学派考古专著 18，伦敦。

第二节 皮耶特拉 - 帕帕流域靠岸处

G. 伊阿寇比，《圣保罗皮耶特拉 - 帕帕河港附近的挖掘，林琴科学院院士的古纪念碑》，第 39 卷，1943 年，第 1-178 页。

F. 黛拉，圣保罗皮耶特拉 - 帕帕河港的壁画。罗马，A. 多纳蒂（编辑），罗马绘画。《起源于拜占庭时代的罗马绘画》，1998 年马尔泰拉戈，第 283-286 页。

N. 法贾尼、R. · 帕里斯、M.T. · 迪萨尔奇纳（编辑），罗马国家博物馆 - 马西莫宫。马赛克，米兰，2012 年，第 177-178 页，表格 27.1，第 175-178 页；N. 法贾尼、C. 加斯帕里、R. 帕里斯（编辑），系列，米兰，2013 年，第 466-470 页，第 341-343 号表格。

第三节 城市中的河岸港口

卡莱赛迪 · G，泰斯塔西奥河岸的发掘，《国立林琴科学院收到的关于古迹的报告》，第七卷，1956 年，第 1 页，第 19-52 页。

莫凯贾尼 · 卡帕诺、C – 梅内吉尼 · R，泰斯塔西奥河岸，《罗马市政考古委员会公报》，（XC）1，1985 年，第 86-95 页。

A. 孔蒂诺、G-J. 伯格斯、L. 达利山德罗、V. 德利昂纳第斯、S. 岱拉 · 利卡、R-A. 寇科 - 梅尔力诺、R. 塞巴斯蒂亚尼（2018 年）：《埃米利亚港的来世》，FOLD&R 法斯蒂在线杂志。

卡坡蒂菲罗、A– 夸兰塔，P.（编辑），玛莫拉塔路 2 号的发掘阿文提诺山，文化遗产和活动部，罗马考古遗产特别监督处，罗马市政府，米兰，2011 年。

G-J. ·博格斯、V. ·德利昂纳第斯、S. ·岱拉 · 利卡、R. 寇科、梅尔力诺 · M.、R. 塞巴斯蒂亚尼，F. 黛拉，《Porticus una extra portam Trigeminam: 关于埃米利亚港口的新思考》，第 18 卷，考古国际大会（2013 年 3 月 13-17 日），梅里达，2013 年、2014 年，第 913-917 页。

第一部分　维苏威火山脚下的那不勒斯海湾：佛莱格瑞海岸的港口

第一节：大型商用军事港口综合系统

E. 斯科纳米格利奥，尤利乌斯港：地中海海洋考古新数据，6，2009 年，第 154 页。

P. 卡普托，《奥古斯都和坎帕尼亚的尤利乌斯港》，维罗纳，2014 年，第 36-37 页。

P.A. 吉安弗洛塔，《尤利乌斯港: 航拍照片，直接分析和多部位平面图》，考古区域，2012 年 6 月，第 89-98 页。

A. · 贝尼尼、L. 兰泰里，《古罗马米塞诺港：新的发现，在古代和中世纪地中海港口避难的军用船只》，巴里，2010 年，第 109-117 页。

第二节 巴亚：皇宫、水下宫殿和艾比达菲奥海岬的温泉浴场

J. H. 达姆斯，《那不勒斯湾传奇和其他古罗马坎帕尼亚的随笔》，第二部分等。巴里，2003 年。

G. 迪卢卡，Nullus in orbe sinus Bais prelucet amoenis（拉丁语）。《对复杂架构的思考，也称为巴亚的“阿姆布拉提奥”“索斯安德拉”及“小温泉”》，搁浅船只考古公报，84，2009 年，第 149-168 页。

P. 米涅洛 - C. 卡帕尔迪，《来自贝亚特里托里古罗马别墅的第二部分和第三部分风格的壁画》，I. 布拉干蒂尼（等），皮斯塔诺古罗马别墅壁画会议记录，那不勒斯，2007 年，那不勒斯，2010 年，第 387-394 页。

P. 米涅洛，《巴亚卡斯特洛古罗马别墅：背景的重新考察》，MEFRA，122，2010 年，第 439-450 页。

P. 米涅洛、M. 迪马尔科、F. 瓜尔达西奥内，《巴亚的古罗马别墅：最近的发现和思考》，L. 奇卡拉、B. 费拉拉编辑，基提翁 · 里地奥斯。《和乔瓦娜 · 格雷科一起学习历史和考古学》，大希腊研究中心的笔记 22，2017 年，第 795-810 页。

第四单元　浮海而行：商品与运输

第三部分　艺术品：海底博物馆

珍贵文物：塞罗内海岬铜像的 3D 还原

G. 安德阿斯、A. 科奇亚洛，博达德勒塞罗内铜像，布林迪西水下考古研究，1992 年，考古公报，1992 年副刊；

G. 德帕尔玛、P. 菲奥伦蒂诺，布林迪西铜像，里亚切铜像修复知识，A. 梅鲁克 · 瓦卡罗、G. 德

帕尔玛（编辑），罗马，2003 年，第一册，第 97-117 页。

博达德勒塞罗内铜像，从大海到布林迪西省博物馆，A.· 马林纳佐编辑，巴里 2010 年。

K. 马尼诺，亚得里亚海古青铜器：博达德勒塞罗内波吕丢凯斯雕像（布林迪西），罗马希腊雕塑古典传统和创新元素，国际会议公报（塞萨洛尼基，2009 年 5 月 6 日 -9 日）T. 史蒂芬多 - 厄斯、P. 卡兰阿斯达斯、D. 达马斯克斯编辑，塞萨洛尼基，2012 年，第 467-476 页；

K. 马尼诺，博达德勒塞罗内铜像（布林迪西）：研究新数据和假设，学生论坛集，萨兰托大学考古遗产专业学院三十年研究会议记录（卡瓦利诺，2010 年 1 月 29 日 -30 日），R. 丹德里亚、K. 马尼诺 第 10.1 卷，“历史和考古学”文集，加拉蒂纳，2012 年，第 319-332 页；

K. 马尼诺，博达德勒塞罗内铜像 希律阿提克斯组，考古代表作。展览回顾、调查、比较、目录（罗马，2013 年 5 月 20 日至 11 月 5 日），M.G. 贝尔纳蒂尼（编辑），L. 罗莉 · 盖蒂，罗马，2013 年，第 219-223 页。

P. 莫论诺，埃米利乌斯 · 鲍鲁斯铜像，里亚切铜像修复知识，A. 梅鲁克 · 瓦卡罗（编辑），G. 德帕尔玛，罗马，2003 年，第一卷，第 119-128 页。

第四部分　往昔之景：钱币及纪念章上的船舶及港口

S. 巴尔比 · 迪卡洛、G. 安杰利 · 布法利尼，《锡耶纳大地上的人和硬币》，比萨，2001 年。

G. 安杰利 · 布法利尼，《教皇的港口》，地中海 II。《地点和记忆》，展览目录（塔兰托，1989 年 10 月 13 日至 11 月 15 日），罗马，1989 年，第 119-125 页。

F. 巴尔托洛蒂，《罗马教皇的年度勋章。从保罗五世到保罗六世，1605 年 -1964 年》，里米尼，1967 年。

G. 卡内瓦，C.M. 塔拉瓦里尼（编辑），《古代环境地图册。安齐奥和海神》，罗马，2003 年。

意大利的货币系统。《对于在意大利和意大利人在其他国家铸造的中世纪和现代硬币整体编目的首次尝试》，第一卷至第二十卷，1910 年 -1943 年。

E. 费里齐，《尼禄大帝古罗马小银币中的克劳迪乌斯港》。《一些肖像元素》，第 63 册意大利钱币学年鉴（2017 年），第 387-396 页。

C. 吉劳迪，L. 帕洛利，G. 里奇，C. 塔塔，“港口（罗马 - 菲乌米奇诺）。克劳迪乌斯港和图拉真港的沉积充填是在台伯三角洲古、中古环境演化的背景下进行的。”中世纪考古第 33 卷（2006 年），第 49-60 页。

S. 凯伊，L. 帕洛利（编辑），《港口和海岸：最近的考古学研究》，伦敦，2001 年。

V. 曼努奇（编辑），《图拉真港博物学考古遗址。方法和项目》，罗马，1992 年。

UNIT II WHERE LAND AND SEA ROUTES MEET: PORTS OF ROMAN ITALY

2a. The Ports of Rome - From the Sea to the City, Sailing up the Tiber

2a.1.The Ports of Claudius and Trajan

S. Keay et al. 2005. Portus. An Archaeological Survey of the Port of Imperial Rome. Archaeological Monographs of the British School of Rome 15, London.

S. Keay, L. Paroli eds. 2011. Portus and its Hinterland. Recent Archaelogical Reserch. Archaeological Monographs of the British School of Rome 18, London.

2a.2. The Pietra Papa River Dock

G. IACOPI, Scavi in prossimità del porto fluviale di S. Paolo, località Pietra Papa, in Monumenti Antichi dei Lincei, vol. 39, 1943, pp. 1-178. [Excavations near the river port of S. Paolo, in Pietra Papa, in Ancient Monuments of the Lincei.]

F. TELLA, Affreschi dal porto fluviale di San Paolo, località Pietre Papa. Roma, in A. Donati (a cura di), Romana Pictura. La pittura romana dalle origini all'età bizantina [Frescoes from the river port of San Paolo, in Pietra Papa, Rome, in: A. Donati (edited by), Romana Pictura. Roman painting, from its origins to the Byzantine age.], Martellago 1998, pp. 283-286.

N. FAGIANI, in R. Paris, M.T. Di Sarcina (a cura di), Museo Nazionale Romano [National Roman Museum]. Palazzo Massimo alle Terme. I mosaici [The mosaics], Milan 2012, pp. 177-178, card 27.1, pp. 175-178 N. FAGIANI, in C. Gasparri, R. Paris (edited by), Palazzo Massimo alle Terme. Le collezioni [The collections], Milan 2013, cards nn. 341-343, pp. 466-470.

2a.3. The River Port in the City

Cressedi, G., Sterri al Lungotevere Testaccio, «Notizie degli scavi di antichità comunicate all'Accademia Nazionale dei Lincei» [Excavations at the Lungotevere Testaccio, "News of the ancient excavations communicated to the Accademia Nazionale dei Lincei"], VII, 1956, 1, pp. 19-52

Moccheggiani Carpano, C. - Meneghini R., Lungotevere Testaccio, «Bullettino della Commissione Archeologica Comunale di Roma» [Lungotevere Testaccio, "Bullettin of the Municipal Archeological Commission of Rome"], (XC) 1, 1985, pp. 86-95

A. Contino, G.-J. Burgers, L. D'Alessandro, V. De Leonardis, S. Della Ricca, R.-A. Kok-Merlino, R. Sebastiani (2018): "The afterlife of the Porticus Aemilia" FOLD&R the Journal of Fasti Online.

Capodiferro, A. - Quaranta, P. (edited by), Gli scavi di via Marmorata – 2 . Alle pendici dell'Aventino, Ministero per i Beni e le Attività Culturali, Soprintendenza Speciale per i Beni Archeologici di Roma, Roma Capitale [The excavations of Via Marmorata - 2. On the slopes of the Aventine, Ministry of Cultural Heritage and Activities, Special Superintendency for he Archeological Heritage of Rome, Rome Capita], Milan 2011.

Burgers G-J., De Leonardis V., Della Ricca S., Kok R., Merlino M., Sebastiani R., Tella F., Porticus una extra portam Trigeminam: nuove considerazioni sulla Porticus Aemilia, Actas del XVIII [Porticus una extra portam Trigeminam: new considerations on Porticus Aemilia, Actas of the XVIII], Congreso Internacional de Arquelogía Clásica (May 13th-17th, 2013), Merida 2013, Merida 2014, pp. 913-917.

2b. The Gulf of Naples Beyond the Vesuvius: The Ports of the Phlegraean Coast

2b.1. The Vast Integrated Merchant and Military Port System

E. Scognamiglio, Porto Giulio: nuovi dati, in Archeologia Marittima Mediterranea [Porto Giulio: new data, in: Mediterranean Maritime Archeology], 6, 2009, pp. -154.

P. Caputo, Il Portus Iulius, in Augusto e la Campania [The Portus Iulius, in: Augustus and Campania], Verona, 2014 pp. 36-37.

P. A. Gianfrotta, Portus Iulius: foto aeree, analisi diretta e mappatura multibeam, in Archeologia Aerea [Portus Iulius: aerial photos, direct analysis and multibeam mapping, in: Aerial Archeology], 6, 2012, pp. 89-98.

A. Benini, L. Lanteri, Il porto romano di Misenum: nuove acquisizioni, in Ricoveri per navi militari nei porti del Mediterraneo Antico e Medievale [The Roman port of Misenum: new acquisitions, in: Recovery of military ships in the ports of the Ancient and Medieval Mediterranean], Bari 2010, pp. 109-117.

2b.2. Baia: The Imperial Palace, the Nymphaeum, and the Baths of Punta Epitaffio

J. H. D'Arms, Romans on the Bay of Naples and other Essays of Roman Campania, II ed. Bari 2003.

G. Di Luca, Nullus in orbe sinus Bais prelucet amoenis. Riflessioni sull'architettura dei complessi c.d."dell'Ambulatio", "della Sosandra" e delle "PiccoleTerme" a Baia, [Nullus in orbe sinus Bais prelucet amoenis. Reflections on the architecture of the so-called "dell'Ambulatio", "della Sosandra", and "PiccoleTerme" complexes in Baia], in BABesch, 84, 2009, 149-168.

P. Miniero - C. Capaldi, Affreschi in II e III stile dalla villa romana di Baia in località Tritoli [, Frescoes in II and III style from the Roman villa of Baia in Tritoli , in I. Bragantini (ed.), Atti del X Congresso AIPMA [Proceedings of the 10th AIPMA Congress], Naples 2007, Naples 2010, 387-394.

P. Miniero, La villa romana nel Castello di Baia: un riesame del contest [The Roman villa in the Castle of Baia: a review of the context], in MEFRA, 122, 2010, 439-450.

P. Miniero, M. Di Marco, F. Guardascione, Ville romane in Baiano sinu: recenti rinvenimenti e riflessioni [Roman villas in Baiano sinu: recent discoveries and reflections], in L. Cicala, B. Ferrara (edited by), Kithion Lydios. Studi di storia e archeologia con Giovanna Greco, Quaderni del Centro Studi Magna Grecia [Studies of history and archeology with Giovanna Greco, Notes of the Magna Grecia Studies Center] 22, 2017, 795-810.

UNIT IV ALONG WATERWAY: GOODS AND TRANSPORTATION

4c - Works of Art: A Museum at the Bottom of the Sea

4c.1. Bronze Decorations of the Nemi Ships

ANDREASSI G., COCCHIARO A., Bronzi di Punta del Serrone. Ricerche archeologiche subacquee a Brindisi 1992, in Bollettino di Archeologia, Supplemento 1992; [Bronzes of Punta del Serrone. Underwater archaeological research in Brindisi 1992, in Archeology Bulletin, Supplement 1992].

DE PALMA G., FIORENTINO P., I bronzi di Brindisi, in I bronzi di Riace. Restauro come conoscenza [The bronzes of Brindisi, in: The Riace bronzes. Restoration as knowledge], (edited by) A. Melucco Vaccaro, G. De Palma, Rome 2003, vol. I, pp. 97-117.

I Bronzi di Punta del Serrone. Dal mare al Museo Provinciale di Brindisi [The bronzes of Punta del Serrone. From the sea to the Provincial Museum of Brindisi], (edited by) A. Marinazzo, Bari 2010.

MANNINO K., Bronzi antichi dall'Adriatico: una statua di Polydeukion da Punta del Serrone (Brindisi), in Classical Tradition and Innovative Elements in the Sculpture of Roman Greece, Proceedings of the International Conference [Ancient bronzes from the Adriatic: a statue of Polydeukion from Punta del Serrone (Brindisi), in: Classical Tradition and Innovative Elements in the Sculpture of Roman Greece, Proceedings of the International

Conference (Thessaloniki, May 6th-9th, 2009), (edited by) T. Stefanidou-Tiveriou, P. Karanastasi, D. Damaskos, Thessaloniki 2012, pp. 467-476.

MANNINO K., I Bronzi di Punta del Serrone (Brindisi): nuovi dati e ipotesi di ricerca, in Gli allievi raccontano, Atti dell'Incontro di Studio per i Trent'anni della Scuola di Specializzazione in Beni Archeologici – Università del Salento [The Bronzes of Punta del Serrone (Brindisi): new data and research hypothesis, in: The students' testimonies, Proceedings of the Study Meeting for the Thirty Years of the School of Specialization in Archaeological Heritage - University of Salento] (Cavallino, January 29th-30th , 2010), (edited by) R. D'Andria, K. Mannino, vol. 10.1, Collana "Storia e Archeologia" ["History and Archeology" series], Galatina 2012, pp. 319-332.

MANNINO K., Un gruppo di Erode Attico fra i bronzi di Punta del Serrone (Brindisi), in Capolavori dell'Archeologia. Recuperi, ritrovamenti, confronti, Catalogo della mostra [group of Herod Atticus among the bronzes of Punta del Serrone (Brindisi), in: Masterpieces of Archeology. Recoveries, findings, comparisons, Catalog of the exhibition] (Rome, May 20th –November 5th, 2013), (edited by) M.G. Bernardini, L. Lolli Ghetti, Rome 2013, pp. 219-223.

MORENO P., Statua in bronzo di Emilio Paolo, in I bronzi di Riace. Restauro come conoscenza [Bronze statue of Emilio Paolo, in: The Riace bronzes. Restoration as knowledge] (edited by) A. Melucco Vaccaro, G. De Palma, Rome 2003, vol. I, pp. 119-128.

4d. Images of Memories: Ships and Ports on Coins and Medals

BALBI DE CARO S., ANGELI BUFALINI G., Uomini e monete in terra di Siena [Men and coins in the land of Siena], Pisa 2001.

ANGELI BUFALINI G., I porti dei papi, in Il Mediterraneo. I luoghi e la memoria, Catalogo della mostra [The ports of the popes, in: The Mediterranean. Places and memories, Catalog of the exhibition] (Taranto, ottobre 13th - November 15th, 1989)], Rome 1989, pp. 119-125.

BARTOLOTTI F., La medaglia annuale dei Romani Pontefici. Da Paolo V a Paolo VI, 1605-1964 [The annual medal of the Roman Pontiffs. From Paul V to Paul VI, 1605-1964], Rimini 1967.

CANEVA G., TRAVAGLINI C.M. (aedited by), Atlante storico-ambientale. Anzio e Nettuno [Historical-environmental atlas. Anzio and Nettuno], Rome 2003.

Corpus Nummorum Italicorum. Primo tentativo di un catalogo generale delle monete medievali e moderne coniate in Italia e da italiani in altri paesi. [First attempt at a general catalog of medieval and modern coins minted in Italy and by Italians in other countries], voll. I-XX, 1910-1943.

FELICI E., Il Porto di Claudio nei sesterzi di Nerone. Alcuni elementi iconografici, in Annali dell'Istituto Italiano di Numismatica 63 [The Port of Claudius in Nero's sesterces. Some iconographic elements, in: Annals of the Italian Institute of Numismatics], (2017), pp. 387-396.

GIRAUDI C., PAROLI L., RICCI G., TATA C., "Portus (Fiumicino-Roma). Il colmamento sedimentario dei bacini del porto di Claudio e Traiano nell'ambito dell'evoluzione ambientale tardo-antica e medievale del delta del Tevere", in Archeologia Medievale 33 ["Portus (Fiumicino-Rome). The sedimentary filling of the basins of the Ports of Claudius and Trajan in the late-ancient and medieval environmental evolution of the Tiber delta", in: Medieval Archeology 33], (2006), pp. 49-60.

KEAY S., PAROLI L. (edited by), Portus and its hinterland: recent archaeological research, London 2011.

MANNUCCI V. (edited by), Il parco archeologico naturalistico del porto di Traiano. Metodo e progetto [The naturalistic archaeological park of the port of Trajan. Method and project], Rome 1992.